Refeudalization and the Crisis of Civilization

To discuss the civilization crisis and processes of refeudalization, this volume brings the dialogue of two of the most creative approaches, in Olaf Kaltmeier and Edgardo Lander, to rethink capitalism in the 21st century.

In Chapter 1, Edgardo Lander urgently assesses the current state and political legacy of the "Pink Tide" governments in his chapter "Crisis of Civilization." Reviewing the past two decades of the new millennium, Lander critiques the failure of these governments to provide alternatives to extractivism and economic dependencies. In Chapter 2, Olaf Kaltmeier takes issue with the state of social inequality in the region, highlighting the concentration of wealth within the upper 1% of society in Latin America. Comparing the current economic situation with the ancient regime, the discussion centers around new phenomena like billionaires as president, increased luxury consumption, an emerging culture of distinction, and the intensification of land and spatial segregation. Finally, Hans-Jrgen Burchardt connects the arguments through interviews where both authors sum their efforts to open the issues to future dialogue.

Refeudalization and the Crisis of Civilization provides an accessible and thought-provoking political diagnosis from the Global South which departs from the oft idiosyncratic and cyclical debates of the Global North to offer a new vocabulary for social change. It will create interest in scholars and students of global studies, sociology, and political science.

Olaf Kaltmeier is a Professor of Iberoamerican History at Bielefeld University. He is the director of CALAS, the Maria Sibylla Merian Center for Advanced Latin American Studies in the Humanities and Social Science, and the founding director of the Center for InterAmerican Studies (CIAS) at Bielefeld University. He has done research and teaching in Mexico, Ecuador, Chile, Bolivia, Peru, Argentina, and the USA.

Edgardo Lander is a retired Professor of Social Sciences at the Universidad Central Venezuela (UCV) in Caracas. He served on the Organizing Committee of the World Social Forum held in Venezuela in 2006. As part of the Venezuelan delegation, he participated in negotiations on the Free Trade Agreement of the Americas, which was ultimately defeated. Other positions include Fellow of the Transnational Institute (Amsterdam); member of the academic advisory board of CALAS (Maria Sibylla Merian Center for Advanced Latin American Studies); participant of the Rosa Luxemburg Foundation's Latin American Working Group on Alternatives to Development, at its regional office in Quito; and Visiting Professor in the Masters Program in Political Ecology and Aternatives to Developmemt at the Universidad Andina Simón Bolívar in Quito, Ecuador.

Coping with Crisis - Latin American Perspectives
*Edited by CALAS - Maria Sibylla Merian Center for
Advanced Latin American Studies:
Editorial board: Olaf Kaltmeier,
Sarah Corona Berkin,
Hans-Jürgen Burchhardt,
Gerardo Gutiérrez Cham*

This series is published in cooperation with the Maria Sibylla Merian Center for Advanced Latin American Studies in the Humanities and Social Sciences (CALAS). As a Center for Advanced Latin American Studies, CALAS seeks to foment research of interest in the social sciences and humanities in Latin America, applying historical, scientific, and systematic approaches and employing transdisciplinary and transregional dialogue.

Coping with Crisis - Latin American Perspectives combines three types of publications.

- Volumes from four main research groups: Visions of Peace: Transitions Between Violence and Peace in Latin America; Confronting Social Inequality: Perspectives on Wealth and Power; Coping with Environmental Crises; and Regional Identities in Multiple Crises.
- Translated short monographs titled "Afrontar las crisis desde América Latina."
- Anthologies and monographs authored by CALAS senior fellows' and research group investigations.

Refeudalization and the Crisis of Civilization
Political essays on Latin America
Olaf Kaltmeier & Edgardo Lander

Refeudalization and the Crisis of Civilization
Political Essays on Latin America

Olaf Kaltmeier and Edgardo Lander

NEW YORK AND LONDON

First published 2023
by Routledge
605 Third Avenue, New York, NY 10158

and by Routledge
4 Park Square, Milton Park, Abingdon, Oxon, OX14 4RN

*Routledge is an imprint of the Taylor & Francis Group,
an informa business*

© 2023 Olaf Kaltmeier and Edgardo Lander

Translated by Matti Steinitz and Eric Rummelhoff

The right of Olaf Kaltmeier and Edgardo Lander to be identified as authors of this work has been asserted in accordance with sections 77 and 78 of the Copyright, Designs and Patents Act 1988.

All rights reserved. No part of this book may be reprinted or reproduced or utilised in any form or by any electronic, mechanical, or other means, now known or hereafter invented, including photocopying and recording, or in any information storage or retrieval system, without permission in writing from the publishers.

Trademark notice: Product or corporate names may be trademarks or registered trademarks, and are used only for identification and explanation without intent to infringe.

ISBN: 978-1-032-31255-2 (hbk)
ISBN: 978-1-032-31266-8 (pbk)
ISBN: 978-1-003-30885-0 (ebk)

DOI: 10.4324/9781003308850

Typeset in Times New Roman
by KnowledgeWorks Global Ltd.

SPONSORED BY THE

Contents

List of figures   x

Introduction: Refeudalization and the Crisis of Civilization   1

1 Crisis of Civilization: Experiences of Progressive Governments
   and Debates in the Latin American Left   5

   Introduction 5
   The Terminal Crisis of the Modern Colonial Pattern of
       Civilization 8
       Accelerated Destruction of the Conditions That Have
           Made Possible the Creation and Reproduction of
           Life 9
           The Intergovernmental Panel on Climate Change
               (IPCC) 10
           Planetary Boundaries 12
           Biocapacity and Ecological Footprint 13
           The Anthropocene and the Sixth Great Extinction 14
       Present and Future Socio-Environmental Impacts of
           Global Climate Change 16
       How Do the Powers That Be Respond to These
           Challenges? 18
       What Would Have to Be Changed for Nothing to
           Change? 19
       The Green Economy 24
       Geoengineering 27
       Anthropocene or the Age of Plutocracy? The Profound
           Inequalities in the Distribution of Wealth and
           Political, Communicational, and Military Power That
           Characterizes the Present Post-Democratic World 28
       Who Decides the Future of the Planet? 30

viii   *Contents*

Progressive Latin American Governments in
   the Face of the Civilizational Crisis 37
   Constituent Processes 40
   Ecuador Mineral-State? 52
   Bolivia: From Buen Vivir to Extractivist
      Developmentalism 56
   The TIPNIS Road 58
   Venezuela: The Paroxysm of Extractivism 62
   Extractivism and the Utopian Prospects of
      Transformations That Were Announced 66
   Extractivism, Geopolitics, and Latin American
      Integration 67
Debates of the Left on Current Anti-Capitalist
   Struggles in Latin America 71
   The Emergence of New Forms of Anti-Systemic
      Politics 73
   Other Forms of Politics and Seizure of Power by
      Progressive Governments 79
   Socialism of the 21st Century 81
   Foro de São Paulo 82
   Perspectives of the Foro de São Paulo on Today's
      World 83
   The Primacy of Geopolitics 87
   China's Role as a Blind Spot 88
   Dichotomous Perspectives on Political Ethics 89
   Nicaragua 93
   Venezuela 95
   The Crisis of the Left 98
   A Final Insistence on the Left 101
Bibliography 106

2 The Refeudalization of Society: Social Inequality
   and Political Culture in Latin America   122

Global Refeudalization or Latin American
   "Feudal Mania?" 122
The 1% and the Refeudalization of
   the Social Structure 132
   Refeudalization of the Social Structure
      in Latin America 135
   The Moneyed Aristocracy in Latin America 142
   From Class to Estate 148

Contents ix

The Refeudalization of the Economy 155
   Landlordism and Extractivism 156
   The New Robber Barons 163
   Robbery by Omission: From Panama to Paradise 166
Consumer Identities: Between Luxury and Debt
   Bondage 170
   Consumption, Luxury, and Prestige 174
   A New Debt Bondage 178
Of Citadels, Fortresses, and Walls 180
   Castles in the City 181
   From Gentrification to Retro-Colonial Archipelago 188
Millionaires in Power 192
   The Body of Money 198
   Identity Politics and Political Rationalities:
      Racism and the Right to Kill 201
From Refeudalization to a New Communism? 209
Bibliography 215

Understanding Multiple Crises: Interview with
Olaf Kaltmeier and Edgardo Lander   225

Index   235

List of figures

2.1	Great Gatsby Curve, Corak (2012)	150

Images

2.1	Santa María Reina de la Familia Church in the town of Cayalá, Guatemala.	185
2.2	San Luís Shopping Center, Quito.	186

Introduction: Refeudalization and the Crisis of Civilization

Hans-Jürgen Burchardt and Jochen Kemner

In light of current political developments, a new chapter of progressive governance is emerging in Latin America. Consequently, this is a good juncture to reflect on the first phase of the Pink Tide that started at the onset of the 21st century: what has been achieved? What has been neglected? What should be done differently? What should be done better?

We remember at the turn of the century—from Venezuela (Chavez) to Argentina (Kirchners), Brazil (Lula da Silva/Rousseff), Bolivia (Morales), Ecuador (Correo), Uruguay (Vazquez/Mujica), Paraguay (Lugo), and at times even Chile (Bachelet)—majority left-leaning or self-identifying progressive governments came to power and were able to shape policy for more than a decade. The turn to leftist governments was a result of the deep social—as well as economic—discord that austerity policies and neoliberal privatization programs of the 1990s created in their societies. They were strongly supported by movements that fought against social hardships, but also against centuries of marginalization, as seen in the indigenous movements.

For more than a decade, many of these governments benefited from globally high commodity prices, which allowed them to reduce social distortions; the region saw a significant decline in (extreme) poverty, some noticeable reductions in social inequality, and substantial overall growth in social upward mobility. The prospect of a good life for all seemed to become a reality, spreading optimism throughout the region and beyond.

The end of the commodity boom, beginning in 2014, signaled the decline of the Pink Tide. As a backlash to the unfolding worsening of conditions, some progressive governments became more authoritarian, others were ousted from office as a result of electoral defeats or through coup-like actions. Latin America experienced a shift to the right that encompassed almost the entire continent.

Now there are signs of the beginning of a new wave, reaching its zenith with the return of Lula da Silva to the presidency in Brazil. With Castillo in Peru, Boric in Chile, and above all, Petro in Colombia, the left has taken power in highly contested elections in countries where it had traditionally enjoyed little success or—as in Colombia and before with López

DOI: 10.4324/9781003308850-1

2   Introduction: Refeudalization and the Crisis of Civilization

Obrador in Mexico—had never been able to win democratic elections. For the first time in its history, the six largest Latin American economies (Brazil, Mexico, Argentina, Chile, Colombia, and Peru) are now governed by leftist heads of state. What can be expected from this latest course change?

The chapters by Olaf Kaltmeier and Edgardo Lander brought together in this volume, which were written as part of the research program "Coping with Crisis" of the Maria Sibylla Merian Center for Advanced Latin American Studies (CALAS), provide important ideas for the understanding of the current social dynamics as well as the challenges that Latin America faces at the beginning of the third decade of the 21st century. They focus on the two major challenges that the region has to confront: the social inequalities that have shaped Latin America since colonial times and the increasingly manifest effects of the global environmental crisis and climate change. Both authors are concerned with identifying elements to overcome the accelerated destruction of the natural environment as well as the processes of social disintegration.

Latin America is thus confronted with the double challenge of finding answers to the "terminal multidimensional civilizational crisis of our time" (Lander), under conditions of worsening social disparities that are an expression of an ongoing "refeudalization process" (Kaltmeier). Lander argues that the left in charge of the government in the early 21st century in Latin America failed to recognize the true dimension of the civilizational crisis threatening the planet, which manifested itself first and foremost in massive environmental degradation. These governments did not succeed in developing new political and social responses in order to effectively confront these challenges. As an alternative to capitalism, they continued to rely on a state-centered and development-oriented paradigm, which inhibited truly progressive politics and instead exacerbated the crisis. Lander points toward the lack of (self-) critical reflection on the experiences of progressive governance that he sees as a clear expression of why the left has lost its attraction in Latin America. Instead, its main pundits stick unwaveringly to old unfruitful recipes without considering alternatives and other perspectives, such as those of the new social movements that have gained prominence in the last couple of decades.

In turn, Kaltmeier, when making the case that Latin America points toward refeudalization, does not imply that this means a return to colonial, pre-modern conditions of the *ancien regime,* but a reemergence or revival of social articulations that were never really overcome in the region with its colonial continuities and legacies. This holds true for the immense gap in the social structure, the orientation of central sectors of the economy toward the success of commodities, social norms, cultural and (consumer) values, socio-spatial segregation, and the increasing entanglement of economic and political power in the hands of the money

Introduction: Refeudalization and the Crisis of Civilization 3

aristocracy, the "1%" at the top of the social fabric. However, parallel to these five dimensions that characterize a primarily economically determined refeudalization, Kaltmeier also considers phenomena of change in everyday life, social dynamics, and representational politics.

Despite the different foci of the two social analyses, some overlaps can be identified that give us clues about the requirements of successful progressive governance in the region. Both authors state accurately that the Pink Tide initially generated general improvement in the living conditions of the population. These developments were based on a deepening and broadening of the commodity-based economic model, today often referred to as neo-extractivism, insofar as a larger share of the profits generated through exports of raw products in this model were used to finance social programs that targeted poverty reduction.

Like previous and current neoliberal governments on the continent, however, progressive regimes have deepened Latin America's dependence on commodity exports and thus the region's subordinate integration into the international division of labor, without posing any real challenge to the basic structures of the world market, despite all their anti-imperialist and anti-capitalist rhetoric. Protests and resistance by local, often indigenous, communities or environmental movements against the expansion of, for example, mining projects, oil production, or monocultural agribusinesses, which often helped leftist governments to gain power, were not infrequently met with repression after they stabilized politically.

The failure to use favorable conditions to not only distribute the additional returns from the extractive industries but also to introduce far-reaching structural transformations, by means of fiscal policies or agrarian reforms, led to a situation in which the trend toward the dominance of the 1% over the 99% was not reversed, especially in the social structure, as Kaltmeier points out. As a result of the decline in commodity prices from 2014 and the associated economic crisis, entire segments of the population that had risen in the previous decade have slipped back into poverty. On the contrary, the top 10% were able to maintain their position and even expanded their wealth.

The distinctive commodity orientation of Latin American economies has other consequences as well. For example, it fosters the danger of increasing anti-democratic structures of governance and a political culture that consolidates through hegemonic patriarchal patterns. High commodity revenues can be used to co-opt conflicting parties or veto groups in the event of clashing interests. The resulting clientelism, nepotism, and rampant corruption undermine democratic negotiation processes for consensus-building and weaken social cohesion. This was evident in Latin America both under left-wing governments—as Lander shows with the examples of Bolivia, Nicaragua, and Venezuela—and during the subsequent shift to the right, which Kaltmeier examines in greater detail.

4 *Introduction: Refeudalization and the Crisis of Civilization*

Latin America is also characterized by the strong continuity of its elites, whose economic wealth is often rooted in the 19th century when they gained control of natural resources and have since spread through dynastic accumulation. This does not mean that these elites do not incorporate new groups from other sectors. However, the interdependence between economic and political elites—also a colonial legacy of Latin America, as manifested most recently in the cabinet of the transitional Brazilian president Temer or the "millionaire presidents" Macri and Piñera—is once again intensifying.

The multidimensional civilizational crisis as well as the refeudalization of social and economic relations are, of course, not uniquely Latin American phenomena, nor do they originate in this region. In accordance with the purpose of CALAS, the authors of these chapters are more concerned with discussing specific Latin American responses and ways of coping with the current types of planetary crises and transformative conflicts. The new government of Colombia (Petro/Márquez), with its commitment to a major agrarian and fiscal reform and the goal to foster the transition from an extractive to a productive economy, offers an avenue for a truly transformative program that can both respond productively to the civilizational crisis and, at the same time, address the tendency toward refeudalization in the region. New experiences on how to guarantee a decent life for all can thus be gained without disregarding the safeguarding of nature, the increase of environmental pollution, or the energy transition that is so necessary in Latin America.

1 Crisis of Civilization

Experiences of Progressive Governments and Debates in the Latin American Left

Edgardo Lander

Research Associate: *Santiago Arconada Rodríguez*

Introduction

Humanity is living through a profound crisis, a multidimensional terminal crisis of the modern-colonial pattern of civilization destroying the conditions that make possible the production and reproduction of life on planet Earth. Such is the depth of this crisis that even the options that during the last two and a half centuries appeared as alternatives to capitalism, the most complete expression of this civilizational pattern, are also facing a severe crisis. The political stance of Marxism, the prospects of socialism, and, generally, the more motley spheres of the Left lack credible proposals capable of pointing out *other* directions and options as ways out of the crisis, capable of giving expression to the deep and generalized maladies that extend to the broadest sectors of planet's population. On the contrary, as this systemic crisis accelerates and the impacts of climate collapse spread, as inequalities deepen and insecurity and uncertainty about the future expand, there has been a marked shift toward the extreme right and right-wing options in recent decades. Governments and parties with authoritarian, patriarchal, and xenophobic orientations enjoy growing support in most parts of the world.

In the first two decades of this century, there were significant political/cultural shifts in Latin America, considered at that time the continent of hope against the grain of these global trends, that led to the experiences of the so-called "progressive governments," which seemed to open paths in other directions for humanity. However, after a couple of decades, it is possible to see that, fundamentally, these projects have failed both as processes of anti-capitalist transformation and as alternatives to colonial modernity.

This essay addresses these questions in three sections. First, an analysis is made of the profound civilizational crisis that humanity is experiencing today. It is characterized as the terminal crisis of the modern-colonial

DOI: 10.4324/9781003308850-2

6 *Crisis of Civilization*

pattern of civilization that has as essential its anthropocentric, patriarchal, colonial, classist, and racist character. This societal model of endless growth and continuous assault on the natural environment, with its hegemonic modalities of knowledge, science, and technologies of capitalism, is devastating the conditions for the creation and reproduction of life on planet Earth in an accelerated way, threatening not only human survival but also that of a high proportion of all life. This part analyzes the main diagnoses about the state of the planet and the basic proposals that are being debated/implemented as a response to this profound crisis. It also addresses the implications of the fact that in the hegemonic debates and responses of states, multilateral institutions, corporations, and scientific-technological centers, there is a predominant lack of willingness to question the civilizational assumptions and patterns of basic knowledge and power relations that have led humanity to the present crisis. This results in a radical refusal to explore possible alternatives that would effectively account for the depth of the crisis. The technological and market solutions proposed from these hegemonic perspectives are conceived on the basis of the same market patterns and scientific-technological models that have led us to the present situation. They involve identifying, like in *The Leopard,* what needs to be changed, what responses and images of transformation need to be generated, so as to ensure that nothing really changes, so that the concentration of power and the profound inequalities that characterize the modern colonial capitalist world system will not only be left unchallenged but also consolidated and deepened.

In the second part, some key dimensions of the experiences of the three so-called "progresista" governments of South America (Bolivia, Ecuador, and Venezuela) are critically analyzed. These governments postulated the most radical ruptures not only with the global capitalist regime that is hegemonic today, but also with the fundamental dimensions of the modern colonial world system. These governments emerged at a historical moment when not only the civilizational crisis referred to above was being emphasized, but also when neoliberal globalization was advancing rapidly and the unipolar hegemony of the United States was being consolidated in what was characterized as the "new American century" and the "end of history." The eyes of the world turned to these novel projects of social transformation that seemed to account for and present alternatives to the multidimensional civilizational crisis confronting humanity, to the necessity to overcome anthropocentrism, patriarchy, coloniality, racism, capital's relations of exploitation/domination, and the exclusionary limits of liberal democracy. After these leftist movements and parties took power, significant breaks were announced with the political systems that in different forms had existed on the continent since colonial times. Other social and political subjects entered the political scene as protagonists, particularly those from the indigenous world, and new/ancestral

Crisis of Civilization 7

normative horizons were incorporated, such as those represented by the notions of *buen vivir* and "the rights of nature."

This text does not attempt to provide an overall assessment of these experiences. The critical analysis is based on limited, focused questions: *How have these processes of transformation responded to the complex and multidimensional challenges posed by this crisis of civilization in which the very survival of humanity and life is at stake? To what extent was it possible in these years to take steps, however initial, in the direction of transitions toward alternative forms of production, knowledge, and coexistence with other human beings and nature?*

Contrasting the objectives formulated in the discourses and founding documents of the political processes of these three countries, particularly in new constitutional texts, it is possible to conclude that in the realization of their extraordinarily ambitious objectives, they have fundamentally failed. There were important—albeit temporary—achievements, particularly in the geopolitical sphere and in reducing inequalities and improving the living conditions of the population. However, as has been the case with neoliberal governments in the continent, these progressive governments have deepened extractivism and their subordinate colonial role in the international division of labor and nature. Instead of the voracious and devastating machinery of global capital being confronted, be it from the East or West, it was fed more rapidly. Faced with the resistance of peoples and communities to the systematic advance of mining, energy, and agricultural megaprojects on their territories, the predominant government response has been repression, as has been the case under neoliberal governments.

The interpretation and evaluation of these two decades of experience have produced profound confrontations within the Left, as much in Latin America as globally. In the third part of this text, among these diverse positions, we critically analyze the positions of what is called the official Left, a predominantly state-centric and partisan Left whose most representative expression are the documents and declarations of the Foro de São Paulo, which brought together the vast majority of organizations that define themselves as leftists throughout Latin America. From perspectives that as a whole can be categorized as orthodox, in this official Left, geopolitical dimensions have been prioritized with predominately Manichean views built around the anti-imperialist/imperialist axis, leaving other essential dimensions of the reality of the contemporary world in second or third place: anthropocentrism, patriarchy, racism, colonialism, Eurocentrism .... From these perspectives, there have been few critical or self-critical looks at the experiences of these governments, often expressing unconditional solidarity with leaders and governments of these projects. As the declarations of the Foro de São Paulo clearly illustrate, this official Left, far from recognizing the depth of the civilizational crisis being confronted and what has been the impotence of its

8   *Crisis of Civilization*

forms of doing politics and the historical exhaustion of state-centered, developmentalist, and mono-cultural socialism, has become entrenched in the reaffirmation of abstract principles that no longer account for the multiform complexity of contemporary reality. This Left has closed in on itself in an attempt to defend the indefensible. Apart from recognizing some "errors" and "deviations," the causes of all the ills confronting contemporary society and the problems faced by the "progressive" processes are always on the other side, whether in capitalism, in imperialism, or on the right.

The reflexive and genuinely self-critical inquiry into why all historical experiences of socialism have failed as alternatives to this society in crisis and why socialism has ceased to operate as an imaginary of the future—both desirable or possible—is, fundamentally, marginalized in the debates and concerns of this official Left. This absence of critical/self-critical reflection is, in itself, the clearest expression of the crisis of this Left (of the whole tradition of the Left?) and its (our?) growing inability to recognize other alternatives; the other horizons of the future that through various local and regional experiments are building other ways of doing politics, prefiguring other futures in the present, and, through these means, giving an account of the main dimensions of the crisis we are facing.[1]

This text is written in an expressly polemical tone, as it is intended to convey both the urgency of the issues we are confronting and the urgency of recognizing the need to make a profound break with the ways of thinking and acting that we have inherited. It is conceived as a contribution to the reflections, debates, and controversies that need to be deepened.

The Terminal Crisis of the Modern Colonial Pattern of Civilization

We are facing, as humanity, a profound civilizational crisis: the terminal crisis of the Promethean pattern of civilization of colonial modernity. It is a multiform, multidimensional crisis of a civilizational pattern that in synthetic terms can be characterized as *anthropocentric, patriarchal, colonial, classist, racist, and whose hegemonic patterns of knowledge, science, and technology, far from offering solutions to this civilizational crisis, contribute to deepening it.* The various dimensions of the hegemonic civilizational pattern are by no means independent. On the contrary, they feed back and reinforce each other.

The anthropocentric and patriarchal dogmas of progress and development and the fantasies of the possibility of endless growth in a limited time frame are rapidly undermining the conditions that make the reproduction of life on planet Earth possible. This pattern of development and progress has reached its limit. Despite the fact that a large proportion of the population does not have access to the basic conditions of life (food, drinking water, shelter, etc.), humanity as a whole has already exceeded the limits of the Earth's *carrying capacity*. Without a short-term halt to this uncontrolled growth pattern and a reorientation toward degrowth, *harmony with the rest of life* and a *radical redistribution of access to the planet's common goods*, the continuity of human life is not guaranteed in the medium term.

Each of the main dimensions of this crisis has been deepened by neoliberal globalization during the previous decades. During these decades, the processes of commodification, appropriation, and subjugation of both the natural dynamics of reproduction of life and the cultural practices and forms of knowledge of different peoples of the world to submit them to the demands of the accumulation of capital have advanced by leaps and bounds.

The civilization of scientific-technological domination over the so-called "nature," which identifies human welfare with the accumulation of material objects and with the endless economic growth—whose maximum historical expression is capitalism—has its time counted. The incorporation of new territories for exploitation and appropriation of the knowledge of others, as well as the manipulation of the codes of life (biotechnology) and matter (nanotechnology), accelerate the approach to the limits of a finite planet. At a historic moment in time in which hegemonic civilizational patterns are proving their lack of viability and the monoculture of colonial modernity is approaching its limit, humanity urgently needs the diversity and multiplicity of cultures, ways of knowing, thinking, and living, as sources of alternatives to respond to this civilizational crisis. However, these *others*, as is the case of indigenous and peasant peoples and cultures all over the planet, are being threatened/devastated by the inexorable advance of the logic of commodification of all dimensions of life and the processes of *accumulation by dispossession*.

Capitalism, on its present scale, with its inevitable expansionist logic of devastation, is incompatible with the preservation of life as we know it. This makes it a matter of life and death to put the brakes on this unbridled machinery.

Accelerated Destruction of the Conditions That Have Made Possible the Creation and Reproduction of Life

Although, as we will see below, denialism persists, mainly among sectors linked to the fossil industry and neoconservatives in the United States; between the international academic scientific community and the hundreds of millions of people facing the consequences of climate change around the world today, all doubt has been left behind about the reality and severity of climate change and its anthropogenic determinants.

10   *Crisis of Civilization*

The Intergovernmental Panel on Climate Change (IPCC)

The most comprehensive and thoroughly documented analysis of current planetary-scale climate transformations has been carried out by the IPCC in successive reports, five since 1990.[2] These reports are the result of the work of hundreds of specialists in a wide range of climate-related disciplines from all parts of the world, based on the analysis of all the papers published in specialized scientific journals on these topics and other reports produced by all the scientific research centers devoted to climate-related issues around the world. In each of the successive IPCC reports, they have presented a more severe characterization with higher levels of confidence in climate trends. These reports, far from being alarmist in intent, have a conservative bias. Not only do they require high levels of consensus among the participating scientists for each of their conclusions but also these conclusions pass through the filter of government representatives around the world on whose behalf this group presents its findings. Some of these governments, such as the United States, have gone out of their way to minimize, even deny, the severity of ongoing climatic transformations (Rattani 2018).

Among the main conclusions presented in the latest IPCC report for 2014 are the following:

> Human influence on the climate system is clear, and recent anthropogenic emissions of greenhouse gases are the highest in history.
>
> Warming of the climate system is unequivocal, and since the 1950s, many of the observed changes are unprecedented over decades to millennia.
>
> Each of the last three decades has been successively warmer at the Earth's surface than any preceding decade since 1850.
>
> [...] The more human activities disrupt the climate, the greater the risks of severe, pervasive and irreversible impacts for people and ecosystems, and long-lasting changes in all components of the climate system.
>
> Over the period 1992 to 2011, the Greenland and Antarctic ice sheets have been losing mass (*high confidence*), *likely* at a larger rate over 2002 to 2011.
>
> Glaciers have continued to shrink almost worldwide (*high confidence*).
>
> The annual mean Arctic sea-ice extent decreased over the period 1979 to 2012, with a rate that was very likely in the range 3.5 to 4.1% per decade.

Crisis of Civilization 11

The rate of sea level rise since the mid-19th century has been larger than the mean rate during the previous two millennia (*high confidence*).

Anthropogenic greenhouse gas emissions have increased since the pre-industrial era, driven largely by economic and population growth, and are now higher than ever. This has led to atmospheric concentrations of carbon dioxide, methane and nitrous oxide that are unprecedented in at least the last 800,000 years.

Changes in many extreme weather and climate events have been observed since about 1950

Surface temperature is projected to rise over the 21st century under all assessed emission scenarios. It is *very likely* that heat waves will occur more often and last longer, and that extreme precipitation events will become more intense and frequent in many regions. The ocean will continue to warm and acidify, and global mean sea level to rise.

Climate change will amplify existing risks and create new risks for natural and human systems. Risks are unevenly distributed and are generally greater for disadvantaged people and communities in countries at all levels of development.

Many aspects of climate change and associated impacts will continue for centuries, even if anthropogenic emissions of greenhouse gases are stopped. The risks of abrupt or irreversible changes increase as the magnitude of the warming increases.

Without additional mitigation efforts beyond those in place today, and even with adaptation, warming by the end of the 21st century will lead to high to very high risk of severe, widespread and irreversible impacts globally (high confidence)

(Intergovernmental Panel on Climate Change).

The synthesis report stresses that we have the means to limit climate change and its risks and that we have many solutions at our disposal that would enable continued economic and human development. However, stabilizing temperature rise below 2°C relative to pre-industrial levels would require a radical and urgent change to the *status quo*. Moreover, the longer we wait to act, the greater the cost and the greater the technological, economic, social, and institutional challenges we will face (Intergovernmental Panel on Climate Change 2014).

In addition to the IPCC reports, there are a number of methodological approaches that use the very extensive information made available by

12 *Crisis of Civilization*

sophisticated technological tools available to characterize what is happening on the planet. There is no general consensus about any of these approaches, and some have generated intense controversy. It is not the purpose of this text to characterize these debates or evaluate the relative value of each of them. What is worth noting is that, in general terms, they all agree that the limits of the planet's *carrying capacity* have been exceeded and that life as we know it is in severe danger. It is worthwhile to dwell briefly on some of these widely publicized approaches, as they allow us to confirm that when drastic measures, commensurate with the severity of the crisis that we face as humanity, are not taken in the short term, it is not for lack of information or the existence of reasonable doubts about what is happening.

Planetary Boundaries

The Stockholm Resilience Centre at Stockholm University has developed a model of nine variables that it characterizes as planetary boundaries that should be monitored to ensure the health of the terrestrial ecosystem. Beyond the debates about the possibility of defining measurable objective limits (Brand and Wissen 2018), this approach has the virtue of broadening the gaze to a wider range of dimensions that permit a comprehensive analysis of the planet's situation. These variables are:

1 Climate change
2 Loss of biosphere integrity (biodiversity loss and extinctions)
3 Stratospheric ozone depletion
4 Ocean acidification
5 Nitrogen and phosphorus flows to the biosphere and oceans
6 Land system change (e.g., deforestation)
7 Freshwater consumption and the global hydrological cycle
8 Atmospheric aerosol loading (microscopic particles in the atmosphere that affect the climate and living organisms)
9 Chemical pollution and the release of novel entities (e.g., organic pollutants, radioactive materials, nanomaterials, and microplastics)

These nine dimensions have been represented on a four-category scale:

1 Limit not yet quantified
2 Below boundary (safe)
3 In the zone of uncertainty (increasing risk)
4 Beyond the zone of uncertainty (high risk)

According to the 2015 update, four of these limits have already been exceeded as a consequence of human activity: *climate change*; *loss of biosphere integrity*; *land system change*; and *biochemical flows to the biosphere and oceans.* Two of these, climate change and loss of biosphere integrity, are characterized as core limits that could drive the Earth system to a new state (Stockholm Resilience Center 2015).

Biocapacity and Ecological Footprint

The Global Footprint Network seeks to quantify the pressure exerted by human beings on the systems of reproduction of life on the planet. To do so, it works with two main categories: *biocapacity* and *ecological footprint*. *Biocapacity* or *biological capacity* is defined as the capacity of ecosystems to produce biological materials and absorb the waste generated by humans, under current management schemes and technologies.

The *ecological footprint* is an indicator of the environmental impact generated by human demand on the resources of the planet's ecosystems and the capacity of ecosystems to process waste, relating it to the Earth's ecological potential to regenerate those abilities. In order to synthesize the notion of ecological footprint into a unitary indicator, ecological footprint calculations are made by adding up the number of hectares of average productivity that would be necessary for a given standard of living and consumption, whether individual, local, regional, national, continental, or global. This is done by incorporating the following components: (1) built-up land footprint; (2) carbon footprint; (3) cropland footprint; (4) grazing land footprint; (5) forest land footprint; (6) fishing grounds footprint (Global Footprint Network 2009). Today, by far the largest of all pressures on the planet's biocapacity is the area required to reabsorb the carbon footprint.

According to this perspective and its methods of calculation, if the ecological footprint of humanity as a whole is smaller than the biocapacity of the planet, an ecological reserve exists. If, on the contrary, the ecological footprint is greater than the planet's biocapacity, an *ecological deficit* or an *ecological debt* emerges.

The *planetary equivalent* is the number of planet Earths that would be needed to support humanity's ecological footprint given a particular global ecological footprint, per country, and so on.

According to the Network's calculations, humanity as a whole used less than the total biocapacity of the planet until the early 1970s, accumulating an increasing ecological deficit since then.

> Since the 1970s, humanity has been in ecological overshoot, with annual demand for resources exceeding what the Earth can regenerate each year. Today humanity uses the equivalent of 1.7 Earths to provide the resources we use and absorb our waste. This means that it now takes the Earth one year and six months to regenerate what we use in one year. We use more resources and ecological services than nature can

14   *Crisis of Civilization*

> regenerate through overfishing, overexploiting forests, and emitting more carbon dioxide into the atmosphere than forests can sequester
>
> (Global Footprint Network).

By quantifying the ecological footprint, it is possible to evaluate human pressure, whether on the planet as a whole or on more limited territories, continents, countries, etc. The ecological footprint varies extraordinarily from one region of the planet to another, according to the living standards and consumption levels of the populations. The industrialized countries of the Global North, both in terms of historical accumulation and their current activities, have a much larger ecological footprint than the countries of the Global South and tend to exceed the carrying capacity of their own territories by far.

> If there is a regional or national ecological deficit, this means that the region is importing biocapacity through trade or liquidating regional ecological assets, or emitting waste into global commons such as the atmosphere. In contrast to the national scale, the global ecological deficit cannot be compensated for through trade, and is therefore equal to overshoot by definition
>
> (Global Footprint Network).

The ecological footprint today exceeds the global carrying capacity occurs under conditions of extreme inequalities. As noted above, a significant proportion of the world's population does not have regular access to such basic necessities of life as food, water, shelter, and energy. In contrast, 4.1 planets would be needed for the entire population of the planet to have the current average consumption levels of the U.S. population (McDonald 2015).

The Anthropocene and the Sixth Great Extinction

Another important contribution to the diagnosis and quantification of the planet's environmental situation is the Living Planet Reports, jointly produced by WWF International (Switzerland), the Institute of Zoology of London's Zoological Society, Stockholm University's Resilience Center, the Global Ecological Footprint Network, the Stockholm Environment Institute, and Metabolic in the Netherlands (WWF et al. 2016, 2018). These reports address the planetary environmental crisis by tracking what is happening to the biodiversity and abundance of species in the ecosystems of the planet. The report from 2016 has as its axis of analysis the characterization of the Anthropocene as the world's sixth mass extinction event.

> The size and scale of the human enterprise have grown exponentially since the mid-20th century. As a result, the environmental

conditions that fostered this extraordinary growth are beginning to shift. To symbolize this emerging environmental condition, Nobel Prize winner Paul Crutzen (2002) and others have proposed that we have transitioned from the Holocene into a new geological epoch, calling it the "Anthropocene" (e.g. Waters et al., 2016). During the Anthropocene, our climate has changed more rapidly, oceans are acidifying and entire biomes are disappearing – all at a rate measurable during a single human lifetime. This trajectory constitutes a risk that the Earth will become much less hospitable to our modern globalized society (Richardson et al., 2011). Scientists are now trying to discern which human-induced changes represent the greatest threat to our planet's resilience (Rockström et al. 2009a). Such is the magnitude of our impact on the planet that the Anthropocene might be characterized by the world's sixth mass extinction event. In the past such extinction events took place over hundreds of thousands to millions of years. What makes the Anthropocene so remarkable is that these changes are occurring within an extremely condensed period of time. Furthermore, the driving force behind the transition is exceptional. This is the first time a new geological epoch may be marked by what a single species (homo sapiens) has consciously done to the planet – as opposed to what the planet has imposed on resident species

(WWF et al. 2016).

The main indicator with which Living Planet approaches the study of diversity is the Global Living Planet Index, which monitors 14,152 observations of 3,706 vertebrate species (mammals, birds, fish, amphibians, and reptiles) around the world. According to the results of this monitoring, between the years 1970 and 2012, only 42 years, "the population abundance of vertebrates underwent a 58% decline" with no signs that the rate of annual decline is slowing (WWF et al. 2016, 10).

Between 1972 and 2012, terrestrial populations declined by 38%, freshwater populations by 81%, and marine populations by 36%. "If current trends continue to 2020 vertebrate populations may decline by an average of 67 per cent compared to 1970" (WWF et al. 2016, 12). According to the 2018 report, with data updated through 2014, "species population declines are especially pronounced in the tropics, with South and Central America suffering the most dramatic decline, an 89% loss compared to 1970" (WWF et al. 2018).

According to the Executive Secretary of the UN Convention on Biological Diversity, Ahmed Djoghlaf, 150 animal species are becoming extinct every day, the greatest loss of biological diversity since the dinosaurs disappeared (El País 2007).

16   *Crisis of Civilization*

Present and Future Socio-Environmental Impacts of Global Climate Change

Although global warming has received the most attention and has been most widely documented in recent decades, it does not, on its own, account for the multiple dimensions of global environmental collapse. It is no longer a question of potential impacts in the medium or short term, but of transformations that are altering and destroying the conditions for the reproduction of the lives of hundreds of millions of people in the present. The most important impacts are the following:

1 Increased frequency and intensity of extreme weather events: hurricanes, floods, droughts, heat waves, and forest fires. Hurricane Maria marked a before and after in the lives of the inhabitants of the island of Puerto Rico. A year after it occurred, thousands of homes remained destroyed and without basic services; consequently, there has been a significant migration. This devastation, under conditions of deep public sector indebtedness, is being used to justify draconian austerity and privatization policies that threaten even the University of Puerto Rico.
2 Prolonged droughts, desertification processes, and widespread loss of agricultural and livestock land. In Africa, in particular, this has led to massive climate-related migrations as the conditions for the reproduction of their lives are being destroyed.
3 Rising sea levels are leading to the disappearance of inhabited islands. Hundreds of millions of people, especially in Bangladesh, live in low-lying areas that are threatened with remaining permanently flooded (Ahmed and Meenar 2018). Coastal cities across the globe are at severe risk.
4 The melting of glaciers places the lives of the one-sixth of humanity that depends on rivers originating from them at risk (Jamail 2018). This is particularly threatening for South America, where 99% of all tropical glaciers on the planet are located—glaciers that are extremely sensitive to climate change. There has been a sustained reduction in their volume and coverage over the last 50 years. This is especially serious for Bolivia and Peru, as much of their population lives in arid areas where they are highly dependent on glacier-fed rivers (Rabatel et al. 2013).[3]
5 The accelerated loss of biodiversity, which is a fundamental condition for the preservation of life, becomes even more serious under the conditions of the accelerated climatic changes that are currently taking place. Entire ecological systems can collapse as a consequence of the loss of biological diversity. *Functional extinction* of a species can occur when it, despite retaining relative levels of abundance, ceases to perform interactions with the environment, without which devastating effects on other species can occur (Rabatel et al. 2013).

The ability to adapt to today's changing climatic conditions is significantly limited when biodiversity is reduced. The loss of variety in the seeds for staple foods, such as wheat, corn, soya, and potato, and the oligopolistic control that a few transnational corporations have over them have severe social and political consequences ....

The massive collapse of the insect population on the planet caused by human action has received less attention and has been less systematically studied than the loss in biodiversity and population of other varieties of plant and animal life. However, insects are an essential component of life systems on the planet. Among other functions, they are a fundamental source of food for birds and fish. The loss of pollinators represents a severe threat to the reproduction of both wild and cultivated plants and with it the food security of humanity (Bidau 2018).

6 Massive contamination of land and water caused by the use of agro-toxins in agriculture and the scale, concentration, and methods used in the so-called animal factories, such as the large, industrialized pig farms.

7 Local pollution in the large cities of the Global South, with serious effects on the health of their inhabitants.

8 Rising sea temperatures and acidification cause the deterioration of coral reefs that play a vital role in protecting coastal areas, provide habitat for many marine species, are a source of nitrogen and other essential nutrients for marine food chains, and contribute to the fixation of carbon and nitrogen (Queensland Museum 2010–2019). With a high level of confidence, the IPCC affirms that with a temperature rise of 1.5°C between 70% and 90% of coral reefs would disappear, and 99% in the event of a temperature rise to 2°C (Intergovernmental Panel on Climate Change 2018).

9 According to the 2018 Lancet Report on Health and Climate Change, "current changes in heatwaves, climate change, labor capacity, vector-borne diseases, and food security provide an early warning of the myriad, overwhelming impacts on public health if temperatures continue to rise as expected. Trends in climate change impacts, exposures, and vulnerabilities show an unacceptably high level of risk to the current and future health of the population worldwide" (Lancet 2018).

While there is a complete consensus in the scientific communities about the severity of environmental transformations and their anthropogenic origin, there is not a full consensus on the time frame left for humanity before the continuity of these devastating processes, especially the continued production of greenhouse gases, causes catastrophic and irreversible effects. Such is the complexity of these processes, their non-linear nature, and their feedback dynamics that even the most sophisticated calculation systems are unable to establish precisely what the points of

18 *Crisis of Civilization*

inflexion might be after which everything would change. According to the Potsdam Institute for Climate Impact Research and a number of other recognized institutions working on the issue (Potsdam Institute for Climate Impact Research et al. 2017),[4] the time available to take drastic action is extraordinarily short. According to these institutions, the goal reached in the Paris agreement to prevent the increase in global average temperature from exceeding 2°C, and as much as possible not to exceed 1.5°C above pre-industrial levels, is considered necessary to prevent incalculable risks to humanity. However, this would only be realistic if greenhouse gas emissions peak by 2020 at the latest, and then begin to decline thereafter. According to this report, if this is not achieved the planet is at risk of moving beyond thresholds that would trigger major, and fundamentally irreversible, changes in the Earth system.

How Do the Powers That Be Respond to These Challenges?

In this context of a profound crisis corroding the conditions for the reproduction of life, the imaginaries of progress, development, and end-less growth continue to guide public policies and investment priorities throughout the world system. For multilateral economic and financial organizations such as the International Monetary Fund, the growth of Gross Domestic Product continues to be the main criterion by which the results of economic activity are evaluated, an objective on the basis of which the main economic policy guidelines are formulated. In all coun-tries of the world, government performance continues to be evaluated on the basis of these same criteria. This consensus on the desirability of "strong global economic growth" was ratified in the final declaration of the G20 held in Buenos Aires at the end of 2018 (G20 2019).

In contrast to the multiple alarm signals formulated by the diagnoses referred to above, all the main projections of fossil fuel consumption point to sustained growth well beyond 2020. According to the International Energy Agency, assuming that the commitments of the Paris Agreement are met, oil demand will continue to grow at least until 2040, the last year for which the projection is made (International Energy Agency 2017). In what they call the "advanced economies," a slow reduction in green-house gas emissions should continue, with China's emissions stabilizing for a few years and then, by 2030, beginning to slowly fall. However, these reductions would be more than offset by the sustained increase that would continue to occur in what they call "the rest of the world."

Shell's 2018 Energy Transition report explores trends in greenhouse gas emissions and temperature in three possible scenarios. In only one of these, a scenario in which society takes the necessary actions to com-ply with the Paris Agreements, would it be possible to prevent the tem-perature from rising more than 2°C. "This would require sustained and unprecedented collaboration across all sectors of society, supported by highly effective government policies" (Shell 2018). The withdrawal of the United States from the Paris Agreement turned these goals into a remote possibility.

According to the enterprise BP, the use of fossil fuels will continue to grow until at least 2040, the last year for which estimates are made. Greenhouse gas emissions will also continue to increase (BP 2018, 7, 14).

ExxonMobil's projections indicate that between 2015 and 2040 the world's Gross Domestic Product will double. Between 2015 and 2030, the global middle class, with its corresponding consumption levels, will grow even more. In projections up to 2040, fossil fuel consumption continues to grow steadily until 2040 by which time 60% of the planet's energy needs would be met by oil and gas (ExxonMobil 2017).

What Would Have to Be Changed for Nothing to Change?

Whether explicitly or not, the world's economic, political, and scientific elites have been asking themselves a complex question: How can we respond to the deepening climate crisis without confronting the civilizational patterns that have led to it and challenging the power relations that today control the decisions that define the direction of the planet, without questioning the dominant forms of knowledge of colonial modernity? In other words, what would be necessary to change in order not to change anything at all?

Is it possible to give effective answers from the same economic, state, commercial, and scientific-technological patterns that have led humanity to the present crisis? Would it not be convenient to take Albert Einstein's warning seriously: "We cannot solve problems with the same mentality with which we created them."

Is it possible to propose ways out that allow the survival of human life on the planet without a radical questioning of the project of colonial modernity, that is, in the words of Santiago Castro-Gómez (2000), of the "Faustian attempt to submit the whole of life to the absolute control of man under the sure guidance of knowledge"?

Is it possible to find ways out of the profound environmental crisis without altering the extraordinary inequalities that exist, and without a drastic reduction in the consumption patterns of the richest minorities on the planet, when it is estimated that almost 50% of carbon emissions are a consequence of the activities of around 10% of the global population, that 70% of emissions are generated by 20% of the population (Anderson 2018), and "only 10 countries, with the United States at the head, are historically responsible for two-thirds of the gases emitted and that currently 10 nations are responsible for more than 70% of emissions" (Ribeiro 2018)?

From the viewpoint of the hegemonic powers, the challenge is how to limit the problems facing humanity in such a way that they can be

20   *Crisis of Civilization*

addressed without questioning the foundations of the current pattern of civilization. How to make the diagnosis in such a way that it has technological and market solutions that, far from questioning the capitalist order, reaffirm it?

There is a close, inseparable intertwining of purely ontological and epistemological dimensions that have to do with the central tenets of colonial modernity (subject/object separation, nature as an object, the dogmas of development, progress, endless growth, the imaginaries of total control over human beings and nature) on the one hand, and on the other hand, the political, geopolitical, and economic interests, the places of enunciation, from which diagnoses are formulated and solutions are proposed to the challenges facing humanity today.

A widespread pattern in the responses formulated by contemporary centers of political, economic, and scientific power is the search to reduce the complex interrelation of factors that affect climate change to few if not, preferably, one variable. If it can be synthesized in a single figure, even better. This is an expression of the radical reductionism that confuses reality with quantification. Just as the economy has tried to express the complex economic reality in a figure, the GDP, the studies, debates, and international agreements on climate change, have been moving in the direction of this same reductionist logic. The multiform dimensions of planetary environmental collapse have been reduced to one basic aspect: global warming, understood as the rise in the average temperature of the Earth's surface. This, in turn, has been reduced to a single causal determinant: the emission of greenhouse gases as mainly a consequence of the burning of fossil fuels. A synthetic indicator is then created: the figure for the concentration of greenhouse gas particles in the atmosphere, expressed in parts per million, in what Camila Moreno has called the *carbon metric*.[5] In this way, the crisis of an anthropocentric, patriarchal, and mono-cultural civilizational pattern of endless growth is limited to a technical issue. How to limit, through emission restrictions and capture mechanisms, the concentration of greenhouse gases in the atmosphere? What regulations, what technological responses, and what investments would be necessary for this goal?

As Moreno argues, the way we describe and frame a problem predetermines the type of solutions and responses we can consider. That is, while some dimensions of the problem are illuminated, others are obscured or hidden. While highlighting the relevance and usefulness of particular patterns of knowledge and their technological capabilities, others are denied or destroyed. When it comes to complex issues in relation to which there are different interpretations and divergent interests, a primary area of confrontation and assertion of unequal power relations operates precisely to control the agenda through the definition of the basic questions: How do we understand what is at stake? The extent to which a single interpretation is imposed rules out possible answers from other subjects,

Crisis of Civilization   21

other knowledges, and other perspectives, even though history has shown time and again that many of these other cultures have a greater capacity to live in harmony with nature than modern colonial logic—despite all its scientific/technological sophistication. From an authoritarian mono-cultural perspective, the possibility of other ways of life, other cultures on planet Earth, is denied. Perspectives such as *Sumak Kawsay* and *Suma Qamaña* or the defense of the rights of nature as starting points to initiate the required deep paradigmatic transformations in the relationship of human beings with the rest of the webs of life are not even granted a few moments of attention.

In this way, the diagnoses, debates, and international agreements on climate change have operated as devices that have reinforced exclusion and colonial control over the "others" whose knowledge and experiences are apparently not considered to have anything substantial to contribute to these debates. In this way, an epistemicide is being committed as Camila Moreno points out:

> [...] human-induced climate change is happening and happening fast. [...] by framing the problem in a way that is Carbon-centered, knowledge and possibilities for global communication and political action are created in ways that exclude and destroy knowledge at the same time.

> [...] translating a complex multidimensional ecological and social crisis like climate change into tons of carbon dioxide equivalent (CO_2) - which we can measure, count, own, price, and trade - not only narrows our view of what truly transformative actions could be, but rather allows for actors and interests to continue to operate the current system as they do now
> (Camila, Speich Chassé and Fuhr 2017).

Carbon metrics have enabled the assignment of a monetary value to carbon emissions, and with it the creation of *ad hoc* institutional designs labeled *carbon markets* in which the right to pollute is bought and sold nationally and internationally (Dag Hammarskjöld Foundation 2009; Transnational Institute and Carbon Trade Watch 2007). By compensating poorer countries with payments for limiting their emissions, wealthier countries and companies can maintain or increase their consumption and pollution levels. Those with greater financial resources can thus continue to appropriate a fundamental common good of the planet, the capacity to absorb/retain greenhouse gases. The colonial mechanisms aimed at reducing emissions from deforestation and forest degradation (REDD and REDD+), whereby forest management is shifted from the traditional ways of local forest dwellers to highly sophisticated scientific/technological management controlled by transnationals and large environmental

22 *Crisis of Civilization*

NGOs, constitute a particularly perverse mechanism within the logic of carbon markets (Cabello and Gilbertson 2012).

When the problem is narrowed down in these terms, the most important issues at stake remain invisible or relegated to secondary political spheres. First of all, the crucial issue of the extreme and growing inequalities that characterize today's world is left out of any diagnosis, debate, or agreement. In international climate negotiations, no one seems to have the audacity to argue that only through a radical redistribution of the use of the planet's carrying capacity would it be possible to simultaneously address the issues of the planet's limits and the fact that hundreds of millions of people lack the basic conditions for the reproduction of their own lives.

The fundamental role of the patterns of production, distribution, and food consumption of the agroindustry that produce extraordinary environmental impacts through the reduction of genetic diversity, the massive contamination of water and land with agro-toxins, and the deforestation required for the expansion of the agricultural frontier disappears in a view centered on carbon metrics. According to GRAIN, an international organization dedicated to supporting small farmers in the struggle for biodiverse, community-controlled food systems, "the use of fertilizers, pesticides, machinery and soil destruction cause just over a tenth of greenhouse gases. One of the main causes of soil destruction is that organic matter is no longer returned to the soil" (GRAIN 2010). "Collectively, five meat and dairy corporations are currently responsible for more annual greenhouse gas emissions than ExxonMobil, Shell and BP" (GRAIN 2018). Alternatives such as those that Via Campesina (an international coalition of small farmers, agricultural workers, fishers, landless, and indigenous peoples) has been proposing for years, regarding the contribution that ecological peasant agriculture can make to cooling the planet (Vía Campesina 2015), are not even considered. The experiences and knowledge of the indigenous peoples of the Amazon, who have not only lived for thousands of years in harmony with their environment but who, through their farming practices, have contributed to creating ecological systems of greater biological diversity, are considered unscientific, by which these voices are excluded even from projects related to their own territories. If the problem of energy consumption is addressed exclusively as an issue of greenhouse gas emissions, there is no need to question the levels of energy consumption that are assumed to inevitably continue to grow in a sustained manner. Consequently, all forms of energy generation that contribute to limiting emissions are considered suitable alternatives.

From this perspective, attempts have been made to relegitimize nuclear energy (Public Citizen; Union of Concerned Scientists 2018). Even the prominent environmentalist James Lovelock, creator of the Gaia hypothesis, has argued that nuclear energy is the only option to save the planet (McCarthy 2004).

Crisis of Civilization 23

The virtues of wind and solar energy as clean energy sources are high-lighted, without incorporating the consequences of large-scale mining in the Global South into the analysis. The fact that these sources do not produce emissions in their energy generation phase is celebrated, but the limits on the realization of aspirations that exist today in communities around the world for access to energy as a right and the democratic, local, and sovereign control of energy production and management as a result of the mega wind and solar installations controlled by large corporations is left out of the debate.

Large hydroelectric dams are promoted as clean energy, despite their devastating environmental impacts, including massive emissions during the construction phase. Rivers have fundamental functions in the preservation of ecosystems all over the planet.

> In many places, connected, free-flowing rivers are crucial for carrying sediment downstream, bringing nutrients to floodplain soils, maintaining floodplains and deltas that protect against extreme weather events, and providing recreational opportunities or spiritual fulfilment
>
> (WWF et al. 2016, 36).

And yet, according to the 2016 Living Planet Report, nearly half of the total volume of the planet's rivers has been altered by regulating or fragmenting their flows. If the 3,700 large irrigation or hydroelectric dams that have been planned or are under construction were completed, 93% of the natural flow of the planet's rivers would be affected (WWF et al. 2016, 34). Opposition to large dams that displace populations from their territories is currently one of the most widespread pockets of resistance throughout the Global South, particularly in Latin America (Gómez 2014; Gómez Fuentes and Copitz Ahahí 2015; RED-DESC n.d.).

In the name of environmental protection, from a perspective focused on the effects of burning fossil fuels, agrofuels have been promoted as ecological. In this way, food production is being replaced by the production of fuel for vehicles, despite the fact that more than 800 million people suffer from chronic malnutrition. The food sovereignty of indigenous peoples is under particular threat. With the expansion of the monoculture frontier for this purpose, processes of deforestation and the loss of forest biodiversity are accelerating, thus contributing to the acceleration of the climate transformations that they are supposed to be trying to limit (Global Forest Coalition 2008). After years of the European Union promoting biofuels as friendlier to the planet than fossil fuels, recent research has concluded that palm oil-based fuels are three times more harmful to the environment than fossil fuels. In addition to greenhouse gas emissions, there are the impacts of deforestation, peatland destruction, impacts on

24   *Crisis of Civilization*

biodiversity, and population displacement (Malins 2017). Based on these results, the Norwegian parliament has decided to ban the import of palm oil from 2020 (Chow 2018).

One of the most notorious examples of the blocking of alternatives that operates as a consequence of reductionist diagnoses, such as that of carbon metrics, is the way in which electric cars are incorporated into the debate and policies on climate change. There are multiple economic, social, and cultural impacts the global spread of individual automobile use has had all over the planet. The pressure on territories generated by large-scale metal mining required for its production, especially in the Global South, is extraordinary; it has contributed to the unviable expansion of cities (*urban sprawl*), produces over a million deaths per year due to automobile accidents, takes the city away from pedestrians and alters spaces for shared socialization, contributes to the increase in the number of cardiovascular diseases due to people walking less, aids the celebration of social inequalities insofar as cars become symbols of prestige and ostentation, aids in blocking the establishment of efficient public transport systems, and, as a result of congestion, significantly increases the time that city dwellers have to spend on their daily commute. When they operate with internal combustion engines, they contribute to urban pollution and global warming through the emission of greenhouse gases. When the "problem" of the automobile is reduced exclusively to the latter, to the emission of greenhouse gases, a technical solution is possible: the introduction of electric cars. All other dimensions of individual car culture are excluded from the debate. By presenting them as "green," governments and automobile corporations re-legitimize the individual car as the normal mode of transport in modern society. Through subsidies and other public incentives, the shift from internal combustion to electric cars has been encouraged as a way to increase demand and boost economic growth (Brie and Candeia 2012). According to projections released by the Global Economic Forum in Davos, it is estimated that by 2040 the number of mobile cars will have doubled compared to their current state (World Economic Forum 2016). Despite all the celebrations about the virtues of the electric car, ExxonMobil estimates that by 2040, approximately 80% of cars will still be running on fossil fuels (ExxonMobil 2017).

The Green Economy

The most ambitious strategic proposal that has been formulated from the economic, political, and scientific centers of today's hegemony has been the green economy. These are formulations by which means, in the name of preserving life on the planet, the doors are opened to take advantage of the environmental crisis to create a new sphere of capital accumulation through deepening the control and commodification of nature.

Crisis of Civilization 25

Following the same course of previous legitimizing theoretical constructions, like *sustainable development* (United Nations General Assembly 1987)—an epistemological theoretical device created to seek and save the dogma of development in the face of the growing evidence that humanity was being led toward a precipice—in preparation for the United Nations Conference on Sustainable Development, Rio +20, held in Rio de Janeiro in 2012, the United Nations Development Programme (UNDP) produced a document, with the contribution of experts from all over the world, of more than 600 pages in which the environmental problems facing the planet are explored in great detail. With the proposal of the green economy, it seeks to define a new conceptual framework within which the debates, negotiations, and policy-making processes of all countries and multilateral agencies should take place (United Nations Environment Programme 2011).

The concept of a green economy intends to achieve the magic of enabling both the continuation and even acceleration of economic growth and the protection of the planet. It is an extraordinary synthesis of techno-fix and market solutions to address the crisis that humanity is experiencing. It is a sophisticated effort to demonstrate that it is possible to solve the problems of the environmental crisis of the planet without altering the global structure of power in the world system, nor the existing relations of domination and exploitation in it. Throughout the report, it is argued that only with the same market mechanisms and scientific and technological patterns, with the same logic of sustained growth, will it be possible to save life on the planet. With this, they seek to overcome the so-called myth that there is a trade-off between economic progress and environmental sustainability.

According to the UN Environment Programme (UNEP), the transition to a green economy can relaunch the global economy with growth rates that are much higher than would be possible under the current model. It would generate more and better jobs, reduce poverty, achieve greater levels of equity, and meet the Millennium Development Goals, all in a way that would be sustainable, that is, recognizing the value of nature, reducing the emission of greenhouse gases and the pressure on the natural environment, thus, allowing its recovery. All this, of course, by creating new and profitable areas of investment that would make it possible for global capital to emerge from its current crisis and increase its rates of profit. Accordingly, it is not about questioning the possibility of sustained economic growth, nor the notion of progress, but of reorienting investment and technological innovation in the direction of the green economy. By displaying a stubborn inability to at least imagine that another world is possible, it is argued that the most important determinant of the current crisis has been the misallocation of capital. It is, therefore, about market failures. They argue that during the last decades, most investments were made in real estate, fossil fuels, and financial assets. Comparatively little

26 Crisis of Civilization

has been invested in renewable energy, energy efficiency, public transport, sustainable agriculture, protection of ecosystems and biodiversity, and soil and water conservation. The problem would then lie in the fact that the market has been operating by the wrong signals. The proposed solution is therefore aimed at creating other signals for the markets so that activities that contribute to the preservation of life are more profitable than those that harm it.

The realization of these severe "market failures" and their extraordinarily dangerous consequences for life on the planet did not lead UNEP to even think about the possibility that these signals may be the result of the growing power of financial markets in the definition of public policies, of the growing subjugation of all other social logic, be it democracy, equity, solidarity, or even the preservation of life, to a single criterion: the maximization of short-term profit for capital. According to the report in question, the problem is much narrower, a problem that can be solved without the need for structural transformations in the operation of the system, let alone taking the civilizational order into consideration. Viewed through this lens, the only problem is that "markets" have been operating on the basis of "failures of information," the non-incorporation of the cost of "externalities," and on the basis of inadequate public policies such as "perverse or environmentally harmful subsidies." The solutions proposed in the report are therefore a set of "necessary policy guidelines" to change the regulatory context, incentives, and conditions of access to information in which markets operate.

The transition to the green economy and its new technological bases would require investments in the order of billions of trillions of dollars, amounts that only global financial capital and large transnational corporations can count on. Thus, the future of the planet would depend on the states, through tax policies, regulations, incentives, and investments, to redirect this sum of private investments from the "brown economy" to the "green economy."[6]

Also problematic are the processes of financialization of nature-based, among others, on the notion of the tragedy of the commons formulated by Garrett Hardin (1968). Many currents of liberalism defend the idea that, in order to protect nature, it is indispensable to assign it both an owner and a monetary value. *Environmental services, carbon markets,* and the aforementioned *REDD* and *REDD+* are the main instruments through which the environmental crisis is exploited to create new spheres of capital appreciation and advance in the centralized corporate and state control of the planet's *common goods*, imposing mercantile logics on the territories of aboriginal peoples and peasants. In this way, the operation of other cultural logics regarding the relationship with the natural environment that for millennia has allowed human coexistence with the rest of the webs of life is hindered or prevented.

Geoengineering

The search for technological solutions to the environmental crisis, based on the arrogance that makes people believe that it is possible to have full control over all of nature's processes, finds one of its most extreme expressions in geoengineering.

This Promethean notion of man as master and owner of nature (man in a masculine sense, because it is a patriarchal civilizing pattern) seeks to bring to its full realization the dream of Francis Bacon who, from the very origins of modernity, conceived of knowledge as power, as the ability to subdue, control, and bend the forces of nature. Genetic engineering (manipulation of the codes of life) and geoengineering are the most extreme and dangerous examples of operating within these imaginaries and the incapacity to even imagine options outside this framework. According to the ETC Group:

> Geoengineering is the intentional, large-scale intervention in the Earth's oceans, soils and/or atmosphere, most often discussed in the context of combating climate change. Geoengineering can refer to a wide range of schemes, including: blasting sulphate particles into the stratosphere to reflect the sun's rays; dumping iron particles in the oceans to nurture CO2 -absorbing plankton; firing silver iodide into clouds to produce rain; geneticallyengineering crops so their foliage can better reflect sunlight.

> [...]

> Equally unsurprising is that once the smog clears, the major private sector players in geoengineering will likely be the same energy, chemical, forestry and agribusiness companies that bear a large responsibility for creating our current climate predicament – in effect, the same folks who geoengineered us into this mess in the first place.

> [...]

> Opting for geoengineering flies in the face of precaution. Even some of those who would like to see large-scale investment in the field are quick to acknowledge that we do not know enough about the Earth's systems to risk intentional geoengineering, or even to risk real-world geoengineering experiments.

> [...] In other words, geoengineering uses new technologies to try to rectify the problems created by the use of old technologies, a classic techno-fix

(ETC Group 2010, 3).

28   *Crisis of Civilization*

Once some of these complex global technological systems were in place, they would have to be permanently monitored and maintained, since they are artificial technological regimes with no capacity for self-regulation. This would require centralized technocratic controls, denying any possibility of democratically determined and decided choices about the future of the planet. All this is frighteningly close to the dystopias of environmental authoritarianism.

These technological delusions have another consequence. On the basis of blind confidence that the technological solutions required to limit and counteract the damage being done to the planet will be available in the short term, action on the structural causes of the planetary crisis can continue to be postponed. Without international regulation of any kind, in disregarding the precautionary principle, hundreds of geo-engineering experiments and projects are being carried out all over the planet. According to systematic monitoring by the ETC Group and the Heinrich Böll Foundation, between 2012 and the present, the number of geoengineering activities has increased from 300 to 800, a record that is necessarily partial. This includes carbon sequestration projects, solar radiation management, weather alteration, and other approaches. This information has been systematized into an interactive map of the activities around the world.[7]

Guided by unbridled instrumental rationality, detached from all ethical considerations, these sorcerers' apprentices are gambling with the future of life. Given the extraordinary power of the technological instruments at our disposal, it is becoming more and more urgent to incorporate into human action the warning given decades ago by the German philosopher Hans Jonas (1984) on the increasing ethical responsibility of humans in the technological age with the view that 'the technological capacity of humans to produce changes in nature will always be greater than the scientific capacity to foresee the effects of these alterations.'

Anthropocene or the Age of Plutocracy? The Profound Inequalities in the Distribution of Wealth and Political, Communicational, and Military Power That Characterizes the Present Post-Democratic World

It would be inexplicable that humanity continued to advance in apparent somnambulism in the direction of environmental devastations that had been foreseen, publicized, and experienced by hundreds of millions of people, were we not living in a capitalist, post-democratic society, characterized by levels of concentration of wealth like never before in the history of humanity. A very small proportion of humanity today has the capacity to direct major decisions about the present and the future of the planet drawn from their conceptions of the world and their short-term economic and political interests. In the words of Silvia Ribeiro:

> Environmental problems are serious, with strong and unequal social impacts, and climate change is one of the main ones. But they are not caused by "humanity as a whole." Rather than the age of Anthropocene, as some call it, we live in the age of plutocracy, where everything is defined so that the very few rich and powerful in the world can maintain and increase their profits, at the expense of everything and everyone else. This absurd social, economic, environmental, and political injustice requires many weapons to maintain itself, and one of them is conceptual warfare. Inventing concepts that hide the causes and characteristics of reality, that divert attention from the need for real and profound changes and better yet, that serve to make new businesses out of the crises
>
> (Ribeiro 2016).

These deep and growing inequalities exist between continents, between countries and within countries, between men and women, and between different human groups that have been hierarchized by the political/ epistemological device of the racialization of all populations on the planet throughout the time of colonial modernity.[8] Although, measured in terms of monetary income, global poverty has declined in recent decades; inequalities have simultaneously increased.

Oxfam is the international social activist organization that has most systematically dedicated itself to studying and denouncing the growing inequalities that characterize contemporary societies. According to the 2018 report on global inequalities, 42 people have the same wealth as the 3.7 billion people with the least wealth and the richest 1% continue to possess more wealth than the rest of humanity (Oxfam International 2018).

According to Credit Suisse, North America, roughly 6% of the world's global population, has more than 36% of the world's wealth; while India, around 16% of the world's population, has about 3%; and Africa, about 13% of the total population, has less than 2%. While 36 million people, or 0.7% of the world's population, own 45.5% of the global wealth; 3,474 million people, 70.1% of the total population, own only 2.7% of global wealth. This wealth is, in turn, highly concentrated geographically. The United States has 43% of the total number of millionaires on the planet. According to Credit Suisse, 51% of people who own more than US$50 million, a total of 75,000, are residents of the United States (Credit Suisse Research Institute 2017).

The *World Inequality Report* (*2018*) reports that, during the post-war decades, inequalities tended to fall around the world but that, since 1980, there has been a sustained increase in inequalities with a trend

30   *Crisis of Civilization*

toward a pattern of high inequality, even in countries such as Russia and China, which four decades ago had significantly lower levels of inequality. Between 1980 and 2016, the bottom 50% of income earners received 13% of total growth, while the top 1% of income earners received 27% of total growth. Between the years 1980 and 2016, in the United States, the share of the richest 1% of the population in total income rose from 10% to 20%, while the share of the bottom 50% of income fell from over 20% to 13%. According to the report, the relationship between public and private wealth is a "crucial determinant" of the level of inequality in countries. Since 1980, in virtually all countries, the share of wealth in the hands of the public sector has declined while that in private ownership has increased. In the case of China, the weighting of public capital in the economy as a whole was halved between those years, while in the United States and the United Kingdom, public net wealth (public assets minus public debt) has turned negative (Alvaredo, Chancel, Piketty, Saez, and Zuman 2018).

Who Decides the Future of the Planet?

In addition to the obvious consequences in terms of the levels of exclusion and inequalities that result from this brutally unequal appropriation of the *commons*, the impacts of the global strengthening of economic, and therefore political, power in this small minority of the super-rich, the so-called Davos class, on the climate crisis have been extraordinary in terms of the functioning of political systems and decision-making processes.[9]

Despite the displacements that have occurred as a result of the emergence of new economic sectors and their corresponding large corporations such as Apple, Samsung, Microsoft, Facebook, and Google, the hydrocarbon and automotive corporations ExxonMobil, Petrochina, Shell, Chevron, Sinopec, BP, Total, Toyota, Volkswagen, General Motors, and Ford continue to be among the largest corporations in the world, and, thus, continue to have an extraordinary capacity for political influence. This capacity to influence the public agenda and government decisions is particularly notable in the case of the United States, where it has led to public policies that, far from slowing environmental devastation, are accelerating it.

When the environmental crisis became a major focus of world public opinion, international negotiations began to take place, and demands for national regulations and international agreements to limit climate change grew louder, alarm bells started ringing in the hydrocarbon industry corporate groups, such as Exxon, and a broad and well-funded effort to prevent policies that would limit their profit margins was deployed. Using the same arguments that the tobacco industry had been using to deny their negative health effects, despite their own research that strongly demonstrated the opposite, the big oil companies carried out a multi-million dollar campaign to deny the link between greenhouse gas emissions and climate change or demonstrate that the negative impacts of climate change were being irresponsibly exaggerated (Fahey 2012).

Exxon was an active participant in the most important coalition of business organizations that sought to influence climate change debates on an international level, denying its existence and opposing any regulation aimed at reducing greenhouse gas emissions. This so-called *Global Climate Coalition* was active between 1989 and 2001 (Wikipedia 2018).

Among the right-wing institutions that continue to this day to play an active role in producing materials and propagating climate change denialist positions is the Heartland Institute, whose stated mission is to "discover, develop, and promote free-market solutions to social and economic problems" (The Heartland Institute). In addition to well-funded public meetings with extensive media outreach, its *Science and Environmental Policy Project* produces materials through which they seek to "scientifically" demonstrate the falsity of global warming. One of the areas in which this institute has devoted the most effort is the promotion of what they call the Nongovernmental Panel on Climate Change. This is defined as an international group of international academics and scientists totally independent of governments and all political pressure and influence. According to the Heartland Institute, it differs sharply from the International Panel on Climate Change, which is sponsored by governments and accused of being politically motivated and predisposed to believe that climate change is a problem that requires a solution (The Nongovernmental Panel on Climate Change 2017). The critique of what this group considers to be the distortions of the IPCC reports is synthesized in publications such as *Nature, Not Human Activities, Rules the Climate*, and *Climate Change Re-considered II. Biological Impacts* (Idso et al. 2014; Singer 2008).

Beyond this type of intervention on specific aspects of the climate debate, or in those referring to environmental regulation, the growing concern about what they were seeing on the horizon as a threat, not only to their economic interests but also to the future of capitalism, has led some conservative business sectors in the United States to develop a multidimensional, long-term strategy aimed not only at influencing governmental decision-making processes and the content of the media but, even more ambitiously, at waging a cultural war aimed at altering the shared meanings of society. This is properly speaking a strategy aimed at the creation of a new Gramscian-style hegemony with a "libertarian" content, that is, a demand for a minimal state and the full pre-eminence of mercantile relations in society as a whole. The most systematic, best funded, and, undoubtedly, most successful efforts in this direction have been led by the brothers Charles G. and David Koch. Between them, they have one of the largest fortunes in the world, estimated at over one hundred

32   *Crisis of Civilization*

billion dollars, based on a wide range of economic activities, the most important of which are associated with fossil fuels (International Forum on Globalization). They have spent hundreds of millions of dollars over the decades to fund universities, research centers, scholarship programs, "libertarian," and right-wing think tanks such as the Cato Institute and the Heritage Foundation, and the media. They have supported and fostered diverse groups across the country on issues such as the fight for a ban on abortion, teaching evolution in school as just another theory on the same level as the so-called *creationism*, the fight against government intervention/regulation in all areas of collective life, opposition to the expansion of the public health care system, and defense of religious freedom. They have also widely funded election campaigns for candidates at all levels of the state structure who would be willing to defend the interests and free market ideology of the Kochs.

These systematic and sustained efforts are beginning to bear fruit in the national political arena with the emergence of the movement known as the Tea Party, on the fringes, and within the Republican Party. From the beginning, this movement, which presents itself as a spontaneous grassroots popular rebellion against the country's elites and against the interference of Washington in collective life, was able to count on the political support and very generous contributions from Americans for Prosperity, the Kochs' main political activist organization, and others from the wide range of organizations operated by the Kochs alone or with their corporate allies. Bolstered by intense grassroots activism in the 2010 Republican Party primaries and appealing to so-called "libertarian," anti-elite, and anti-state positions across the country, the so-called Tea Party revolution led to significant rightward shifts in the Republican Party.

One of the arguments that has been used most effectively in this battle is the claim that environmental protection policies constitute an expansion of state intervention, that is, an unacceptable interference in the exercise of individual and corporate freedom, threatening the fundamental individualistic values of American society. To confront environmental regulations, which usually imply additional costs for polluting economic activities, the language of "environmental taxes" has been developed. Promoted by the close alliance between the Tea Party movement and Americans for Prosperity, there has been a strong campaign to get "every elected official" at every level of government in the United States to sign a statement pledging not to support any environmental protection initiative that raises taxes or government revenues. Of the 85 newly elected Republican representatives in the U.S. House of Representatives in 2010, 76 had taken this oath as candidates, 57 of whom received financial support from the Koch organizations for their election campaign.

All of this is taking place in the context of an extraordinary increase in the role of money in the U.S. political system. In that country where the power of money has historically operated in a stark form, in 2010, the Supreme Court adopted a decision that extraordinarily increased the power of corporations over the entire political system.[10] Based on the unusual assumption that corporations have the same rights as individuals, this Court reversed restrictions that were more than a century old, as well as constitutional doctrines that had been reaffirmed by various decisions of previous courts and Congress throughout history. It ruled that placing limitations on corporate and union spending in election-eering was a constitutional violation of free speech as provided by the First Constitutional Amendment. Given the exorbitant costs of election campaigns in the United States, this decision further strengthened the power of lobbyists to buy legislative and executive decisions that favored their interests. The provision was celebrated by the U.S. right wing as a restoration of the basic principles of the republic, whereas it has been described as a severe attack on democracy by politically liberal and left-ist sectors.[11]

This background sets the stage for the Trump administration's aggressive policies of promoting fossil fuels and dismantling environmental regulations. In his election campaign, Trump repeatedly denounced the institutional legal framework for environmental protection that had been created in the United States during the previous half-century and offered to begin dismantling it as soon as he became president.

From the first days of his administration, Trump sought to differentiate himself as radically as possible from the environmental policies promoted by the Obama administration in the energy and environmental sphere. Republican control of both houses of Congress gave him an extraordinary margin of freedom to advance this agenda. On the first day of his presidency, the White House website announced that Obama's *Environmental Action Plan* would be eliminated (Temple 2017). Shortly after his inauguration, he firmly issued the executive order *Promoting Energy Independence and Economic Growth* (The White House 2017a), which defines "the national interest to promote clean and safe development of our Nation's vast energy resources, while at the same time avoiding regulatory burdens that unnecessarily encumber energy production, constrain economic growth, and prevent job creation [...] the prudent development of these natural resources is essential to ensuring the Nation's geopolitical security." All key executive departments were instructed to review in the very short term all regulations that could potentially limit energy production in order to "suspend, revise, or rescind" these regulations. At the same time, a wide range of presidential regulatory actions relating to energy and climate issues were repealed.

In all ministries and other governmental institutions that had some relation to energy and environmental issues, only those who shared this agenda of accelerated deregulation and support for the fossil industry were promoted by Trump to leading posts.

34   *Crisis of Civilization*

In June 2017, six months into his presidency, Trump launched the energy component of his global strategy called "America First." To significant share of the energy industry, Trump presented his energy plan "Unleashing American Energy." In this presentation, Trump detailed his conceptions of the relationship between energy and the environment and announced what his main energy policies would be in order to achieve not only energy independence but also *energy dominance* for the United States. It is worth quoting in detail:

> Our country is blessed with extraordinary energy abundance, which we didn't know of, even five years ago and certainly ten years ago. We have nearly 100 years' worth of natural gas and more than 250 years' worth of clean, beautiful coal. We are a top producer of petroleum and the number-one producer of natural gas. We have so much more than we ever thought possible. We are really in the driving seat. And you know what? We don't want to let other countries take away our sovereignty and tell us what to do and how to do it. That's not going to happen. (Applause.) With these incredible resources, my administration will seek not only American energy independence that we've been looking for so long, but American energy dominance.
>
> […]
>
> This vast energy wealth does not belong to the government. It belongs to the people of the United States of America. (Applause.) Yet, for the past eight years, the federal government imposed massive job-killing barriers to American energy development.
>
> […]
>
> I'm dramatically reducing restrictions on the development of natural gas. I cancelled the moratorium on a new coal leasing—and you know what was happening—the new coal leasing on federal lands, it was being so terribly restricted.
>
> […]
>
> We have finally ended the war on coal.
>
> […]
>
> We're ending intrusive EPA regulations that kill jobs, hurt family farmers and ranchers, and raise the price of energy so quickly and so substantially.

Crisis of Civilization   35

In order to protect American jobs, companies and workers, we've withdrawn the United States from the one-sided Paris Climate Accord. (Applause.)

[…]

Today, I am proudly announcing six brand-new initiatives to propel this new era of American energy dominance.

[…]

The golden era of American energy is now underway. And I'll go a step further: The golden era of America is now underway. Believe me (Applause.)

(Trump 2017).

This language and these priorities in relation to climate change and energy policy are expressed in all their radicalness in the Trump administration's first national security document for the year 2017. The concept of climate change is not once mentioned in this 68-page document, and the expansion of energy production and economic growth take full precedence over environmental protection. The concept of *energy security* is essentially replaced by that of *energy dominance*:

For the first time in generations, the United States will be an energy-dominant nation. Energy dominance—America's central position in the global energy system as a leading producer, consumer, and innovator—ensures that markets are free and U.S. infrastructure is resilient and secure. It ensures that access to energy is diversified, and recognizes the importance of environmental stewardship.

Climate policies will continue to shape the global energy system. U.S. leadership is indispensable to countering an anti-growth energy agenda that is detrimental to U.S. economic and energy security interests

(The White House 2017b, 22).

To achieve these objectives, the document states that it is necessary to confront this anti-growth agenda and achieve a reduction of greenhouse gas emissions, not through onerous regulations, but through technological innovations.

As Michael Klare notes, "[…] the expansion of the fossil fuel industry and its exports has been transformed into a major component of American foreign and security policy" (2018).

These are not just policy statements and doctrinaire documents. The Trump administration years saw a very wide-ranging decision on a vast

36   *Crisis of Civilization*

spectrum of energy and environmental fields stemming from these doctrinal orientations.

It is not possible to present an exhaustive list of the Trump administration's policies and regulatory modifications. The list is very extensive and new decisions have been added every week. Based on the systematic tracking of environmental decisions by two teams at Harvard University and Columbia University, New York Times reporters had identified 57 environmental rules that had been overturned or were in the process of being overturned as of the end of January 2018 (Popovich, Albeck-Ripka, and Pierre-Louis 2018).

The implementation of the Trump administration's energy and environmental policies will have extraordinary impacts not only for the United States but also for life on the planet. By "unleashing" the energy production of even the most polluting sources such as coal and fracking and withdrawing the United States from the Paris Agreement in order to achieve global energy dominance, the administration of the most powerful country on the planet is undermining the viability of the modest agreements for limiting greenhouse gas emission that had been agreed to in multilateral negotiations. These policies are further reducing the chances that atmospheric temperatures can be prevented from rising more than 2°C above the pre-Industrial Revolution average, a threshold beyond which, as noted above, it is estimated that planetary environmental transformations of both a catastrophic and irreversible nature could occur.[12]

The United States is not alone in this commitment to unlimited fossil energy growth. At COP 24 in Poland in December 2018, it was joined in this stance by delegations from the other two major oil producers, Saudi Arabia and Russia, and also by Kuwait (Hanley 2018).

Trump's policies have already had a significant impact on the increase in global bank financing of the exploitation of the most polluting fossil fuels. According to a report by the Rainforest Action Network on the relationship between the global financial system and the fossil industry of 2018,[13] financing by global banking for the exploitation of extreme fossil fuels (coal, tar sands, Arctic, and ultra-deep sea mining, and liquefied natural gas), which had fallen after the Paris Agreement, rose again in the first year of the Trump administration. Financing for oil sands grew by 11% between 2016 and 2017.[14,15] After the Paris Agreement, financing for coal mining remained stable, but outside of China, it doubled in 2017. Both US and European banks significantly increased the financing of coal mining between 2016 and 2017 (Rainforest Action Network 2018).

In Trump's ambitions to regain full U.S. hegemony in the contemporary world system, the extreme risks to life posed by this government's energy and environmental policies are being complemented by an increasingly aggressive foreign policy and an extraordinary increase in the military budget to 700 billion U.S. dollars (Superville 2018).

The Republican Party and the Trump administration today represent a dangerous radicalization of each of the major negative dimensions of civilization in crisis: anthropocentrism, progress, development, patriarchy, racism, xenophobia, homophobia, militarism [...].

Noam Chomsky is right when he states that the Republican Party, now led without much resistance by Donald Trump, has become the "most dangerous organization in human history," and that the world has never seen an organization so deeply dedicated to the destruction of planet Earth (Oppenheim 2017).

The year 2018 was particularly critical from the point of view of the planetary environmental crisis. Multiple scientific reports that were released throughout the year, only some of which have been cited in this text, present increasingly alarming diagnoses of the planet's situation. The IPCC presented the report requested by the Climate Change Conference/COP 23 held in Paris on the implications of a 1.5°C temperature rise. The report was approved by all governments, including the United States, in Incheon, South Korea, in October 2018. According to this report, based on two years of analysis of 6,000 scientific papers, a temperature increase of 1.5°C, which during the Paris Agreement negotiations in 2015 had been assumed to be relatively safe, actually poses severe risks. They conclude that unprecedented changes are required in the short term and that we are far from taking the necessary measures. They affirm that greenhouse gas emissions would need to be reduced by 45% from 2010 levels by 2030, 12 years from now, and reach net zero emissions by 2050 if a global climate catastrophe including the total destruction of coral reefs, the disappearance of Arctic ice, and the destruction of communities living on islands in different parts of the planet is to be avoided (Intergovernmental Panel on Climate Change 2018).

And yet, regardless of these debates, greenhouse gas emissions continue to grow, with an estimated global increase of 2% in 2018 (Global Carbon Budget 2018). The years 2015, 2016, 2017, and 2018 have been the four warmest years on record.

Against this backdrop, some of the super-rich, who have built themselves bunkers to survive the catastrophe that they assume to be inevitable, worry about how to maintain the obedience of their employees and armed guards when, with the collapse, money loses its efficacy as an incentive (Rushkoff 2018; Zibechi 2018).

Progressive Latin American Governments in the Face of the Civilizational Crisis

The reflection on the experiences of the three so-called "progresista" governments from Bolivia, Ecuador, and Venezuela is carried out in this text based on the challenges that the civilizational crisis facing humanity today poses for any project of societal transformation. The question posed is a

38   *Crisis of Civilization*

narrow one: *how have these processes of transformation responded to the complex and multidimensional challenges posed by this civilizational crisis when what is at stake is the very survival of humanity and life itself?* This is not an arbitrary question, for at least two reasons. First, what may have been considered "revolutionary" or transformative in another historical moment may no longer be so in the contemporary world. The evaluation of the depth of a process of social transformation cannot, therefore, be based on abstract, universal, ahistorical criteria, rather it depends on power structures, relations with the rest of so-called "nature," the means of production, and the cultural practices and imaginaries that characterize the historical pattern of domination being confronted. As argued above, this is the classist, anthropocentric, patriarchal, racist, colonial, and mono-cultural pattern of power that has led humanity to the current crisis of civilization. Second, this approach is justified by the fact that, to an important extent, overcoming these multiple dimensions of the hegemonic pattern of power of the capitalist world system is, at least partially, among the main objectives enunciated in the founding documents of these processes of change, their rich constitutional debates, and the final content of the new constitutions of these three countries.

Consequently, without ignoring the importance of other essential issues, the focus will not be on an evaluation of the management of these governments from the point of view of the impact of their social policies aimed at improving the living conditions of the population or their implications in the geopolitical sphere. The emphasis is placed on those dimensions that have to do directly with the way in which these political processes account for and respond to the main challenges of the civilizational crisis that humanity is experiencing today. This is not done with the expectation of magical solutions that could alter, in the short term, the dominant civilizational features and patterns of power, but by asking to what extent these projects have pointed toward confronting and questioning those patterns, today hegemonic, in the transition toward solutions to the current civilizational crisis.

While most of the world was experiencing losses on the Left, the profound disenchantment with the idea of socialism that, for many, was produced by the fall of the Berlin Wall, the collapse of the Soviet bloc, "the end of history," the economic, cultural, and military hegemony of the United States, the announcement of the New American Century[...] Latin America appeared as the *continent of hope* in the form of the so-called progressive governments.

What were the historical prospects of the proposed transformations, the main strategic orientations, the imaginaries of change present in these new progressive governments and the social forces that represented their political/social support bases? The so-called "progressive" processes are in no way characterized by unitary political ideological and/or programmatic content.

Crisis of Civilization 39

According to Raúl Zibechi (2010), in Latin America, "the political-social reality [was] shaped not by a single scenario but by three": the struggles to overcome U.S. domination, capitalism, and development. That is, the simultaneous presence of anti-imperialist and anti-capitalist tendencies and pathways and the search for alternatives to development. It would make sense to add to these, at least, two other prospects. The first would be that of national popular projects, which give priority to industrialization, democratization, inclusion, and redistribution, which could be characterized as pending tasks of the imaginary—all present in these societies—of the construction of democratic nation-states of social welfare, with greater or lesser levels of populism. And, second, the prospect of the modernization of the state.

These are not historically exclusive alternatives, nor are they easily complementary, but instead involve trends and options that have been complexly intertwined and confronted in these political processes.

As Arturo Escobar (2007) has pointed out, the names used to refer to these processes of change illustrate this extraordinary complexity: "Socialism of the twenty-first century, plurinationality, interculturality, substantive democracy, citizen revolution, endogenous development focused on *buen vivir*, cultural and territorial autonomy, decolonial projects in the direction of post-liberal societies [...]"

The simultaneity of these projects gives rise to tensions and conflicts in these processes of change, shaping the different axes that articulate the conflicts of their societies. Even though these different projects for change may be simultaneously present in public discourse and appear in some way articulated in the proposals of the governments of these countries, at different times, one axis or another may acquire particular relevance or urgency. This not only means that certain processes and confrontations of other dimensions are placed on a lesser plane, but also that they may lose visibility, either in the public debate or the priorities of the government.

A fundamental axis of the political struggles from these years was built around the conflicts between popular democratic processes, on the one hand, and privileged national sectors and transnational interests, on the other. These conflicts arose over such key issues as the national control of common goods that were in the hands of transnationals or the struggles over land distribution and the search for greater levels of equity. These confrontations can be understood in either the code of the classic opposition between Left and Right or that of a national popular struggle against an exclusionary social order. These agendas often appeared in association with the prospects of socialism.

However, these confrontations only account for part of the basic contradictions present. In the cases of Ecuador and Bolivia, in addition to these popular national struggles, other political-civilizational logics have been present that gave priority to the decolonization of the mono-cultural

40 Crisis of Civilization

liberal state on the way to the construction of a new *Plurinational State* and the cultural patterns of *buen vivir* or living well based on other productive modalities, other forms of knowledge, other forms of authority, and other ways of relating to the rest of the networks of life.

In the national popular logic, and in the prospects of socialism, national sovereignty, democratization, and redistribution of wealth have priority. This has been associated with the development of a stronger sovereign state with a presence throughout the national territory, capable of formulating and implementing public policies in favor of the popular sectors, and increasing social spending: education, health, employment, social security, the fight against poverty, and subsidies for the neediest families. In the logic of decolonization, priority is given to plurinationality, the right to differences, the sovereignty of indigenous peoples over their own territories, the autonomy of peoples, communities and movements, legal pluralism, the rejection of developmentalism/extractivism, as well as the recognition of the rights of Mother Earth. The struggle for decolonization points toward a profound civilizational transformation that questions not only capitalism but also the patterns of production and knowledge of the dominant Western culture, which is synthesized in the notion of *buen vivir*.

Constituent Processes

The coexistence of diverse normative outlooks regarding the desired society finds its expression in the appearance of important tensions present in the constitutional texts themselves, tensions that tend in all cases to become more accentuated over time in the years of the progressive governments.[15] Alongside other orientations that are also present (strengthening of state-centrism, the goal of modernizing the state, the imaginaries of the social welfare state...), there are three fundamental axes or dimensions contained with greater or lesser weight in these constitutional texts that, while addressing fundamental alternatives to colonial modernity, announce the aspiration for profound ruptures with the last century of the socialist tradition. It is these novel and radical axes that defined their foundational potential, rupturing the political traditions of colonial modernity in the continent. The centrality of these axes in the constitutions of Ecuador and Bolivia is extraordinary, with less weight in the case of Venezuela.

These axes, which represent other utopian outlooks, are the following: in the first place, the *confrontation with anthropocentrism* expressed in the recognition of the rights of nature, the defense of Mother Earth. This shows an extraordinary ontological and epistemological rupture with the fundamental assumptions of colonial modernity: the subject/object separation; the conception of nature as an object to be appropriated, manipulated, and used by human beings for their own material well-being. In the

Crisis of Civilization 41

face of the predatory patriarchal anthropocentric logic of endless growth, development, and progress and a conception of human happiness based on the accumulation of material goods, notions of balance and harmony with the rest of the webs of life are incorporated. These *other* worldviews of indigenous peoples, Afro-descendants, and peasants that differ from colonial modernity, although not characterized in the texts in a coherent way, leave a powerful alternative imprint on the documents in the cases of Ecuador and Bolivia.

Second, the postulation of *plurinational states* and *interculturality* foregrounds the need for a radical break with more than five centuries of mono-cultural state authoritarianism, colonial as well as republican. Unlike limited liberal multiculturalism, this poses a radical questioning or even a rupture with said mono-cultural order. Plurinationality and interculturality formulate transformative outlooks that, while recognizing the current geographic borders of national states, postulate the goal of building effectively plural states, not only with the presence of different languages but also epistemological plurality, different forms of ownership, different modes of production, different legal regimes, and different public authorities, as an expression of the extraordinary historical and structural heterogeneity of these societies.

Third, there is the stipulation of other modalities for the exercise of democracy, beyond the limits of a liberal democracy that has historically been characterized in the continent as exclusive, racist, classist, and patriarchal. Unlike the socialist experiments of the 20th century, the starting point is the implicit or explicit recognition that the basic rights and freedoms that have been possible in liberal democracy have not been a gift from the bourgeoisie, but rather the result of historical struggles carried out over centuries by the subaltern sectors for the expansion of their rights. Consequently, the replacement of this "class democracy" with the democracy of another class, or the democracy of the nomenclature from the socialist experiments of the last century, was not proposed, but rather the deepening of democracy through the incorporation of other modalities and other traditions: *participatory democracy, community democracy,* and *plebiscitary democracy*. In the cases of Ecuador and Bolivia, this implied the recognition that liberal democracy has been the expression of only one of the various historical/cultural traditions existing in those countries, the recognition that there have been and still are, in other cultural traditions, other modalities of exercising public authority and decision-making.

Another fundamental axis of the transformational outlooks to move beyond colonial modernity is the confrontation with patriarchy, which, however, has a limited and ambiguous presence in the discourses and in the foundational texts of these political processes.

The distance between the normative outlook of 15–20 years ago and the current reality of these progressive governments is enormous.

42 *Crisis of Civilization*

The radical spirit of these documents captures, in its complexity and tensions, the struggles, spirit, and transformative imaginaries that were present in the years in which these constituent texts were produced. In order to approach what happened in these experiences, it makes sense to dwell on their content.

The Venezuelan Constitution of 1999 states in its preamble that:

> The people of Venezuela, exercising their powers of creation and invoking the protection of God, the historic example of our Liberator Simon Bolivar and the heroism and sacrifice of our aboriginal ancestors and the forerunners and founders of a free and sovereign nation; to the supreme end of reshaping the Republic to establish a democratic, participatory and self-reliant, multiethnic and multicultural society in a just, federal and decentralized State that embodies the values of freedom, independence, peace, solidarity, the common good, the nation's territorial integrity, comity and the rule of law for this and future generations; guarantees the right to life, work, learning, education, social justice and equality, without discrimination or subordination of any kind; promotes peaceful cooperation among nations and furthers and strengthens Latin American integration in accordance with the principle of nonintervention and national self-determination of the people, the universal and indivisible guarantee of human rights, the democratization of imitational society, nuclear disarmament, ecological balance and environmental resources as the common and inalienable heritage of humanity
>
> (University of Minnesota Human Rights Library).

In a country with a numerically smaller indigenous population than other countries on the continent, the characterization of the country as multiethnic and multicultural is reinforced in chapter VIII, which is devoted extensively to the rights of indigenous peoples:

> Article 119. The State recognizes the existence of native peoples and communities, their social, political and economic organization, their cultures, practices and customs, languages and religions, as well as their habitat and original rights to the lands they ancestrally and traditionally occupy, and which are necessary to develop and guarantee their way of life. It shall be the responsibility of the National Executive, with the participation of the native peoples, to demarcate and guarantee the right to collective ownership of their lands, which shall be inalienable, not subject to the law of limitations or distrait, and nontransferable, in accordance with this Constitution and the law
>
> (University of Minnesota Human Rights Library).

Crisis of Civilization   43

For the demarcation of indigenous peoples' lands the twelfth Transitional Provision of the Constitution establishes a period of two years. The protection of the environment is defined in the following terms:

> Article 127. It is the right and duty of each generation to protect and maintain the environment for its own benefit and that of the world of the future. Everyone has the right, individually and collectively, to enjoy a safe, healthful and ecologically balanced life and environment. The State shall protect the environment, biological and genetic diversity, ecological processes, national parks and natural monuments, and other areas of particular ecological importance. The genome of a living being shall not be patentable, and the field shall be regulated by the law relating to the principles of bioethics.
>
> It is a fundamental duty of the State, with the active participation of society, to ensure that the populace develops in a pollution-free environment in which air, water, soil, coasts, climate, the ozone layer and living species receive special protection, in accordance with the law.
>
> Article 129. Any activities capable of generating damage to ecosystems must be preceded by environmental and socio-cultural impact studies. The State shall prevent toxic and hazardous waste from entering the country, as well as preventing the manufacture and use of nuclear, chemical and biological weapons. A special law shall regulate the use, handling, transportation and storage of toxic and hazardous substances. In contracts into which the Republic enters with natural or juridical persons of Venezuelan or foreign nationality, or in any permits granted which involve natural resources, the obligation to preserve the ecological balance, to permit access to, and the transfer of technology on mutually agreed terms and to restore the environment to its natural state if the latter is altered, shall be deemed included even if not expressed, on such terms as may be established by law
>
> (University of Minnesota Human Rights Library).

The 2009 Constitution of Bolivia (República de Bolivia. Asamblea Constituyente 2009) defines the plurinational and communitarian character of the country in the following terms:

> In ancient times mountains arose, rivers moved, and lakes were formed. Our Amazonia, our swamps, our highlands, and our plains and valleys were covered with greenery and flowers. We populated this sacred Mother Earth with different faces, and since that time we have understood the plurality that exists in all things and in our diversity as human beings and cultures. Thus, our peoples were

44   *Crisis of Civilization*

formed, and we never knew racism until we were subjected to it during the terrible times of colonialism.

We, the Bolivian people, of plural composition, from the depths of history, inspired by the struggles of the past, by the anti-colonial indigenous uprising, and in independence, by the popular struggles of liberation, by the indigenous, social and labor marches, by the water and October wars, by the struggles for land and territory, construct a new State in memory of our martyrs.

A State based on respect and equality for all, on principles of sovereignty, dignity, interdependence, solidarity, harmony, and equity in the distribution and redistribution of the social wealth, where the search for a good life predominates; based on respect for the economic, social, juridical, political and cultural pluralism of the inhabitants of this land; and on collective coexistence with access to water, work, education, health and housing for all.

We have left the colonial, republican and neo-liberal State in the past. We take on the historic challenge of collectively constructing a Unified Social State of Pluri-National Communitarian law, which includes and articulates the goal of advancing toward a democratic, productive, peace-loving and peaceful Bolivia, committed to the full development and free determination of the peoples.

The pluricultural character is reaffirmed in Article 8 in the following terms:

The State adopts and promotes the following as ethical, moral principles of the plural society: ama qhilla, ama llulla, ama suwa (do not be lazy, do not be a liar or a thief), suma qamaña (live well), ñandereko (live harmoniously), teko kavi (good life), ivi maraei (land without evil) and qhapaj ñan (noble path or life).

The 2010 Law on the Rights of Mother Earth "aims to recognize the rights of Mother Earth, as well as the obligations and duties of the Plurinational State and society to ensure respect for these rights." It is based on the following mandatory principles: "harmony; collective good; guarantee of regeneration of Mother Earth, respect and defense of the Rights of Mother Earth; non-commercialization; and Interculturality" (Plurinational State of Bolivia 2010).

The Preamble of the Constitution of Ecuador (Republic of Ecuador, Constituent Assembly 2008) states that:

We, the sovereign people of Ecuador, recognizing our millenary roots, forged by women and men of different peoples, celebrating

Crisis of Civilization 45

nature, Pacha Mama, of which we are a part and which is vital for our existence, invoking the name of God and acknowledging our diverse forms of religiosity and spirituality, appealing to the wisdom of all the cultures that enrich us as a society,

We decided to build a new form of citizen coexistence, in diversity and harmony with nature, to achieve the good living, the *sumak kawsay*.

Article 57 recognizes, among others, the following collective rights:

Freely maintain, develop and strengthen their identity, sense of belonging, ancestral traditions and forms of social organization.

Maintain possession of ancestral lands and territories and obtain their free adjudication.

Participate in the use, usufruct, administration and conservation of the renewable natural resources found on their lands.

Free, prior and informed consultation, within a reasonable period of time, on plans and programs for prospecting, exploitation and commercialization of non-renewable resources found on their lands that may affect them environmentally or culturally.

Participate in the benefits that these projects bring and receive compensation for the social, cultural and environmental damage they cause.

Conserve and promote their biodiversity and natural environment management practices.

Conserve and develop their own forms of coexistence and social organization, and of generation and exercise of authority, in their legally recognized territories and community lands of ancestral possession.

Create, develop, apply and practice their own or common law.

Not to be displaced from their ancestral lands.

Maintain, protect and develop collective knowledge; their sciences, technologies and ancestral knowledge; genetic resources containing biological diversity and agrobiodiversity; their traditional medicine, including the right to recover, promote and protect ritual and sacred sites, as well as plants, animals, minerals and ecosystems within their

46 *Crisis of Civilization*

territories; and knowledge of the resources and properties of fauna and flora ... Any form of appropriation of their knowledge, innovations and practices is prohibited.

To develop, strengthen and promote the system of bilingual intercultural education, with quality criteria, from early childhood stimulation to higher education, in accordance with cultural diversity, for the care and preservation of identities in line with their teaching and learning methodologies.

Build and maintain organizations that represent them, within the framework of respect for pluralism and cultural, political and organizational diversity. The state shall recognize and promote all their forms of expression and organization.

The territories of peoples in voluntary isolation are of irreducible and intangible ancestral possession, and any type of extractive activity shall be prohibited in them. The State shall adopt measures to guarantee their lives, ensure respect for their self-determination and their will to remain in isolation, and guarantee the observance of their rights. Violation of these rights shall constitute the crime of ethnocide, which shall be punishable by law.

Ancestral, indigenous, Afro-Ecuadorian and mountain peoples may establish territorial districts for the preservation of their culture ... Communes with collective ownership of land are recognized as an ancestral form of territorial organization.

This Constitution incorporates, for the first time in constitutional history and in an express form, the recognition of the Rights of Nature, dedicating the seventh chapter to it.

Art. 71. Nature or Pacha Mama, where life is reproduced and fulfilled, has the right to full respect for its existence and for the maintenance and regeneration of her life cycles, structure, functions and evolutionary processes.

Any person, community, people or nationality may demand from the public authority the fulfillment of the rights of nature. In applying and interpreting these rights, the principles established in the Constitution shall be observed, as appropriate.

The State shall provide incentives to natural and legal persons, and to the collectives to protect nature, and will promote respect for all the elements that make up an ecosystem.

Given the profound ruptures established in these texts, it is clear that they could never be thought of as the formal juridical design of a new society, but as utopian horizons of other possible futures, as agendas and normative political platforms from which to confront, simultaneously, the themes of alternatives to development, planetary limits, the impossibility of the logic of endless growth on a limited planet, the recovery/construction of multiple cultural alternatives to the monoculture of capital, and the radicalization of democracy beyond the narrow historical confines of its liberal representative form. They also contain fundamental challenges to hegemonic Eurocentric and colonial patterns of knowledge that display a deeply anthropocentric and patriarchal character. Their contents express the protagonistic role of peoples, subjects, communities, and social organizations, especially from the indigenous world, which, until then, had been fundamentally marginalized in politics within these countries.

In order to approach the experiences that arose from these constitutional floors, it is important to begin by recognizing that these texts in no way expressed a new intercultural hegemony in these societies. They are the result of a correlation of forces at a particular juncture where the prevailing order in each of these countries was weakened or delegitimized.

Around 15–20 years on, most of the expectations generated by these rich normative prospects have been foiled. No one claimed that these transformations were easy, nor that these extraordinarily ambitious goals—a plurinational state, rights of nature—were short-term objectives. What was at stake was the initiation of a complex transition in other directions to the suicidal course taken by the hegemonic powers that are today leading humanity to the precipice. However, the political Left in government did not manage to detach itself from the imaginaries of development, progress, and endless economic growth as the fundamental axes for social transformation. Perhaps they never considered it, or even believed in it, beyond the discursive sphere.

Given the profound environmental crisis that threatens life on the planet, any transformative anti-capitalist project must necessarily have as its constitutive focus an active response to this threat to life. However, in none of these experiences were significant steps taken in the direction of a transition to another productive model compatible with the preservation of life. In each of the countries, there was a deepening of their subordinate colonial role in the international division of labor and nature, although this occurred with the partial reorientation of the destination of exports from old to new empires. In each case, the process of prioritizing economies that were completely focused on extractivism was deepened. The extractive model has been the basic axis of public policies, blocking the possibility of advancing in the direction of the transformative objectives that were enunciated in the constitutions and other legal texts referring to other non-predatory modalities of relationship with nature,

48   *Crisis of Civilization*

plurinationality, and the deepening of democracy. Extractivism, as a priority, forces the opening of all territories to its exploration/exploitation, for a sprawling dynamic of accumulation by expropriation. Through its massive exports of minerals, energy, and agro-industrial products, the continent of predominantly progressive governments, far from placing obstacles to stop or even slow down the unbridled operation of the devastating machinery of global capital, has compounded its active contribution to the process.

It is not possible to move in the direction of overcoming the authoritarian mode of the liberal mono-cultural state, as well as the recognition of the rights of indigenous peoples and their effective autonomy in their own territories, if the main focus of the economic policy is the exploitation of so-called "natural resources" found in these territories. The improvement in the living conditions of the majority of the population that took place during these years was extraordinarily fragile. These governments had considered it necessary to take advantage of this new condition in which the prices of the primary goods exported were growing faster than those of the industrial goods imported in order to maximize their short-term fiscal revenue. They made the expansion of primary exports the main focus of their economic policy, at least for the short and medium term. Responding to the demands of populations whose living conditions had been deeply affected by the decades of neoliberalism, and in search of legitimacy in the eyes of their voters to give continuity to the processes of change, short-term policies of increased public spending had priority. Taking advantage of the rise in the demand and price of primary goods—the so-called commodity boom—and greater state control of the benefits of these activities, both through property and higher tax rates, the fiscal income of states with progressive governments increased significantly. The presence of the state was recovered, increasing social spending substantially. Access to food, education, health services, and social security improved. Unemployment rates and levels of poverty, critical poverty, and inequality, measured in terms of monetary income, decreased. These are undoubtedly formidable achievements after decades of neoliberal policies that had impoverished the population, increasing the exclusion of the popular sectors and thus increasing inequality in what was already the most unequal continent on the planet.

These were distributive policies sustained by extraordinary revenues based on high commodity prices that historical experience had shown could not be sustained over time. In the tensions between the search for alternatives to development and distributive clientelist policies, the latter consistently prevailed. These policies were for some years the fundamental bases of the legitimacy of these governments in popular sectors, particularly in urban areas, but at the same time a main source of their weaknesses as transformative projects.

The Latin American debate on extractivism has been shaped by fundamental differences, not only about the nature of the transition to a post-capitalist society but also about the type of post-capitalist society being postulated. Central to these debates have been, either implicitly or explicitly, profound disagreements about *development, alternatives to development,* or *post-development.* The critical view of neo-extractivism generally starts from a critique of the hegemonic civilizational model, the civilizational pattern of endless growth, and sustained subjugation or permanent war against the rest of nature. This includes capitalism, but, as the historical experience of 20th-century socialism showed, it goes beyond capitalism.[16] Those who defend extractivism, on the contrary, argue that only thanks to the resources provided by extractive activities will it be possible to overcome capitalism. They see extractivism as a transitional stage, a stage that would allow both satisfaction of the immediate needs of the population and accumulation of a level of wealth and scientific-intellectual capacity to consider, later on, its transcendence. The most systematic defense of extractivism in the Latin American debate in recent years has been made by the Vice-President of Bolivia, Álvaro García Linera. His interventions reaffirm confidence in the virtues of development, based on a radical inversion of the profound meaning of the notion of *Vivir Bien* [Living Well].

The following texts illustrate his main arguments:

> [...] at first, is it not possible to use the resources provided by the primary export activity controlled by the State to generate the surpluses that allow the satisfaction of the minimum living conditions of Bolivians and the guarantee of an intercultural and scientific education that generates an intellectual critical mass capable of assuming and conducting the emerging processes of industrialization and knowledge economy? (García Linera 2013, 109).

> By what means can extractivism be overcome? By ceasing production? By closing the tin mines? The gas wells? by going backwards in the satisfaction of the basic material means of existence, as its critics suggest? Is this not rather the route to an increase of poverty and the direct road to the restoration of the neoliberals? Is not tying the hands of the revolutionary process for the sake of extractivist rejection what the conservative forces want most in order to asphyxiate it? (ibid., 110).

> [...] the thoughtless critics in favor of non-extractivism [...] in their political liturgy mutilate the revolutionary forces and governments of the material means to satisfy the needs of the population, generate wealth, and distribute it with justice; and from this create a new non-extractivist material base that preserves and expands the benefits of the laborious population. (ibid., 107-108)

50 *Crisis of Civilization*

Behind the recent anti-extractivist criticism against revolutionary and progressive governments, we can identify the shadow of conservative restoration. (ibid., 110)

That is what *Vivir Bien* consists of: using science, technology, and industry to generate wealth. Otherwise, how could we build roads, health posts, schools, produce food, satisfy the basic and growing needs of society? But at the same time, we need to preserve the fundamental structure of our natural environment for us and the generations to come, who will have in nature the realization of their infinite capacities to satisfy their social needs. (ibid.)

In contrast to the critique of extractivism in its civilizational dimensions of an assault on Mother Earth, García Linera considers it to be a "technical system for processing nature" compatible with any type of society.

[Extractivism is a set of] technical systems for processing nature through labor, and they can be present in pre-capitalist, capitalist, or communitarian societies.

Critics of extractivism confuse the technical system with the mode of production, and this confusion leads them to associate extractivism with capitalism, forgetting that there are non-extractivist societies, the industrial ones, which are fully capitalist! There can be capitalist, non-capitalist, pre-capitalist, or post-capitalist extractivist societies. And likewise, there can be non-extractivist capitalist, non-capitalist, or post-capitalist societies

(García Linera 2013, 107).

It seems to be beyond consideration that the imperial way of life of those supposedly non-extractive societies of the Global North is only possible on the basis of the appropriation of the wealth produced by the extractive practices of the Global South.[17] Capitalism is a global system, not a national regime.

The extractivist productive model is neither a mere "technical relationship with nature," nor can it be understood as a stage to be overcome later. As Fernando Coronil points out:

The process of value creation involves at the same time the production of objects and the transformation of social relations [...] production encompasses the production of commodities and also the formation of the social agents involved in that process and, therefore, unites in a single field of analysis the material and cultural orders within from which human beings form themselves while constructing their world

(Coronil 2002, 46–47).

As is evident from the Venezuelan experience, rentier extractivism not only produces oil, but also shapes a model for the organization of society, a type of state, a political regime, cultural patterns, and collective subjectivities and imaginaries. These can by no means simply be reversed when, at a later stage of the processes of change, it is decided that the economic conditions have been reached that would allow for the abandonment of extractivism.

> [...] These rents contribute to similar patterns of internal specialization and external dependence that consolidate the role of Third World nations as what I call nature-exporting societies. Even when these nations try to break their colonial dependence on primary commodity exports by implementing development plans aimed at diversifying their economies, they usually rely on the currency earned from primary commodity exports to do so, thereby intensifying their dependence on primary commodities. Paradoxically, in seeking to exploit their comparative advantage, these nature-exporting nations often reassume their colonial role as sources of primary commodities, a role now rewritten in terms of the neoliberal rationality of globalizing capitalism. For them, postcolonialism is followed by neocolonialism
>
> (Coronil 2002, 7).

Extractivism became a shared conception among the countries of UNASUR (Rodríguez Araque 2014) and ALBA.

> Declaration of ALBA from the Pacific Coast. XII Summit of Heads of State and Government of ALBA-TCP. Guayaquil, July 30, 2013
>
> On the other hand, we express the right and the need for our countries to take advantage, in a responsible and sustainable manner, of their non-renewable natural resources, which have the potential to be used in a sustainable manner.
>
> We are convinced that the main social imperative of our time - and of our region - is to combat poverty and misery. In this sense, we reject the extremist position of certain groups that, under the slogan of anti-extractivism, systematically oppose the exploitation of our natural resources, requiring that this can be done only on the basis of prior consent of the people and communities living near that source of wealth. In practice, this would mean that it would not be possible to take advantage of this alternative, ultimately jeopardizing the social and economic successes achieved so far
>
> (ALBA 2013).

52 *Crisis of Civilization*

Ecuador Mineral-State?

In the case of Ecuador, the multiple tensions and confrontations with the imaginaries of change were expressly manifested from the very beginning of the process. The National Development Plan presented by the government in 2009 (*National Plan Nacional para el Buen Vivir 2009–2013*) addresses the complex and contradictory task of designing, from centralized state management, a transition toward a society dedicated to the philosophy of *Buen Vivir* [Good Living]. As in Bolivia, the plan proposes in an initial phase to deepen extractivism as a condition for producing wealth and responding to the needs of the population. It is about "medium and long-term planning guidelines, with an outlook of 16–20 years." The first phase, called "Accumulation for the Transition and Deepening of Distribution," is defined in terms of "accumulation, in the sense of dependence on primary goods to sustain the economy [...]." The plan is marked by serious tensions between the objectives of *Buen Vivir*, plurinationality, and interculturality, on the one hand, and options for modernization, on the other, in which the fundamental solutions for the country would be provided by research and development, technological innovation, and the creation of specific niches such as biotechnology and nanotechnology in which Ecuador, thanks to its immense biodiversity, could have comparative advantages.

Alberto Acosta (2009) has argued and documented that, as in almost all countries whose economy is centered on the exploitation/export of primary goods, oil exploitation in Ecuador has produced extreme economic distortions, severe social impacts, and environmental devastation and has not contributed to the well-being of the population. The new constitution was supposed to be the starting point for a break with this extractive model. However, this has not been the case.

The conflict over oil exploitation in the Yasuní-ITT National Park-Indigenous territory, became the most emblematic expression of the conflicting visions of the desired society present in Ecuador in recent years. The Yasuní-ITT initiative to leave the oil in the ground in exchange for the partial international funding of revenues that the Ecuadorian state would have obtained from its exploitation had become an international touchstone as a project of collaboration and global socio-environmental justice and received extraordinary support from the country's population (Martínez 2009). This support found expression in the massive canvassing conducted by the Yasunidos collective to demand the holding of a national referendum to decide whether to exploit these hydrocarbon reserves. As an expression of the clear choice for extractivism, the Correa government, through procedures described as manipulated, carried out by the supposedly autonomous National Electoral Council, invalidated enough signatures to rule that the minimum required had not been collected and decided that the requested referendum would not be held (Friends of the Earth International 2014). In December 2018, a commission appointed by the new transitional National Electoral Council concluded that irregularities had been committed and that the Yasunidos had indeed collected the signatures required to hold the referendum (El Comercio 2018).

The socio-environmental impacts of oil production in Ecuador have been devastating. In its operations in the Ecuadorian Amazon, the U.S. company Chevron-Texaco, between 1964 and 1990, produced massive levels of contamination/destruction of water, land, and vegetation with severe impacts on the inhabitants of the area. In its lawsuit, demanding compensation for the damage caused, the Ecuadorian government claims that the company deliberately applied obsolete techniques that it no longer used elsewhere in order to increase its profits:

> In Ecuador, Chevron-Texaco produced one of the most serious environmental crimes in history. The transnational oil company is responsible for the spill of no less than 15.8 billion liters of oil and 28.5 million gallons (108 million liters) of crude oil in the Amazon. More than 2 million hectares of the Ecuadorian Amazon were affected by almost 30 years of contamination at the hands of a single company, which acted with impunity in violation of the minimum patterns of environmental protection and which today refuses to recognize it: Texaco (now Chevron)
> (Republic of Ecuador, Ministry of Foreign Affairs and Human Mobility 2015).

Despite these precedents, and the lack of conditions to guarantee that they would not be repeated, the Correa government opted to open up new areas of the Amazon to oil exploitation in territories that overlapped with the indigenous territories of the Shuar, Achuar, Kichwa, Shiwiar, Andoa, Waorani, and Sápara peoples, despite opposition from these peoples and lack of the free, prior, and informed consultation to which the Ecuadorian state is obliged by both national and international norms (Salva la Selva 2013).

With the profoundly asymmetrical relations that were established between Ecuador and China during the Correa administration, new forms of colonial subordination were created, forcing the country to continue deepening extractive activities for many years, since a large proportion of the massive loans granted by China to Ecuador had to be paid in oil. Some of these loans for large infrastructure works, such as hydroelectric dams, in addition to acts of corruption, resulted in technically deficient structures that were lacking adequate geological studies and long-term water availability. The most emblematic case in this regard is the Coca Codo Sinclair dam, the largest engineering work in the

54   *Crisis of Civilization*

history of Ecuador, built in the immediate vicinity of an active volcano: the Reventador (Pacheco 2018).

Ecuador is a country with no mining tradition. However, due to the limitations of the country's existing hydrocarbon reserves and the profound transformations that were operating in the global mineral market, expressed in accelerated increases in demand and prices, as well as in more efficient technologies for identifying and extracting low-grade mineral deposits, previously considered unprofitable, successive governments, both in the neoliberalism of the previous decades and the Correa government, carried out legal and institutional reforms aimed at attracting transnational mining companies. This took place within very different constitutional framings (Sacher 2017).

In line with positions for the protection of nature that were being debated within its halls, in 2008, the Constituent Assembly approved a *Constitutional Mining Mandate* (Republic of Ecuador. Constituent Assembly 2009). This established, among other things, a six-month moratorium on large-scale mining exploration activities, which held that mining could not affect water sources and springs, restricted mining in protected areas, and prohibited monopolies. In view of the fact that most of the mining concessions that had been granted up to that time lacked investment projects and that they had essentially become the basis for speculative activities of buying/selling these rights, it was also decided that concessions that had not carried out environmental impact studies and prior consultation processes, or that did not comply with the law in terms of tax and patent payments, would be extinguished.

And yet, the following year the Correa government passed a new *Mining Law* (República del Ecuador. Asamblea Nacional 2009), which, although it was much more favorable from a fiscal and environmental point of view than legislation from the neoliberal era, did not comply with important aspects of the restrictions and regulations on mining activity planned in the *Constitution* and the *Constitutional Mining Mandate*. Relations between the Confederation of Indigenous Nationalities of Ecuador (CONAIE) and President Correa, having already soured during the debates of the Constituent Assembly due to their conflicting positions on plurinationality, which Correa opposed, broke down with the approval of the *Water Law*, the *Organic Law on Food Sovereignty,* and the *Mining Law.* The latter authorizes large-scale mining in the country and disregards the right of indigenous peoples to prior consultation on mining activities to be carried out in their territories (Resina de la Fuente 2012). CONAIE filed an action of unconstitutionality against this law before the Constitutional Court, on the grounds that it violated multiple articles of the Constitution, International Labor Organization Agreement 169, the American Convention on Human Rights, and the Additional Protocol to the Convention on Human Rights in the Area of Economic, Social and Cultural Rights. This Court decided in favor of

Crisis of Civilization   55

the CONAIE with regard to prior consultation, but ratified the constitutionality of the rest of the law (Republic of Ecuador. The Constitutional Court for the transition period 2010).

During the years of Correa's government, systematic steps were taken in the direction of turning Ecuador into a mining country. In June 2013, the National Assembly approved a set of amendments to the *Mining Law* in response to demands made by mining companies (Sacher 2017, 192–193). In February 2015, the creation of a new Ministry of Mining was decreed (El Telégrafo 2015). In May 2016, "the 'Mining Cadastre' was opened for the new awarding of concessions of areas for geological exploration and the development of new mining projects" (Acción Ecológica 2016a). In this way, an unprecedented expansion of mining is taking place in the country. According to William Sacher, if all applications pending before the Ministry of Mining were to be authorized by mid-2017, 3,688,000 hectares of concessions would be granted, 15% of the national territory (Sacher 2017, 176). The Ecuadorian government, under both Correa and Lenin Moreno, has been taking an increasingly active stance in promoting mining activity, including its participation in the annual meetings of the most important international mining association, the Prospectors and Developers Association of Canada. According to the global mining site, *MINING.com*, thanks to the modification of the legal regulatory framework for mining activity, and a major outreach campaign to investors, in less than a year there were 420 applications for mining concessions, and new mining investments totaling US$4 billion are expected between 2017 and 2020 (Jamasmie 2017). This is how Ecuador is progressing in the direction of what William Sacher has called a *Mineral-State*, "a state that puts a significant section of its entire apparatus at the service of promoting mega-mining" (Sacher 2017, 311–314). The largest mining ventures in the country are from Canadian and Chinese companies. Of the five major mega-mining projects in force in 2017 (three gold and two copper), three were Chinese-owned, one Canadian, and the last a Canadian-Swedish company (Sacher 2017, 395–396).[18]

Given the devastating socio-environmental impacts of mega-mining, it will inevitably encounter resistance from environmental organizations, but the resistance will fundamentally come from the indigenous and peasant communities that are threatened or affected. The actions of environmental and human rights organizations have been answered mainly with threats or their closure. *Decree 16* of 2013, and *Decree 739* of 2015, establish very detailed regulation and supervision of every NGO, their goals, their statutes, their internal functioning mechanisms, each of their activities, as well as their accounting. Various grounds for dissolution are established, among them: "Deviating from the objectives for which it was constituted" and "Engaging in partisan political activities, reserved for political parties and movements registered in the National Electoral Council, which interfere in public policies that threaten the internal or

56 *Crisis of Civilization*

external security of the state or that affect public peace" (Correa Delgado 2013).[19] Accusing them of engaging in political activities, the Correa government closed down the Pachamama Foundation, which has a long history of defending communities affected by mining in the Amazon, and attempted to outlaw the most important environmental organization in the country: Acción Ecológica. The outcry, nationally as well as internationally, was so strong that the government had to drop that measure without a result.

Against the resistance of indigenous communities and organizations, the responses have been more aggressive. Two methods have been used to try to demobilize the communities. In the first place, both companies and the government try to divide the communities with offers of various kinds to certain segments or leaders of the communities. They already have a great deal of experience with this and often succeed in their objectives. But if this does not happen, they proceed to criminalize the protest/resistance through the application of some norm of the *Organic Integral Penal Code* (Republic of Ecuador, Ministry of Justice, Human Rights and Worship. Subsecretaría de Desarrollo Normativo 2014). The strategic choice to promote large-scale metal mining has inevitably been accompanied by judicialization and repression (Acción Ecológica 2016b; Ortega and Isabel 2016; Zorrilla 2017).

Rafael Correa clearly summarized the incompatibility between the constitutional principles of *Sumak Kawsay*, plurinationality, and the rights of nature, on one hand, and his modernizing project of the state based on large-scale extractivism, on the other,

> I always said that the greatest danger to our political project, once the right wing was defeated at the polls, was and is leftism, environmentalism, and infantile *indigenismo*; what a pity that we were not wrong about that
>
> (El Universo 2009).

Bolivia: From Buen Vivir to Extractivist Developmentalism

Bolivia has been a mining country since early colonial times, starting with the exploitation of the silver mines of Potosi, with all the social, environmental, and cultural and political institutional consequences that this history has entailed. The 2009 Constitution appears as a potential point of rupture in this profound colonial inheritance/injury, a rupture guided by the radical notions of plurinationality, pluriculturality, political-territorial autonomy of indigenous peoples, community economy, and later, the law of the rights of nature. But how have the profound tensions between this normative horizon proposed in this constitutional text and the clear developmentalist/extractivist choice defended by García Linera in the texts cited above been processed in recent years? In addition to the intensification of hydrocarbon production, which is still the country's main source of foreign exchange, metal mining has expanded extraordinarily in recent years. Beginning in the neoliberal decades, but accelerating during the years of Evo Morales' government, recent years have seen profound changes in mining activity in the country. These transformations have taken place mainly in the massive expansion of the scale of this activity and its greater territorial coverage, the relative weight of the different minerals extracted, the methods of mining exploitation, and the types of capital involved. From an exploitation first historically concentrated in silver and then in tin, there has been a shift toward the predominance of zinc, silver, lead, and gold. This has been accompanied by a broad expansion of mining from the more traditional areas of the Altiplano to the lowlands in the east of the country, especially in Santa Cruz, having already granted mining rights for a large part of the national territory. Open-pit mining has been the predominant form of exploitation (Díaz Cuellar 2017). The total value of mining activity in the country increased from US$1.151 billion in 2006 to US$4.156 billion in 2012 (Díaz Cuellar 2017). Zinc became the most important mineral in terms of both volume and value. Between 2007 and 2016, its production increased from a value of US$673 million to US$1.01 billion (Zaconeta Torrico 2017). Thanks mainly to the expansion of mining activity and the *commodities boom*, between 2006—the first year of Evo Morales' government—and 2014, the value of Bolivian exports increased by more than 300%, from US$4,088 million to US$12,899 million. From that year onwards, with the end of the cycle of high commodity prices, the total value of exports began to fall arriving at US$7.846 billion in 2017, when the country, after several years of being in the black, had for the third consecutive year a deficit in its trade balance. That year was the second consecutively in which the total value of mineral exports exceeded those of hydrocarbons (Instituto Boliviano de Comercio Exterior 2018).

This mining expansion is celebrated by García Linera in the following terms: "Today we export three times more in volume than in 2005, and this already speaks to us of a mining country. Bolivia lives from its gas, but also from mining and we are proud of that." (Diaz Cuellar 2017, 42)

Despite the government's repeated nationalist/anti-imperialist discourse, this increase was mainly due to three mines controlled by transnational companies: San Cristóbal, San Bartolomé, and San Vicente. Between 2006 and 2012, four transnational companies were responsible for 52% of the country's mining exports (Díaz Cuellar 2017, 46). These have been years of huge profits for the mining transnationals. The state, for its part, only controls a minority share of mining production and has had a limited share of the revenues from this activity. The average fiscal pressure from the years 2004 to 2014 was only 8.1% of the gross value of exports (Díaz Cuellar 2017, 57). As "the vast majority of the value and volume of the country's mining production is made up of zinc, silver, and lead that are not refined in the

58 *Crisis of Civilization*

country" (Díaz Cuellar 2017, 60), the historical colonial model has been continued in which the social impacts and environmental liabilities of mining occur in Bolivian territory while most of the profits are made by transnationals abroad.[20]

The socio-environmental impacts of open-pit mining are severe and generally irreversible, beginning with the displacement of people from their land, the destruction of their conditions of cultural reproduction, and, with it, the denial of alternative forms of life to that of the logic of growth of the mercantile economy and the imaginary of progress. In the current conditions of global mining, in which it has become profitable for companies to exploit reserves with very low tenor, it is necessary to remove large quantities of material for each unit of mineral extracted, affecting vast tracts of land. The vegetation layer from wooded mountain slopes is removed, and groundwater and surface water are affected and polluted. Massive amounts of toxic chemicals, such as mercury and cyanide, are used, affecting both water and arable land and the surrounding populations and wildlife (Tejada Soruco 2011).

In this accelerated expansion of the mining frontier, the right to free, prior, and informed consultation has been systematically violated (Bascopé Sanjinés 2017). As has been the case in the rest of Latin America, this expansion of mining activity into indigenous and peasant territories has created multiple processes of resistance to which the Movimiento al Socialismo (MAS) government has often responded with a criminalization of protest and repression (Madrid Lara 2013; Territorios en Resistencia 2014). According to the Observatorio de Conflictos Mineros en América Latina (OCMAL), Bolivia, although it has "a medium-low degree of violence," is one of the Latin American countries with a "high degree of criminalization" of resistance to mining (Gárate 2016; Observatorio de Conflictos Mineros en América Latina 2017).

As in the other countries of the continent, far from achieving the goals of productive transformation and a plural economy, not focused on extractive activities, with the commodity boom the primary export model was consolidated, and the search for other options was blocked.

The TIPNIS Road

The conflicts over the road through the Isiboro Sécure Indigenous Territory and National Park (TIPNIS) became the paradigm case for the existing tensions between development/extractivist views that have been predominate in the government and the conceptions of *buen vivir* established in the constitution. This conflict, in a way, distills the struggles between the models of society that have crossed the Bolivian process in recent years.

The Isiboro Sécure National Park was created in 1965. For decades, it has been an area of continuous conflict between indigenous peoples living

Crisis of Civilization 59

there and various external threats. In opposition to the arrival of settlers to their territories and the opening of the area to logging activities, the first indigenous march to La Paz in defense of their territories took place in 1990. It was expected that, with the environmental and land rights of the indigenous peoples established in the new constitution, the preservation of this national park would be guaranteed. However, the government of Evo Morales rekindled a project promoted by the Initiative for the Integration of the Regional Infrastructure of South America (IIRSA) to build a road through the park and, with funding from Brazil's National Bank for Economic and Social Development (BNDES), signed an agreement to carry out the work, despite the strong opposition of the inhabitants.

The indigenous peoples defending TIPNIS undertook multiple mobilizations and other forms of resistance against the road. Between August and September 2011, the indigenous defenders of TIPNIS organized a 600-kilometer march to La Paz, which was met with popular support both along its route and on its arrival in the capital but repeatedly blocked and repressed by state security forces. After repressing (Servindi 2011) and accusing them of being agents of the United States government and funded by international NGOs, the government of Evo Morales finally gave in and approved Law 180, in which, based on the Political Constitution of the state, the status of the Indigenous Territory and National Park Isiboro Sécure (TIPNIS) "as an indigenous territory of the Chimán, Yuracaré and Mojeño-trinitario peoples, of an indivisible, imprescriptible, unseizable, inalienable, and irreversible nature and as a protected area of national interest" is ratified. This territory is declared an "intangible zone" and provides "that the Villa Tunari-San Ignacio de Moxos highway, like any other, will not cross TIPNIS" (Plurinational State of Bolivia. The Plurinational Legislative Assembly 2011). A few months later the government announced the termination of the contract with the company OAS.

After carrying out (and winning) a consultation with the inhabitants of the area in 2012, considered illegitimate due to the composition of the participants and the manipulation and coercion that accompanied it (Somos Sur 2016), the government allowed a few years to pass before resuming the construction of the road. In 2017, when it considered that it had succeeded in disarticulating and weakening the resistance, it repealed *Law 180* through *Law 969* and with it the intangibility of that territory. Although the text is full of the necessary references to "harmony with Mother Earth," "pluriculturality," "free, prior, and informed consultation," and the "promotion, protection, and conservation of cultural heritage," the objective of this new law is clearly oriented toward "integral and sustainable development"; the "exploitation of renewable natural resources and the development of productive activities" (with the participation of private capital); and "the opening of local roads, highways,

60   *Crisis of Civilization*

navigational fluvial, aerial, and other systems" (Estado Plurinacional de Bolivia. La Asamblea Legislativa Plurinacional 2017). In this way, the road issue is once again placed at the center of the national political debate (Salva la Selva 2017).

Two visions of life have been at stake in these struggles. For the indigenous peoples living in the National Park, it is a question of preserving and deciding on their own ways of life, the defense of their ancestral territories, the protection of forests and waters, and the rights of nature, all of which would be threatened by a highway that would cut the territory in two and would accelerate the entry of *cocalero* settlers, loggers, and the prospecting/exploitation of hydrocarbons. For the government, it is a question of continuing with its basic option of economic growth based on extractivism and infrastructure works that overcome the obstacles to greater physical integration of the country. The exploration/exploitation of hydrocarbons has been severely limited by the inaccessibility of these territories. There are already three blocks tendered for these activities covering 35% of the National Park's territory (Fundación Solón 2018). For the *cocalero* settlers, this is a new agricultural frontier where they can expand their production. Almost all the families living in "Polygon 7," south of TIPNIS, live from coca cultivation (Fundación Solón 2018).

The different policies that the government has implemented in the development of this conflict clearly illustrate the consequences of its choice for extractivist development. By prioritizing the construction of the road despite the opposition of the inhabitants of TIPNIS, it has systematically applied its policy of dividing movements, communities, and loyalties, as well as creating parallel structures that it can control (Prada Alcoreza 2018). Public media has been used to discredit those who oppose its policies. Simultaneously, resistance has been repressed and territories militarized. In relation to their support bases, clear priority has been given to the interests of the growers of surplus coca incorporated into the political economy of cocaine and transporters and participants in the timber industry over the interests of the indigenous peoples of the lowlands. As Raúl Prada Alcoreza has argued,

> The uniqueness of these conquering and colonizing figures is not only that they do so as a "development" project, but that they do so in the name of "anti-imperialism" and, most incongruously, in the name of "decolonization"
>
> (2018).

The initiatives in three energy sectors illustrate the extent to which the policies of the MAS government do not undertake extractivist developmentalism as a transitory phase toward another model of production organization but as a coherent strategic option. This is a definite option that, as noted above, distances itself radically from the outlook of the

Crisis of Civilization 61

movements that initially brought the MAS government to power, as embodied in the constitutional text.

First, there is the nuclear program. In his 2012 accountability message to the Plurinational Legislative Assembly, Evo Morales stated that the peaceful development of atomic energy had become a "strategic priority" of the Bolivian state (Somos Sur 2014), as part of the aspiration to turn Bolivia into "the energy center of South America." This program, questioned for the risks involved, has been handled with very little transparency, and the information released by the government has been changing and often contradictory. The announced measures range from a small reactor for medical and research purposes to a nuclear power plant for electricity generation. Second, the construction of the large hydroelectric dams Chepete and El Bala have been questioned both because of the severe human and environmental impacts they would have and the enormous foreign debt burden they would represent for the country (Fundación Solón 2017a).[21] The two dams, intended for electricity exports, would cost a total of US$8.063 billion and do not have an assured market. It has been estimated that the costs of generating a megawatt-hour (MWh) are considerably higher than the average prices at which Bolivia has sold electricity to Brazil over the last decade (Fundación Solón 2017b). Third, after the government had systematically denounced agrofuels as a threat to food security during its first years (Servindi 2018), in September 2018, it passed the so-called *Ethanol and Additives of Vegetal Origin Act 1098* that authorizes the production of ethanol from sugarcane and biodiesel from soybeans and other oilseeds (*El Deber* 2018). Bolivia is late to these initiatives, which in many parts of the world are being challenged both by the resistance of affected communities and the greater scientific knowledge about their severe environmental impacts.

It is somewhat paradoxical that all this is being done by a government that, in previous years, played such a prominent role in the international negotiations against climate change. It was the country that convened and hosted the World People's Conference on Climate Change and the Rights of Mother Earth (Tiquipaya Summit) held in Cochabamba in 2010 at which indigenous, environmental, academic, and popular organizations from different parts of the world jointly built a peoples' platform in the fight against climate change. It is the government of the country that, despite all the pressure, remained alone in opposing the final agreement of the United Nations Climate Change Conference 2010 (COP 16) held in Cancún, from their judgment that there were no sufficiently strong decisions being taken in the face of the seriousness of climate change. This country was the main promoter of resolution 64/292 of July 28, 2010 through which the United Nations Assembly explicitly recognized the human right to water and sanitation (United Nations, Department of Economic and Social Affairs 2014).

62   *Crisis of Civilization*

Venezuela: The Paroxysm of Extractivism

Venezuela represents an extreme case of the choice for extractivism as a development model. During the Bolivarian government, despite discursive references to the need for alternatives to oil rentierism, there was a systematic deepening of dependence on oil and rentier logic and its corresponding socio-environmental devastation. Due not only to variations in the price of crude oil, the weight of oil, as a proportion of the total value of Venezuelan exports, went from around 63% in 1998 to 96% at the end of Chávez's life (Banco Central de Venezuela 2018).

Through quantifying the heavy and extra-heavy oil reserves in the Orinoco Oil Belt, the imaginaries of abundance from the previous decades were revived. In the 1970s, in another cycle of abundance due to high oil prices, during the first government of Carlos Andrés Pérez, the common sense that Venezuela was a rich country was strengthened. The official discourse in those years called it the *Great Venezuela*, the popular discourse referred to it as *Saudi Venezuela*.

With regard to climate change and the responsibilities of the country with the largest oil reserves on the planet, the gap between the discourse and the policies actually carried out could not be wider. At the negotiations of the United Nations Climate Change Convention Venezuela's representatives presented radical speeches blaming capitalism and the industrialized countries of the North for the high levels of fossil fuel consumption that threaten life on the planet. However, government policy has been to maximize oil extraction. The clearest example of this profound contradiction is found in the so-called *Plan for the Homeland*, the last government program presented by Chávez for the 2012 presidential elections. This program, subsequently approved by the National Assembly as the country's development plan, is organized around five main objectives. Goal number five is to preserve life on the planet and save the human species. However, objective number three is to consolidate Venezuela's role as a *World Energy Powerhouse*. To that end, according to this plan, oil production was to double from three million to six million barrels per day between 2013 and 2019. Fortunately for the planet, these efforts failed miserably. As a result of the collapse of the oil industry, oil production by the end of 2018 had fallen to less than one million barrels per day (OPEC 2018). The so-called *Plan for the Homeland* unambiguously defines the extractivist/rentier character of what is envisioned as a revolutionary oil policy:

> [...] our oil policy must be revolutionary, which has to do with who captures the oil rent, how it is captured and how it is distributed. There is no doubt that it should be the State that controls and captures the oil rent, based on mechanisms that maximize its value, to distribute it for the benefit of the people, seeking the integral social

Crisis of Civilization   63

development of the country, in fairer and more equitable conditions. This is the element that differentiates us from any other oil policy
(Chávez 2012).

Faced with the sustained decline of oil revenues since 2014, the Venezuelan government, instead of seeking alternative options to the rentier primary export logic that has caused so much damage to the country, opted in strategic terms for deepening this logic, now through large-scale mining.[22] As part of the policy for the creation of special economic zones in which labor, environmental, and indigenous peoples' regulations are made more flexible in order to attract transnational capital, in February 2016, President Maduro issued the Orinoco Mining Arc Decree by which 112,000 square kilometers, 12% of the national territory, an area equivalent to Cuba, are opened to international large-scale mining. It is a vast area rich in minerals, including gold, coltan, aluminum, diamonds, and radioactive minerals. The mineral to be exploited on which the government has placed most emphasis has been gold. According to Eulogio del Pino, at that time Minister of Petroleum and Mining and President of PDVSA, gold reserves in the area were estimated at 7,000 tons, which would represent some 280,000 million dollars (Agencia Venezolana de Noticias 2016).

The territory delineated as the Orinoco Mining Arc has socio-environmental and even economic wealth far greater than the potential monetary value of the mining reserves. It is part of the ancestral territory of the Warao, E'Ñepa, Hoti, Mapoyo, Kariña, Piaroa, Pemón, Ye'kwana, and Sanema indigenous peoples, whose material conditions of existence are being devastated by this mining exploitation, not only in flagrant violation of their constitutional rights, but also threatening them with ethnocide. It occupies a portion of the Amazon Rain Forest that plays a critical role in the regulation of the planet's climate regimes and whose preservation is vital to slow the advance of climate change. It is a territory of extraordinary biological diversity that is also the main source of water for Venezuela and the area where the hydroelectric dams that supply more than 70% of the electricity consumed in the country are located. Deepening the extractivist logic, preference has been given to obtaining short-term monetary income, even if this implies massive irreversible socio-environmental devastation. All this is imposed by presidential decree in the total absence of public debate, in a country with a constitution that defines it as democratic, participatory, multiethnic, and pluricultural.

This decree constitutes an open violation of environmental rights and responsibilities established by the Constitution of the Bolivarian Republic of Venezuela, by current environmental legislation and international agreements signed by the country, such as the *Convention on Biological Diversity*. The Law on the Protection and Guarantee of the Habitat and Lands of Indigenous Peoples (2001) and the *Organic Law on Indigenous*

64   *Crisis of Civilization*

Peoples and Communities are also being violated (LPCI, December 2005). These violations include all the norms of prior and informed consultation that are firmly established in both Venezuelan and international legislation (ILO Convention 169), in cases where activities are planned that could negatively impact the habitats of these peoples.

In the Mining Arc project, the participation of "private, state, and mixed companies" is projected. The decree contemplates a wide range of public incentives to these mining corporations, among others, the flexibilization of legal regulations, simplification and speeding up of administrative procedures, the waiving of certain requirements established in the Venezuelan legislation, the provision of "preferential financing mechanisms," and a special customs regime with tariff and para-tariff preferences for their imports. International corporations are also lured with a special tax program that provides for total or partial exemption from the payment of income tax and value-added tax:

> Article 21. Within the framework of the sectorial economic policy, the National Executive may grant total or partial exemptions from Income Tax and Value Added Tax, applicable exclusively to activities related to the mining activity, for the purpose of promoting the impulse and growth of the National Strategic Development Zone of the Orinoco Mining Arc.
>
> Likewise, joint ventures formed for the development of primary activities, provided for in the Decree with Rank, Value and Force of Organic Law that Reserves to the State the Activities of Gold Exploration and Exploitation, as well as those Related and Auxiliary to these, on the deposits located in the National Strategic Development Zone of the Orinoco Mining Arc will enjoy these benefits for the duration of the development of the project
>
> (Maduro Moro 2016).

Possibilities to oppose the negative impacts of large-scale mining in the Arco Minero area are prohibited by the regulations of the decree. In order to prevent the activities of the companies from being hindered by resistance, a Zone of Strategic Development under the responsibility of the National Bolivarian Armed Forces is created in the area:

> Article 13. The Bolivarian National Armed Force, in conjunction with the organized People's Power, and in coordination with the authorities of the Ministry of People's Power with competence in petroleum matters, shall be responsible for safeguarding, protecting and maintaining the harmonious continuity of the operations and activities of the Strategic Industries located in the Orinoco Arco Minero National Strategic Development Zone.

The decree in question expressly establishes the suspension of civil and political rights throughout the territory of the Arco Minero.

> Art. 25. No particular, trade union, association or group interest, or their regulations, shall prevail over the general interest in the fulfilment of the objective contained in the present decree.
>
> Subjects who carry out or promote material actions aimed at hindering the total or partial operations of the productive activities of the Strategic Development Zone created in this decree shall be sanctioned in accordance with the applicable legal system.
>
> The State security agencies will carry out the immediate actions necessary to safeguard the normal development of the activities foreseen in the Plans of the Orinoco Arco Minero National Strategic Development Zone, as well as the execution of the provisions of this article
>
> (Maduro Moro 2016).

The consequences of this "prevalence of the general interest over particular interests" are extraordinarily serious. The term "general interest" is understood to mean mining exploitation as it is conceived in this presidential decree. Any other vision, any other interest, even the appeal to the Constitution, becomes defined as a "particular interest" and, therefore, subject to the "immediate actions necessary to safeguard the normal development of the activities foreseen" in the decree to be carried out by the "security agencies of the state."

What are, or can be, the interests referred to here as "particular"? The decree is worded in such a way as to allow a broad interpretation. On the one hand, it expressly identifies trade unions and trade union interests as "particular." This can undoubtedly lead to the suspension, throughout the area, of the rights of the workers covered by the Constitution and the *Organic Labor Law*. Does this also imply that the "trade union" and, therefore, "particular" rights of journalists to report on the development of the mining activities are also suspended? Are the rights of indigenous peoples, in that case, of particular interests?

At the end of 2018, the large investments from transnationals expected by the government had not yet arrived, mainly due to the lack of legal security for them. However, illegal gold and coltan mining has expanded rapidly with the participation of tens of thousands of miners. This vast expanse of the national territory has become a territory partially on the margins of the state, particularly in the hands of powerful mafia-like components of the armed forces. Armed groups, paramilitaries, members of the ELN, FARC dissidents, and criminal gangs called "unions" control different sectors within these territories and fix the prices at which they

66   Crisis of Civilization

force miners to sell the minerals extracted (Romero and Ruiz 2018; Vitti 2018). All this with the complicity of members of the Venezuelan armed forces. This illegal mining activity operates with high levels of violence, frequent deaths of miners due to territorial disputes, and severe socio-environmental impacts. For gold mining, mercury is used on a massive scale and is already found in high concentrations in mothers and children in the area. Indigenous girls are abducted from their communities to be subjected to prostitution in the mining camps.

This choice for extractivism and the complete openness and creation of the best possible conditions for transnational corporations has been complemented by other decisions taken by the unconstitutional National Constituent Assembly and by President Maduro, through an equally unconstitutional State of Economic Emergency that has been pro-longed since the beginning of 2016: the *Law for the Protection of Foreign Investments* (Bolivarian Republic of Venezuela. National Constituent Assembly 2017); the elimination of income tax for PDVSA and its asso-ciated private, national, and foreign companies (Rodríguez Rosas 2018), as well as the partial privatization of state-owned oil companies, selling them to Chinese firms under conditions that are kept secret and, there-fore, unknown to the Venezuelan population. The new contracts signed with international corporations for oil production are clearly unconsti-tutional and violate the country's sovereignty (Millán 2019; Plataforma Ciudadana en Defensa de la Constitución 2018). This broad opening up to neoliberalism is taking place under circumstances in which the gov-ernment, in the context of a deep crisis, is extraordinarily weak and, therefore, has to accept conditions imposed by external investors or lend-ers, mainly from its "allied" countries, China and Russia. The contradic-tion between the fiery anti-imperialist rhetoric and the auctioning off of the common goods of Venezuelan society to transnational capital could hardly be greater.

Extractivism and the Utopian Prospects of Transformations That Were Announced

The choice of these governments to open extractivism to transnational capital has impeded the possibility of the most radical transformative objectives formulated at the beginning of these processes of having any chance of fulfillment. Neither the recognition of the plurinational state, nor the rights of indigenous peoples over their ancestral territories, nor the right to prior consultation in relation to activities impacting their territories were possible as it was precisely these territories that had to be handed over for exploitation by public, private, national, or foreign companies.

It is paradoxical that in the years when most South American coun-tries had so-called leftist or pro-resistance governments, including some with constitutions based on the notions of plurinationality and pluriculturality—and constitutional and/or legal recognition of the rights of nature—was precisely the historical phase of the accelerated advance of predatory extractivist transnational capital, even into territories that had been relatively isolated before and, therefore, not fully subject to the commodifying logic of capital.

Extractivism as the dominant productive model has been intertwined in these experiences with a state-centric pattern of social organization. The recovery of the state after decades of neoliberal dismantling in favor of the market has resulted in the strengthening of a state from which an avant-garde and/or technocratic political leadership, new versions of Latin American historical *caudillismo* or the irreplaceable leader, impose their will on society as a whole based on the state's view of society and the identification of the state with the general interest of society. In this way, the potential of advancing in the direction of the creation of spheres of autonomy and social experimentation, without which neither the plurinational state nor the collective construction of an alternative society is possible, have been blocked. The potential of deploying the forms of participatory and community democracy envisaged in the constitutional texts have also been blocked.

Extractivism, Geopolitics, and Latin American Integration

With the shift to the Left represented by the so-called progressive governments, important geopolitical changes took place in the subcontinent. Politically coordinated steps were taken in the search for regional autonomy in relation to the historical domination of the United States in the region. The fact that there were self-declared leftist or progressive governments in most of the countries of the subcontinent at the same time was historically unprecedented. The most important expression of this new continental moment was the defeat of the Free Trade Area of the Americas (FTAA), an imperial project that sought to constitutionalize the neoliberal order throughout the American continent.

Thanks to the high income produced by the export of commodities, it was possible to reduce the weight of the foreign debt and the dependence on the Bretton Woods institutions. Military ties with the United States were limited or severed, as was the case of the expulsion of US military forces from the Manta Base in Ecuador and the suspension on sending personnel to be trained at the School of the Americas. Collaboration with the US Drug Enforcement Agency (DEA) ceased. The traditional political and economic alignment with the United States was altered and issues such as climate change and the rights of the Palestinian people were pursued with greater international political independence. The spectrum of trade relations, sources of financing, and external investment expanded dramatically, a process in which China played a leading role.

68 *Crisis of Civilization*

During these years, a set of sub-regional bodies was created. The most important integration and political cooperation organizations were the *Unión de Naciones Sudamericanas* (UNASUR/Union of South American Nations), the *Alianza Bolivariana para los Pueblos de Nuestra América – Tratado de Comercio de los Pueblos* (ALBA-TCP/Bolivarian Alliance for the Peoples of Our America - Peoples' Trade Treaty), the *Comunidad de Estados Latinoamericanos y Caribeños* (CELAC/Community of Latin American and Caribbean States), and *Petrocaribe*, a solidarity agreement for energy cooperation between Venezuela and Caribbean and Central American countries. Of these organizations, UNASUR was the one that simultaneously represented both the greatest potential for autonomous regional political and economic integration and the deep contradictions and transformative limitations of these progressive governments.

This organization was created by the twelve countries of South America. Its constitutive treaty, signed May 23, 2008, defines the purpose of the organization in the following terms:

> The Union of South American Nations aims to build, in a participatory and consensual manner, a space for cultural, social, economic and political integration and union among its peoples, giving priority to political dialogue, social policies, education, energy, infrastructure, financing and the environment, among others, with a view to eliminating socioeconomic inequality, achieving social inclusion and citizen participation, strengthening democracy and reducing asymmetries within the framework of strengthening the sovereignty and independence of states
>
> (UNASUR 2011).

The most outstanding political moment of UNASUR, when the project of South American integration seemed to become a reality, occurred a few months later when there was a profound crisis in Bolivia in which the stability of the government and territorial integrity of the country were at stake, as a consequence of the secessionist threats of the provinces of the so-called Media Luna. Faced with this situation, under the pro tempore presidency of Michelle Bachelet, an emergency meeting of the presidents of the organization's countries was held in Santiago, Chile, where it was agreed:

1 They express their fullest and strongest support for the constitutional government of the President of the Republic of Bolivia, Evo Morales, whose mandate was ratified by a large majority in the recent referendum.

2 They warn that their respective governments strongly reject and will not recognize any situation that implies an attempt at a civil coup, the rupture of institutional order or that compromises the territorial integrity of the Republic of Bolivia (UNASUR 2008).

Crisis of Civilization 69

This meeting was important for two fundamental reasons. First, it effectively managed to initiate negotiation processes with conditions that relegitimized the government of Evo Morales and made it possible to overcome the crisis. Second, for the first time in the history of the continent since its independence, a political conflict with continental repercussions was addressed and resolved by an institution from the region without the participation of the United States, Canada, or the Organization of American States. A milestone that seemed to have clearly marked a before and after.

However, in the area of economic integration, the dominant dynamic has moved in the opposite direction. Despite the many meetings and agreements and high-sounding speeches about continental integration, if each of the countries in the region prioritizes the expansion of exports of one or more primary goods to extra-continental markets, often the same goods to the same markets (oil, iron, copper, soybeans...), mainly to China, there is little room left to be economically complementary and articulate chains of production. In each of the countries of the region, regardless of whether their governments were progressive or neoliberal, over the last three decades, there has been a process of refocusing economies and an increase in the weight of primary goods in total exports (see Table 1.1).

Within the period shown in this graph, intra-regional trade in Latin America shows, with small fluctuations, little variation. In 2015, intra-regional imports for Latin America and the Caribbean as a whole accounted for only 15% of its imports, while intra-regional exports constituted 17% (CEPAL 2017). During the years of progressive governments in Bolivia, Ecuador, and Venezuela, with the exception of imports from Venezuela, both intra-regional imports and exports declined as a percentage of the total (CEPAL 2002, 2010, 2016).

Table 1.1 Change in Primary Resource Export as Share of Total Exports within South America

Country/ year	2000	2002	2004	2006	2008	2010	2012	2014	2016
Argentina	67.5%	69.5%	71.2%	68.2%	69.2%	67.8%	67.9%	67.9%	74.3%
Bolivia	72.3%	84.2%	86.7%	89.9%	92.8%	92.6%	94.7%	94.4%	94.5%
Brazil	42.0%	47.4%	47.0%	49.5%	55.4%	63.6%	65.0%	65.2%	60.1%
Chile	84.0%	83.2%	86.8%	89.0%	88.8%	89.6%	85.8%	85.9%	85.3%
Colombia	65.9%	62.2%	62.9%	64.4%	68.5%	77.9%	82.5%	82.4%	74.5%
Ecuador	89.9%	89.7%	90.7%	90.4%	91.7%	90.2%	91.0%	93.8%	92.5%
Paraguay	80.7%	85.1%	87.3%	84.1%	92.1%	89.3%	91.2%	90.6%	90.6%
Peru	83.1%	83.0%	83.1%	88.0%	86.6%	89.1%	85.4%	85.3%	96.9%
Uruguay	58.5%	63.7%	68.4%	68.7%	71.3%	74.3%	75.9%	76.3%	77.9%
Venezuela	90.9%	86.2%	86.9%	92.7%	95.%	95.7%	98.3%	...	...

CEPAL, *Anuarios Estadísticos de América Latina y el Caribe, 2004-2017.*

70 *Crisis of Civilization*

The process of integration in South America that has advanced the most runs counter to the content of the political discourse on a new integration of progressive governments. It is the one that is led by the guidelines of the Initiative for the Integration of South American Regional Infrastructure (INRSA). This project arose in the year 2000 at the initiative of President Cardoso of Brazil. Its objective was, and still is, to generate infrastructure works in the fields of transport, energy, and telecommunications, in order to facilitate intra-regional and international trade. This proposal came at a time when neoliberalism was at its peak in the continent, and when, with the sole exception of Venezuelan President Hugo Chávez, who was just beginning to define the guidelines for his economic proposal, all the other presidents of the continent were betting on a neoliberal course. As critics have pointed out over the years, this is a project for the development of large-scale physical infrastructure and legal standardization, aimed at deepening the region's subordinate colonial role in the international division of labor and nature (Metiendoruido.com 2016; Servindi 2016). Its main projects, such as the construction of large highways through Amazonia and the Andean mountain range, the dredging of rivers to make them navigable for larger ships, and railroads, aim to overcome the "barriers" represented by mountains and jungles to facilitate the exploitation of "resources" Some of the large hydroelectric dams are intended to supply power for mining. All of this is directly related to the unstoppable momentum of "progress," accelerating with large infrastructure investments the appropriation of territories occupied by indigenous peoples and peasants, equally expanding the massive processes of environmental devastation.

IIRSA and UNASUR were constituted by the same twelve countries that cover the totality of South American territory. These are two models that originated in different geopolitical contexts and that apparently have divergent declared objectives. However, in 2009, UNASUR established complete continuity with IIRSA through the creation of the South American Infrastructure and Planning Council of UNASUR (COSIPLAN), which integrated IIRSA as its technical infrastructure forum.[23]

Given the extraordinary weight of Brazil in South America, the economic and geopolitical interests of that country have played a preponderant role in IIRSA projects through the financing of the BNDES development bank and their implementation by large Brazilian construction companies such as Odebrecht and Camargo Correa. These undertakings were accompanied by extraordinary levels of corruption.

The tension between these two programs for the future of the continent, the neoliberal developmentalist/extractivist program represented by the IIRSA, and the program of radical rupture in the direction of *buen vivir*, the recognition of the rights of nature, and interculturality, is resolved by UNASUR, beyond its speeches and declarations of principles, through facts, in favor of the former.

The precariousness of the dynamics of regional economic integration, the weakness that the interdependence of its chains of production entails—accurately described as interconnection without integration (Zibechi 2016)—was laid bare in the ease with which UNASUR began to be dismembered as the governments of the continent shifted to the right. Six countries (Argentina, Brazil, Chile, Colombia, Peru, and Paraguay) have announced that they will leave the bloc (CNN 2018).

Debates of the Left on Current Anti-Capitalist Struggles in Latin America

Over the last two centuries, the spectrum of anti-capitalist struggles has never been homogeneous, free of debates, or confrontations, from essential founding issues, such as the characterization of capitalism and the models of alternative societies for which they fought, to strategic and tactical debates about the meaning that these struggles, their subjects, methods of organization, and their peaceful or violent nature.[24]

During the English Industrial Revolution, for the first time in history, processes of transforming from a rural, primarily agricultural-based society to an urban, factory-based society took place. Every basic aspect of the life of society as a whole was profoundly altered within a few decades. The enclosure of the commons implied the transformation of what had hitherto been in common use (grazing land, forests, water) into a property for the exclusive use of its private owners. The conceptions and practices of time underwent profound changes. A new regime of discipline was created in which the organization of life ceased to revolve around the rhythms of nature, in terms of agricultural activity, and became organized around the times and rhythms of industrial activity. Simultaneously, the era witnessed the transition from the traditional extended family structure to the nuclear family as well as transformations in the social fabric of the community and the emergence of a new individualism and anonymity in urban life. The logic of commodification began to extend to ever wider areas of collective life.

So profound and accelerated were the transformations that took place in a few decades, and so extraordinary the changes, that broad sectors of society became aware that the world was changing and that new ways of life were emerging before their eyes. This made it possible for what can properly be called a civilizational debate to take place. Different sectors of society experienced and evaluated these dynamics in ways that were not only extraordinarily differentiated but antagonistic. It is possible to identify, in very general terms, three major positions in relation to this great civilizational transformation. The first of these, the bourgeoisie, the so-called industrialists, assumed liberal positions associated with the idea of progress, free trade, and blind faith in the advances of science and technology. Traditional customs and ways of life were seen

72 *Crisis of Civilization*

as obstacles to be overcome. A second position was that which has been commonly characterized as traditionalist or conservative, associated mainly with the feudal class of rural landowners and the church. Beyond the narrative constructed by the victors, this second position was not limited to reactionary landowners. Rather, it constituted a more complex resistance that incorporated the opposition to the commodification of nature and a different understanding of the relationship between humans and nature. They were also opposed to what they saw as a tearing apart of the fabric of society. The third position is the one that can be identified with the subaltern sectors most directly affected by these transformations, mainly the peasants expelled from the lands on which they lived by means of enclosures and the subsequent subjugation to the new and brutal conditions of factory discipline. One of the most important expressions of resistance against the enclosures and the new factory conditions was that which identified the new machinery as the main cause of these processes and turned the confrontation with them into their main form of struggle: the *Luddites*.

The confrontations between these different social sectors and postures around these accelerated transformative dynamics were often violent, with state repression of resistance playing a central role. Only a very small proportion of the population had the right to vote. These were civilizational confrontations insofar as what was at stake, to a considerable extent, was precisely what model of the organization of collective life would end up prevailing.

By the beginning of the fourth decade of the 19th century, most of the resistance had been defeated, and the new free social order of the industrialists had been consolidated. Memories of other ways of life were gradually forgotten. This profoundly altered the content of social struggles, which went from being confrontations for or against industrial society to being disputes inside it. The workers' struggles once resistant to the imposition of the factory regime were now struggles within industrial society: struggles over the working day, working conditions, wages, and the right to union organization.

This was a historic defeat for the resistance and its alternatives. The industrial society's way of life spread to the rest of Western Europe.

These are the conditions in which the anti-capitalist struggles identified with the Left and/or socialism emerge and are structured, discarding other potential historical trajectories. This is the cultural-historical context in which Marxism was born. A process that took place first in Europe and then spread to other continents in the course of imperial colonial subjugation. The trend toward homogenization, which from the perspective of the victorious was supposed to proceed until the disappearance of the vestiges of the traditional past, only partially took place in Europe. Much less in the world subjected to colonial domination, where both the political systems of domination and the Eurocentric

Crisis of Civilization 73

resistances left the majority of the population out as present or future subjects. A political grammar was imposed in most of the Global South that, taking the European experience as a template defined who were the legitimate subjects of political and social action, the demands that could be recognized as valid, and their corresponding forms of organization. For a long time, these others (often the majority of the population) and their own cultures and alternative historical trajectories remained off the radar of institutional politics, both from Eurocentric powers and Eurocentric resistances. These other subjects, other cultures, other histories, other forms of organization, other forms of knowledge, and other non-anthropocentric ways of being and being in nature were not only made invisible, but were placed in a past time: primitive, traditional, or feudal. As liberal industrial society was constructed as the present and the future, as the "modern," everything else was relegated to the past[25]—a time overcome in the teleological meta-narrative of modernity. This past was constructed as negativity from which there was nothing to recover. Entire populations, their experiences, and cultures were denied as realities that had any possibility of having anything to say about the present and the future. These Eurocentric perspectives of denial of the *other* are historically rooted in deep racism. European parochial history, its subjects, and its agents were constructed as the model of universal history.

In the anti-capitalist positions identified with Marxism and utopian socialism, there has been, fundamentally, a common framing in the interpretations of capitalism and its alternatives within the modern, colonial, Eurocentric imaginaries of industrial society. Anthropocentric, patriarchal, and mono-cultural conceptions became hegemonic, with blind confidence in progress and the development of productive forces. The transformation was thought of in terms of a revolutionary vanguard party and the leading role of the state as the privileged sphere of change.

The Emergence of New Forms of Anti-Systemic Politics

From a history that is richer and with diverse tonalities, it is possible to discern some of the major milestones that while shaking the foundations of traditional Eurocentric anti-systemic policies, were opening the way for new forms of political action.

May 1968, in its various expressions in different parts of the world, constitutes a historical moment in which a profound crisis is evident in the dominant forms of politics, especially the anti-systemic politically organized expressions. As Immanuel Wallerstein has pointed out, it was the manifestation of a global crisis in the legitimacy of the main forms that the struggles of the Left had taken throughout the world: the real socialism of the Soviet bloc, European social democracy, and the governments resulting from the national liberation movements, especially on the African continent.

74   *Crisis of Civilization*

[...] by the 1960s one of these three kinds of movements or the other had achieved state power in most countries of the world. However, it was clear that they had not succeeded in transforming the world

(Wallerstein 2002).

Thus, the movements and struggles associated with 1968, including the civil rights movement in the United States and the global resistance to the Vietnam War, not only questioned capitalist society but also the various traditions of the Left. Criticizing the state-centric character of politics and the notions according to which societal changes only would occur after the seizure of state power, issues such as patriarchy, sexuality, racism, ethnicity, patterns of consumption, environmental destruction, democracy, and criticism of authoritarianism in all its expressions, from the state/party level, through the worlds of labor and educational institutions, to the everyday and family level were placed at the center of political activism.

The most significant and lasting consequences of these movements were their contributions to the emergence of profound transformations in the culture, imaginaries, and collective consciousness of a broad spectrum of the planet's population, especially the young.

A second critical moment in the transformations of the hegemonic forms of anti-systemic struggles occurred as a result of the fall of the Berlin Wall and the collapse of the Soviet bloc. The impact on anti-systemic struggles was ambivalent (Lander 2004). On the one hand, the collapse of the Soviet Union signified the end of the bipolar world, the strengthening of the imperial power of the United States, and an extraordinary advance in the process of the commodification of life across the planet. This severely limited the margins of action that the bipolar confrontation had offered for many non-aligned experiences. In this sense, it signified a severe setback for anti-capitalist struggles.

However, on the other hand, it favored the liberation of peoples' imaginations from the subjection to a single alternative to capitalism, from the suffocating weight of a teleological philosophy of history that, from its Eurocentric construction, sought to impose a single historical track on all peoples. It ended up burying the pretensions of the existence of a universal historical subject capable of transforming the existing order and building an alternative one. It contributed to delegitimizing the idea of progress and the belief in the possibility of endless economic growth and the unlimited exploitation of nature as a condition for freedom and human happiness. It made more transparent the authoritarian and mono-cultural character of technocrats or revolutionary vanguards with their pretensions of trying to direct society as a whole from the monopoly of truth. New conditions were opened up for the recognition of the multiplicity of sources of knowledge in critique and resistance to the existing order and the foreshadowing of another possible world. It also contributed to diluting the sense of the classical opposition between *reform* and *revolution* and the corresponding

Crisis of Civilization 75

disqualification of everything that was not considered revolutionary. The assumption that the future is open, not predetermined by the laws of history but the product of human action, radically changes the meaning of these old debates. In summary, these complex political-cultural displacements involved, from exceedingly diverse perspectives and practices, radical questioning of the methods of doing politics that had been hegemonic on the Left, especially state-centrism and the resulting priority given to the idea of taking over the state apparatus (whether by armed or electoral means), as well as the centrality given to parties and vanguards in social transformation. On the basis of what had been the experience of both the socialist camp and social democratic governments, there had been a failure to achieve the profound transformations of society to which they aspired. The notion that it would be possible to transform society from the state was questioned. Consequently, priority was given to cultural transformations and the construction of counter-hegemonies as the preconditions for the very possibility of a post-capitalist society. Social transformations are no longer conceived as projects for the future after the seizure of power. The changes and configurations of another society are imagined and practiced in the here and now.

The search for other democratic, plural forms of political action, other organizational and institutional modalities of struggle, other forms of knowledge production required for social transformation, and the emergence of new alternative subcultures are not only exclusively theoretical issues to be addressed by an intellectual elite but also challenges for collective creation from the multiple societal expressions of social-political action. The plurality of actors and subjects, diversity, democracy, and experimentation are shaping the bases of this other politics that incorporates, among others, diverse conceptions and practices of autonomy and self-government.

The World Social Forum, since its first meeting in Porto Alegre in 2001, is conceived as a space for international collective experimentation and consolidation of these new ways of conducting anti-systemic politics. It is constituted as a plural, diversified, decentralized, non-partisan, non-state, non-confessional space; a place for debate, meeting, exchange of experiences, and collective creation; an environment in which the plurality of participating organizations can, in their diversity, despite their differences, recognize each other. Governments have not participated, the presence of political parties has been limited, and the seizure of state power has not been part of their shared agenda.

> [The Forum] aims to consolidate a globalization of solidarity [...] that respects universal human rights, all citizens of all nations and the environment, based on democratic international systems and institutions that are at the service of social justice, equality, and the sovereignty of peoples. [It] includes those who oppose neo-liberalism

76 *Crisis of Civilization*

and the domination of the world by capital or any form of imperialism and seeks the construction of a planetary society oriented
towards a fruitful relationship between human beings and between
human beings and the Earth

(World Social Forum 2002).

In contrast to the organizational practices and modalities that had been
hegemonic on the Left, all this implies other forms of political action and
new democratic, flexible, pluralistic institutionalism, built by the participating movements and organizations themselves. New forms of solidarity and internationalism are created around a wide range of issues:
free trade agreements; peasant struggles; resistance to war; indigenous
peoples' territorial rights; confronting water privatization. Themes and
issues that previously could be thought of as of sectoral interest (respect
for Mother Earth, the defense of territory, confronting patriarchy, the
search for alternatives to the agricultural-food model based on monoculture and transgenic crops, agro-industry, etc.) are now contributing to
the creation of a new political culture. Concepts such as *Sumak Kawsay*
and *Suma Qamaña* are becoming widely shared references.

The *Charter of Principles* of the Forum establishes that it is a space
for meeting, exchange of experiences, and coordination, but not an
organization that in unitary terms makes decisions and formulates
pronouncements in the name of all. This, however, in no way hindered
the coordination of joint actions between movements that participated
in the Forum, such as the global mobilization against the U.S. war in
Iraq called by the Assembly of Movements of the First European Social
Forum organized in Florence, Italy, in November 2002, and that of the
World Social Forum held in Porto Alegre in January 2003. As a result
of this joint action in which movements and organizations from all over
the world participated, the largest simultaneous day of protest in the history of humanity took place. With an estimated participation of around
30 million people, anti-war mobilizations took place in 600–800 cities
around the world (Bennis 2003).

All these processes made possible a broader willingness to critically
reflect on what had been the experience of socialism in the last century,
beyond analyses that would seek to identify "deviations" or justifications
for what would have been inevitable reactions to the imperial threat, it
also opened up old and new debates about Marxism, including the recognition that Marxism and the prospect of socialism as the society of
the future was but one current, among others, from critical thought and
anti-capitalist struggles.

During the last decades, without necessarily breaking with the Marxist
tradition nor questioning its extraordinary validity for the understanding of the dynamics of capitalist society, there has been a wide range
of conceptual contributions and critical practices that have enriched the

Crisis of Civilization   77

understanding of capitalism and made enormously more complex the challenges of overcoming it. It might be possible to identify two main approaches. One with an emphasis on the formulation of other alternatives for the future and the other that recognizes and makes visible ways of life that have persisted for a long time on the margins of capitalism and which, through this new way of seeing the world, emerge as part of the anti-capitalist heritage.

From the perspective of modernity/coloniality, a radical critique of Eurocentric interpretations of modernity has been formulated by highlighting that, for the majority of the planet's population, modernity has been an experience of colonization, enslavement, extermination, and appropriation of common goods without which the shining side of modernity found in the colonizing North would not have been possible. Analyzing the implications of assuming European parochial history as *universal history*, thus, calls into question hegemonic Eurocentric thinking is a key element of these recent approaches.[26]

Aníbal Quijano formulates a severe challenge to Eurocentric teleological thinking and economic determinism with his conception of the *coloniality of power*. Denying the universal character of economic determinism, even as an ultimate determination he argues that historical existence is determined by five interrelated dimensions whose relative weights and modes of interaction are neither defined nor fixed by universal laws but vary in different historical contexts or moments.

> Every form of social existence that reproduces itself over the long term involves five indispensable basic spheres: sex, work, subjectivity, collective authority, and "nature". The ongoing struggle for control over these spheres gives rise to power relations. From this perspective, the phenomenon of power is characterized as a type of social relation constituted by the co-presence and permanent interactivity of three elements: domination/exploitation/conflict, which affects each and every one of the five basic spheres of all social existence and which is the result and expression of the dispute for control over them: (1) sex, its resources and its products; (2) work, its resources and its products; (3) subjectivity/intersubjectivity, its resources and its products; (4) collective (or public) authority, its resources and its products; (5) relations with other forms of life and with the rest of the universe (everything that in conventional language is usually called "nature").

> The forms of social existence in each of these spheres do not arise from one another, but they do not exist, cannot exist, and cannot operate, separately or independently of one another. For this very reason, the relations of power that are constituted in the dispute for the control of such areas or spheres of social existence, neither are

78 *Crisis of Civilization*

they born, nor do they derive from each other, but they cannot exist, except in an untimely and precarious manner, one without the other. That is, they form a structural complex that certainly behaves as such, but where the relations between the differentiated spheres do not have, cannot have, a systemic or organic character, since each sphere of the respective social existence has specific origins and conditions. The concrete elements and the respective measures and ways in which they are articulated in each sphere and in the joint structure come from the concrete behaviors of people, that is, they are always historical and specific in their origin, in their character, in their movement. In other words, it is always about a certain historical pattern of power

(Quijano 2001).

Another fundamental approach in the critique of teleological Eurocentric thinking is the questioning of development, a political-epistemological construct through which the population of most of the global South was transformed into past, into backwardness, into poverty, which required the modernizing intervention of the North, the United Nations, and Bretton Woods institutions and their funding and experts (Escobar 2007).

As patriarchy is a constitutive, foundational dimension of modernity and the capitalist world system, critical contributions from a wide range of feminist perspectives have been essential. Among these, we can highlight: (1) the characterization of modern science as patriarchal insofar as it is based on imaginaries of subject/object separation and mechanistic conceptions of nature as a passive dead object, available to be subjugated and exploited for the material well-being of humanity. The subjugation of nature that is conceived of as feminine is integral to the power of the scientific method (Merchant 1980); (2) the critique of the radically reductionist character of economic science which, by focusing exclusively on monetary exchanges, leaves most of the processes of wealth creation out of its gaze: nature, peasant subsistence work, barter, household work, and care work (Mies 2008); (3) the characterization of the modern state as a patriarchal institution that is sustained at the center of what has been understood as the masculine in the historical division of society between the public and the private, between production and reproduction (Brown 1995; Pateman 1980; Segato 2018); and (4) the different strands of ecofeminism (Mies and Shiva 2016; Salleh 2007).

The diverse contributions and ruptures that have been produced from the theoretical and activist fields associated with ecological economics and political ecology have been vital (Alimonda, Toro Pérez, and Martín 2017; Leff 2006; Martínez Allier 2009), a line of thought to which positions identified with Marxism such as eco-socialism have contributed significantly (Löwy 2012).[27]

Crisis of Civilization 79

Several fundamental currents of a radical questioning of the Eurocentric modalities of anti-capitalist struggles come from *other* traditions, histories, and cultures, which have not been fully subjected to the logic of capital and the ways of life of modern industrial society. In contrast to perspectives that seek the sources of capitalism's transformations in its internal contradictions, these are struggles in resistance to the expansion of capitalism in territories and interstices not fully colonized by it, which seek to preserve, recover, and reconstruct their own heritage, which has been de-drawn, distorted, debilitated, defending—interculturally, without essentialisms—other non-commodified ways of life. This covers a wide spectrum, from indigenous and peasant resistances in many different parts of the world (Kothari and Joy 2017) to forms of solidarity-based economies (Coraggio 2011), experiences of collective recovery/construction of the commons (Bollier and Helfrich 2012), and de-growth proposals (D'Alisa, Demaria and Kallis 2015), especially from Europe.

Other Forms of Politics and Seizure of Power by Progressive Governments

In the decades prior to the beginning of the era of progressive governments, there was extraordinary socio-political activism in Latin America, characterized fundamentally as the broadening of the sphere of politics and the blurring of boundaries of the central axis of articulation: Left/Right. The modalities of the political organization changed and new social subjects became central actors. The paradigmatic examples of this new phase of popular struggles in the continent were the *Caracazo* (1989); the Inti Raymi Indigenous Uprising in Ecuador (1990); the First Indigenous March for Territory and Dignity in Bolivia (1990); the Zapatista uprising in Mexico (1994); and the Cochabamba Water War (1999–2000). None of these struggles were led by political parties nor did they have the seizure of power as their reference point. On less visible scales, throughout the continent, there are simultaneous local struggles in defense of territories and experiments in establishing other ways of living.

Progressive governments come to power in the context of these profound shifts in the conceptions and practices of anti-capitalist struggles, and on the basis of these dynamics of popular mobilization/organization. However, once installed in the state and adopting a state perspective, an extraordinary recovery of old forms of anti-capitalist politics takes place. An epistemology proper to the state's view of reality is assumed, from the perspective of centralized power (Scott 1998). This perspective is well synthesized by Álvaro García Linera in the following terms:

> The State is the only thing that can unite society, the only thing that gathers the synthesis of the general will; that plans the strategic

80 *Crisis of Civilization*

framework and is the engine of the locomotive. The second is light private investment; third is foreign investment; fourth is small business; fifth is the rural economy; and sixth is the indigenous economy. This is the strategic order in which the country's economy has to be structured

(García Linera 2007).

There is an intensified re-emergence of an orthodoxy that seemed to have been left behind by the extraordinary shifts in the politics of the previous half-century: partisanship/vanguardism, state-centrism, patriarchy, anthropocentrism, monoculture, and faith in progress. Step by step, the main contents of civilizational transformations present in the constitutional texts that were previously analyzed are being put aside, giving priority to the strengthening of the state, to the preservation of power in the name of the "Revolution" or "socialism." As has been argued in the second part of this text, in Ecuador and Bolivia, a deep rift developed between the government and the movements and communities that brought them to power.

It is possible to characterize schematically the confrontations that have taken place in the Left, or more broadly in the anti-capitalist camp, regarding the so-called progressive governments, in the following terms. On the one hand, there are those, mainly in the party-affiliated Left—at least for the first stage of the process of change—who have given priority to anti-imperialism, the rejection of the economic policies of neoliberalism, the recovery of the state, national sovereignty, the short-term overcoming of poverty/inequality, and economic growth. In general, they tend to have non-problematized views on issues such as patriarchy, interculturality, territorial autonomies, or the strategic implications of a productive model centered on extractivism.

On the other hand, there are a variety of plural, non-state perspectives that, without ignoring the importance of all of the above, affirm the need to confront equally and simultaneously the racism, patriarchy, coloniality, and anthropocentrism characteristic of colonial modernity. Varying widely, without denying the importance of the state in the contemporary world system, they reject state-centrism without ignoring the complex challenges of political action within, alongside, and against the state. They assume that if the dynamics of the destruction of life on the planet and the wide range of cultures that characterize humanity are not stopped in the very short term, no transformation will be possible. From these perspectives, it is assumed that the theoretical instruments and policies from the last century that seemed sufficient to confront capitalism—centered on class perspectives, forms of property, and the guiding role of the state—are no longer sufficient for the world in which we live. Today we have to confront not only the forms of economic and political domination of capitalism but also the geo-culture of modernity. These are civilizational challenges and, therefore, much more demanding: a patriarchal global system that is destroying both the material conditions that make life on the planet possible and the extraordinary diversity of the memories and cultures of the peoples who inhabit it. Within this current, a radically critical perspective prevails the notion that the accentuation of the extractivist model can be considered as a way to overcome capitalism.

In these oppositions, there are also profound differences regarding the agents of the processes of transformation. In the first bloc, the clear priority is given to the state as the guiding agent of the processes of change and to the party as the disciplinary/electoral tool that guarantees permanence in government, while for the other bloc, the required transformations shall primarily involve social movements and organizations, peoples and communities and account for the multiple expressions of the fabric of society and cultural changes.

These divergences in the interpretations of the political processes of the last decades have also led to a deep division in the field of Latin American academia.

The "progressive" governments and their defenders argue that it is (or was) necessary to take advantage of the context of high demand and commodities prices to accumulate the resources required to make the social, productive, and infrastructure investments that would make it possible, in a later phase, to overcome extractivism. This would necessarily require greater state control over the exploitation of raw materials, either through nationalization or higher taxes, in order to gain a greater share of the income that had previously benefited transnational corporations.[28]

Socialism of the 21st Century

When the Bolivarian process was declared as a socialist project by President Hugo Chávez at the World Social Forum in Porto Alegre in January 2005, this was done, fundamentally, without memory or historical consciousness (Lander 2018). The major issues that had led to the failure of 20th-century socialism as an alternative to capitalism and the hegemonic pattern of civilization, which were pointed out at the beginning of this chapter, were not debated: not anthropocentrism, Eurocentrism, its mono-cultural universalist character, patriarchy, blind faith in progress and the so-called productive forces of capitalism, nor the tendencies toward authoritarianism that led to Stalinism were problematized. The substantive debates held in Venezuela in previous decades were forgotten because the idea of socialism had disappeared from the political horizon. Its protagonists had died, moved away from politics, or adopted neoliberal positions. The publications that compiled these debates were not being reprinted and/or had ceased to circulate.

82   *Crisis of Civilization*

By calling itself "21st century," it seemed to imply that this new project of society would not be similar to the experience of 20th-century socialism, the Soviet experience in particular. However, to the extent that there was no critical debate on these issues, there was no reflection about the question of whether it was possible to disentangle this project of change from its heavy heritage, its rootedness in the conceptions and practices of the socialism that actually existed. In the absence of the will and/or capacity to address these vital questions, it was not possible to imagine 21st-century socialism being significantly different from that of the 20th-century. To the young people who enthusiastically joined this political project in the first decade of the 21st century, the idea of socialism came uncontaminated, only as a promise of the future, without any historical burden.

A worrying sign that the proposal for 21st-century socialism had not seemed to have learned much from the experience of Soviet socialism came when Chávez called for the formation of a single party in 2006. Chávez announced that, in order to advance in this process of building socialism, it was indispensable to overcome the existing political and organizational fragmentation among the forces that formed part of the government. To this end, he announced that it was necessary to form a single party. He suggested the name of the United Socialist Party of Venezuela, the PSUV (Chávez Frías 2006), and the adoption of a hierarchical structure called democratic centralism as its organizing principle, "understood as the subordination of the whole organization to the leadership; the subordination of all militants to its organisms; the subordination of the lower organisms to the higher ones; the subordination of the minority to the majority [...]" (PSUV 2009). In the total absence of any debate on the historical experience of single parties in socialist regimes, the merger between state and party began as soon as the PSUV was created.

Foro de São Paulo

This renewed socialist orthodoxy was not limited to Venezuela. Its most systematic, coherent, and representative expression is recorded in the declarations and documents of the Foro de São Paulo, a space of party convergence founded on the initiative of the Brazilian Workers' Party (PT) in São Paulo in 1990, which today groups together the great majority of political organizations that define themselves as leftist throughout Latin America. While it is not an organic vertical body with the capacity to promote and/or impose common policies on its participating organizations, and although it has not had the kind of political influence of the Comintern in the times of Lenin and Stalin, the number of political parties and organizations that belong to this Forum is still very broad, organizations that even tend to have political differences within their respective countries. The successive declarations produced by the annual

Crisis of Civilization 83

meetings in different parts of the continent since its foundation are formulated on behalf of all members. In these declarations, in addition to a reaffirmation of principles, a pronouncement is made in relation to the most relevant issues of the current situation.[29] The Foro de São Paulo assumes itself to be "[...] the convergence of political parties and movements from the whole spectrum of the Left; protagonists of the most diverse forms of struggle." The Foro de São Paulo defines the struggle against imperialism as its main point of agreement. "Within our plurality and diversity, the political parties and movements that are members of the Foro de São Paulo agree on the struggle against imperialism, which in the last two decades of the twentieth century took the form of neoliberal capitalism" (Foro de São Paulo 2000). This Forum constitutes the clearest expression of what could be called an "official" state- and party-based Left in Latin America.

Perspectives of the Foro de São Paulo on Today's World

The first critical issue in the perspectives of this Left and its positions in relation to the so-called progressive governments has to do with the characterization of the global context in which they operate. How are the civilizational challenges that have been described in this text integrated with the here and now of geopolitical reality within which they take place? This is a Left that seems to remain anchored in the Cold War, seeing the world through reductionist visions articulated around the central axis of confrontations between imperialism/anti-imperialism, imperialism identified with the United States and its European allies. Geopolitics reigns over all the other dimensions of reality,[30] leading to erasing or ignoring, for example, the strong internal socio-environmental conflicts that occur due to the progressive intensification of extractivism.

The most urgent issue facing humanity in our times, the need to curb endless growth on a limited planet and the reality of the climatic transformations that are destroying the conditions for the reproduction of life on the planet, is either not addressed or is addressed only in terms of general references that seem intended to meet only the requirement of being politically correct. In conditions in which the planet is reaching its boundaries and, as has been pointed out, drastic reductions in greenhouse gas emissions are essential in the very short term to avoid climate transformations that threaten life as we know it, the annual declarations of the Foro de São Paulo, for example, show no concern whatsoever about the fact that the *Plan de la Patria* presented by Chávez in 2012 offered to double the country's oil production from three to six million barrels per day by the year 2019.

Neo-developmentalism and extractivism being the main civilizational challenges of our time, with their consequences for climate change, their impact on the territories of indigenous peoples and peasants, their effects

84   *Crisis of Civilization*

on water, deforestation, the destruction of biodiversity as well as their direct impacts on the exercise of democratic rights, the official Latin American Left has limited itself to general statements, taking care not to question the policies of progressive governments:

> Today the planet is threatened by the widespread deterioration of the environment and by climate change, the product of the savage exploitation of natural resources. Yet, the industrialized countries refuse to adopt the measures agreed upon in the international fora that will keep us from continuing along the road to disaster
>
> (Foro de São Paulo 2008).

> The environmental crisis is an integral part of the capitalist crisis. The defense of the environment must take into account the interests of workers, sustainability and national sovereignty because the right wing and imperialism have used the environmental banner to attack leftist governments in Latin America and the Caribbean
>
> (Foro de São Paulo 2013).

> The SPF fights for the environment, natural resources, the seas, the forests, and the water. Moreover, it fights against the disastrous impacts of increased greenhouse gases, on the road to COP 20, in Lima in December 2014, and COP 21, in Paris in December 2015, on climate change, aiming at a global agreement that may mitigate it, besides driving a sustained and sustainable, and renewable productive economy and culture, with solidarity and Living Well practices, and against primary exporting economies subordinated to the world market
>
> (Foro de São Paulo 2014).

From these statements on climate change and on primary exporting economies, the following can be highlighted. In the first place, the responsibility lies elsewhere, "the industrialized countries refuse to take the measures agreed upon in international fora that would prevent them from continuing on the path of disaster." This completely ignores the fact that the deepening of extractivist policies promoted by all progressive governments, far from contributing to slowing down "the road to disaster," has actively contributed to accelerating it. Second, as has repeatedly appeared in government speeches in response to the critical remarks that have been made about their extractivist policies, especially by well-known international environmental organizations, they consider that "imperialism has used the environmental banner to attack leftist governments in Latin America and the Caribbean." Third, there is talk of the need to overcome "the type of primary-export economies subjected to the world market," but there is no recognition that these

Crisis of Civilization 85

"progressive," "friendly" governments, all without exception, have deepened these policies.

The Nicaraguan Canal is celebrated, despite the widespread resistance it has faced in that country, especially from the affected peasants. From a perspective that gives full priority to developmentalism, it is stated that "sustained economic growth [...] will have substantial reinforcement with the construction and implementation of the interoceanic canal" (Foro de São Paulo 2014).

At the same time, the annual declarations of the Foro de São Paulo make no reference whatsoever to the large and emblematic developmentalist/extractivist projects that have been important focal points of popular resistance against the policies of progressive governments among which the following stand out: fracking in Vaca Muerta in Argentine, Belo Monte dam in the Brazilian part of Amazonia, the TIPNIS highway in Bolivia, the decision to exploit the Yasuní oil reserves in Ecuador, and the Arco Minero of the Orinoco in Venezuela. It seems that they are talking about another continent and making an effort to ignore the collective subjects of the most vigorous recent social struggles in Latin America as referents of social transformation.

In the absence of a comprehensive reflection on the significance of patriarchy, the confrontation of it seems to be limited to problems, which, while important, do not account for the complex range of issues at stake in patriarchy. The highlighted issues are equality between men and women at work and in public service and violence against women, as well as sexual harassment.

> Violence has also struck women, who are subjected to femicide, domestic violence, sexual harassment, workplace violence, and aggression by attacking troops and puppet governments. We stand for the eradication of violence against women. [...] it is necessary to continue to develop the struggle of women to overcome sexist practices and ideologies that even within our own organizations and parties continue to exist as manifestations of discrimination that must be eradicated for a new relationship between the genders under conditions of equal opportunity
>
> (Foro de São Paulo 2000).

A new economic and social model, as an alternative to the neoliberal model, that breaks and overcomes the capitalist system, must have a vital attribute: to break with the still existing patriarchal systems of social and political organization. Within this framework, the FSP is committed to full equality for everyone and demands the guarantee of their Human Rights no matter what their gender, sexual orientation or gender identity. Furthermore, the FSP is committed to public policies and affirmative actions in favor of Afro-descendants.

86 *Crisis of Civilization*

[...]

We, the members of FSP parties, recognize that in order to achieve a truly fair and equitable society the presence and participation of women in the different sectors of society is essential. It is necessary to change the traditional roles and patterns that have been historically assigned and assumed in different forms by men and women, from the point of view of breaking down the domination of patriarchies; conditions must be created for the total emancipation of women, eliminating the gender gaps that still exist in the hinterlands of our countries. The policies and strategies of our parties have to ensure, *de jure* and *de facto*, the empowerment of women in conditions of equality, with equal participation both in the public and private spheres. The recognition of the feminist agenda continues to be a challenge for left-wing parties and revolutionaries, as a transversal axis for incorporating the women's agenda and a correct gender approach for policies, programs and actions that are being designed in the struggle against the right wing, oppressive, predatory and patriarchal capitalism, and the imperial counter-offensive of our times

(Foro de São Paulo 2015).

None of these documents mention such essential issues for combating patriarchy as women's sovereignty over their own bodies, the implications of fundamentalist attacks on the so-called "gender ideologies," LGBT rights, or the differentiated impacts of extractivist policies on women. Nor is there any concern about the extent to which the leaderships and hyper-leaderships that have emerged in the continent actually reinforce patriarchal cultural patterns in society as a whole.

The Forum's declarations repeatedly celebrate the creation of organizations for Latin American integration. However, there is no reference to the fact that the extractivist and primary export orientation of all progressive governments block, as argued in the second part of this text, the possibilities of the productive integration of the continent since they put the countries in competition with each other in the face of the world market. Nor is there any mention of the extraordinary vulnerability created by the dependence on the inevitable fluctuations in commodity prices on the international market.

When the PT and Inácio Lula da Silva won elections in 2002, the Foro de São Paulo highlighted, as a central aspect, the fact that it was a moral triumph against corruption, "a meeting point between ethics and politics":

In Brazil, hope overcame fear and allowed a victory of the "yes we can" against one-dimensional thinking. It was a moral triumph against corruption, a meeting point between ethics and politics, a will for change that reached all the confines of this immense country and radiates to

Latin America and the Caribbean, opening up special perspectives for the political and social struggles that our peoples are carrying out against the harmful consequences of neoliberal policies, aggravated in the last period (Foro de São Paulo 2002). Three years later, "the relentless fight against corruption by Lula's governments" is highlighted (Foro de São Paulo 2005).

However, this moral superiority the Left claimed, this meeting between ethics and politics, began to crack when the corruption occurred, on varying scales, in all progressive governments, highlighting the corrupt practices in Brazil's Petrobras and Odebrecht companies for their impacts far beyond national borders and the massive corruption that has characterized the Ortega-Murillo and Maduro governments. In the documents of the Foro de São Paulo, far from calling attention and demanding that drastic measures be taken, investigating its causes, and considering corruption as a serious challenge that has to be faced by leftist governments, these issues are placed in the background. The accusations on this matter are denied or attributed to right-wing or imperialist attempts to destabilize. To wash the hands of the PT, the corruption of the semi-state Petrobras is attributed to "career officials" of the company. It does not seem to be a matter that requires further investigation, since it would appear that it is in the nature of the Left to be honest. In 2016, what Lula declared when he won the elections 14 years earlier was ratified: The "left promotes transparency and honesty in the use and management of public resources" (Foro de São Paulo 2016). The Left's claim to represent ethics and morality, which remains untouched after all the scandals, has contributed to its profound discreditation in the eyes of the population and facilitated the return of the right. This double pattern and double discourse undermine an essential dimension of what the Left would hope to claim as its own particular legacy.

The Primacy of Geopolitics

Many distortions occur as a result of the primacy of geopolitics. It operates on the basis of a Manichean view of reality: the good guys and the bad guys. By continuing to identify imperialism only with the United States, there is little room for the recognition of the profound rearrangements that have taken place in the world system over recent decades, in particular, the emergence of China as an imperial power. Consequently, anyone with confrontational practices or discourses with the United States is identified as a friend or ally. Dictatorial governments capable of massacring their populations on a large scale in order to remain in power, as has been the case of Bashar Hafez al-Assad in Syria, the patriarchal authoritarianism that exists in the Islamic Republic of Iran, or the authoritarian capitalist regimes of China, Russia, Belarus, are defended or implicitly considered as anti-imperialist allies. The extraordinarily

88 *Crisis of Civilization*

popular anti-dictatorial revolts of the Arab Spring were viewed with suspicion, and expressions of solidarity were almost non-existent.

China's Role as a Blind Spot

Based on the primacy of this geopolitical view centered on the United States that has guided the policies of progressive governments in Latin America, there seems to be a blind spot regarding the significance of the growing presence of China on the continent.

Leaving behind the imaginaries of socialism and the Cultural Revolution and despite the tight political control still exercised by the Communist Party, China is today not only a capitalist country but also an imperialist one that reproduces the classic center-periphery relations of the old empires. During the last two decades, it has been the most dynamic engine of capital accumulation on a global scale. This dynamic is clearly illustrated by the rapid emergence of multi-billionaires in China in recent years. Twelve years ago, there were 16 multi-billionaires in China; by 2017, this figure had risen to 373, one-fifth of the world's billionaires. In 2017, two multi-billionaires were created every week. In that year alone, their wealth increased by 39%, rising to US$1.12 trillion (Widrig 2018).

The accelerated growth of the industrial base over the last four decades has generated an extraordinary demand for primary goods, minerals, energy, and agro-forestry, massively increasing the need for imports of these goods, mainly from Africa and Latin America. Today, China is the largest or second-largest trading partner of most South American countries. China is by far the main source of investment and external financing. These relations have been decisive in strengthening Latin America's colonial export-oriented role in the international division of labor and nature. They have been the fundamental driving force behind the intensification of the extractivist model for the export of nature as much in countries with "revolutionary" and "reformist" governments as those with neoliberal ones. According to CEPAL:

> [...] only five products, all primary, accounted for 69% of the value of regional shipments to China in 2015. The dynamics of Chinese foreign direct investment in the region reinforce this pattern, as almost 90% of such investment between 2010 and 2015 went to extractive activities, particularly mining and hydrocarbon production
>
> (CEPAL 2016).

Chinese financing does not impose the structural adjustment conditions characteristic of the loans from the Bretton Woods Institutions, but they are by no means unconditional credits. They are primarily aimed at securing access to primary goods. Their infrastructure funding (ports, railways, hydroelectric dams) is aimed at guaranteeing the exploitation and export of these goods. In the cases of Venezuela and Ecuador, a high proportion of the credits are payable in oil, thus consolidating over time the oil-rentier economy in these countries.

As has been widely documented, the behavior of Chinese transnationals, public or private, has been no different from U.S. transnationals in labor relations or respect for the environment. (International Federation for Human Rights et al. 2018). These types of relationships, far from contributing to the achievement of the utopian prospects enshrined in the constitutions of these countries, have hindered them. China has demonstrated, beyond the rhetoric, that far from being a supportive ally of processes for change, it prioritizes its own economic and geopolitical interests, regardless of the political orientation of the governments with which it negotiates. Resistance to the advances of the processes of accumulation by dispossession from Chinese companies has been more difficult because, unlike the transnationals of American and European origin, whose behavior is widely understood, it has taken quite some time to recognize similar behaviors in these new companies from a "friendly" country.

In its statements, the Foro de São Paulo recognizes in theory the risks of substituting the United States for China in order to continue with the same primary export model:

> At the outset, we must avoid two mistakes. The first one would be to lose sight of the fact that the main problem in Latin America and the Caribbean remains the economic and political hegemony of the United States and its European allies. And changing the model, including the neoliberal influences, is the only secure way to avoid the risks of a Latin American re-primarization. The other mistake would be not to perceive the risks of turning the Latin American region into an exclusive exporter of raw materials. Such a situation could lead to a pure and simple substitution of the US for China in our trade relations
>
> (Foro de São Paulo 2000).

However, to the extent that as a result of decisions taken by these governments, this risk becomes a reality that deepens the colonial role of these economies in the world market, there has been no questioning of these policies.

Dichotomous Perspectives on Political Ethics

The Left represented in the Foro de São Paulo seems to have some lenses to look at and evaluate what happens in countries with conservative, right-wing, or neoliberal governments and others to look at and evaluate

90   *Crisis of Civilization*

what happens in countries with "friendly" governments. In its characterization of progressive governments, there seems to be a suspension of ethical judgment. Governmental policies that the Left had always denounced and confronted as bourgeois, anti-popular, and at the service of external interests seem to acquire a different meaning if they are carried out by progressive governments. In this friend-enemy Manichaeism, the meaning of the policies does not seem to depend on their content, but on those who implement them and the discourses with which they are accompanied. "Militarism and the criminalization of social protest" carried out by right-wing governments are denounced (Foro de São Paulo 2009), but nothing is said about the criminalization of protest in progressive governments or about the growing militarization of Venezuelan society.

The handing over of territory and their natural resources to transnational corporations, which was previously seen as subordination to global capital, becomes an acceptable policy when it is part of the programs of progressive governments, which legitimize it in the name of increasing public spending to improve the living conditions of the population.

It would also seem that the policies of openness to foreign investment and the legal norms for the protection of these investments, which were so radically confronted in their ALCA format, cease to be problematic in this new context. Restrictions on freedom of the press, control of the media, and the persecution of journalists are no longer seen as authoritarian and are reinterpreted as the defense of popular conquests. The repression and criminalization of struggles, resistances and popular mobilizations, the application of anti-terrorist laws, and even the submission of popular activities to military jurisdiction do not seem to generate major concerns, if all this is framed in a discourse of defense of the homeland, or of the revolution, against "subversive action of agents of imperialism." The idea of revolution, that the world is being radically changed in favor of the wretched of the Earth, that the Left is acting as a force of good against evil, has ended up operating as a Machiavellian device in which the end justifies the means.

Solidarity that is understood and practiced as unconditional uncritical solidarity with governments, not with the people, can only have perverse consequences. The blackmail of not giving arms to the enemy and contributing to strengthening the right-wing obliterates critical thinking, denying and hiding the problems until it is no longer possible to confront them. By not accepting that the struggle to transcend capitalism in which everyone has a responsibility is one and the same, the difficulties and obstacles that are faced are taken out of the debate, making it impossible to learn from the experience of one struggle in order to feed the others. By unconditionally supporting "friendly" governments, one is not only supporting but also strengthening and consolidating the most negative aspects of the processes of change by giving them the legitimacy of the international Left.

Crisis of Civilization 91

A clear example of this type of solidarity was the successive meetings of the Network of Intellectuals and Artists in Defense of Humanity in Caracas starting in 2004. Instead of taking advantage of the extraordinary opportunity of a meeting of left-wing political figures and intellectuals from different parts of the world to reflect and debate the complex challenges and obstacles that necessarily arise in any attempt at anti-capitalist change, to share difficulties and experiences and in this way enrich the Bolivarian process with reflections from other parts of the world, these meetings were limited to unconditional support for the Bolivarian process and the celebration/exaltation of the figure of Chávez. The external threats and those of the right-wing opposition were denounced, but there was no critical look at the internal limitations of the process itself, even the most obvious ones. In the face of the apparent consensus of the international Left according to which everything was going so well, the Venezuelan government confirmed time and again that it was on the right track and that there was no need for any possible rectifications.

Far from learning from the historical experiences of the cult of personality, the government actively participated in promoting it. Nor was it pointed out, for example, where the deepening of oil rentier dependence would inevitably lead. This was not for lack of training or because Venezuela was a unique experience of the petro-state but because of the conception of what solidarity was.

If they had had the disposition—the courage?—to have a frank debate on the Cuban experience, given the extraordinary weight that Cuba was having as a model to be followed by the Bolivarian process, it would have been possible to critically reflect on the unfeasibility, both economically and politically, of the insistence on directing the whole of society from a party-state. After decades of this model, it was evident that in Cuba this generated extraordinary inefficiencies and inhibited initiatives and possibilities for individual and collective experimentation in ways of approaching the production of life that were beyond the iron-clad control of the state. The distortions generated by this model of control led to the widespread search for alternative ways of privatizing the commons to solve day-to-day issues and gain access to goods outside of official institutional channels. This is, in terms of the established legal norms: corruption. If the achievements and internal limitations of this experience, beyond the condemnation of the U.S. blockade, had been critically analyzed, perhaps the political leadership of the Bolivarian process would have been more willing to take on the challenges of experimenting with options for the organization of production beyond the Manichean opposition between the state and the market, and the mechanical identification of socialism with statism would have been avoided. This led to the nationalization of large sectors of the Venezuelan economy that, as a result of a precarious management capacity and high levels of corruption, contributed in a very blatant way to the dismantling of the

92 *Crisis of Civilization*

productive apparatus and the severe economic and humanitarian crisis that the country has been experiencing since 2014.

As a consequence of this same logic of acritical unconditionality, Latin American bears a historical responsibility for the situation in Cuba today. For many years, it was assumed that as long as the U.S. blockade was in force, Cuba could not be criticized. This failure to critically reflect on Cuba, in a historical moment where the collapse of the Soviet bloc opened up new questions about alternatives to that failed model, had a boomerang effect. It implied renouncing the ability to critically think about the process that Cuban society was undergoing in order to contribute to the enrichment of what was a limited public debate inside Cuba. A high proportion of the Cuban population felt that society had reached a kind of impasse and that there was a need to explore alternatives, and not necessarily the reopening to the hegemony of mercantile relations. But this concern found no channels of expression in the Cuban political system. And also outside, the Latin American Left abdicated its responsibility and disengaged itself. It contributed nothing and limited itself to unconditional solidarity with the Cuban government and party. This, in turn, contributed to hindering the possibilities for debates on and experimentation with other alternatives inside Cuba. The process of drafting and debating a new constitution in the year 2018 is done on a more incipient floor with options much more restricted than if those debates on and experimentation with alternatives beyond the party-state had begun many years ago. Today, as in China and Vietnam, capitalist relations are advancing in Cuba, creating new and substantial inequalities (Padura 2018).

As in the case of the Soviet Union, in the *gulag* era, the Left is abdicating its ethical and political intellectual responsibility to seek and tell the truth. At that time, in a conscious and informed way, an important part of the intelligentsia and the global Left, but particularly the European Left, with different arguments (to support the struggles of the Soviet people, not to give arms to imperialism, not to demoralize the struggles of the republican side in the Spanish Civil War), was systematically denying what was happening in the Soviet Union, even though millions of people were dying. Denunciations to this effect were rejected as imperial propaganda. The global Left, but especially the European Left, paid for this heavily when Nikita Khrushchev exposed Stalin's crimes at the 20th Congress of the Communist Party of the Soviet Union in 1956. This was accentuated by the fall of the Berlin Wall (1989) and the subsequent collapse of the Soviet bloc. Many decades have passed, and although there was a great variety of positions within the Left in relation to the Soviet bloc, the Left continues to pay for the consequences of not being able to clearly disassociate itself from the authoritarianism of that historical experience in many parts of the world.

Today, we are witnessing two dramatic experiences of the failure of projects for change that generated huge expectations from all over the

Crisis of Civilization 93

world in Latin America: Nicaragua and Venezuela. The reality of the transition from these projects for change to the current reality of deeply corrupt authoritarian governments has not been incorporated into the analyses of broad portions of the Left. Far from seeking to understand what happened in these countries and why it happened and trying to draw lessons to strengthen anti-capitalist struggles, the discourse of unconditional solidarity remains unchanged.

Nicaragua

The Nicaraguan government, headed by the Ortega-Murillo couple, ceased to be a leftist government years ago, despite the continuity of its radical discourse and the fact that they have continued to appear in photos with presidents of the continent's progressive governments. Prominent historical figures of Sandinismo such as Ernesto Cardenal, Mónica Baltodano, Alejandro Bendaña, Sergio Ramírez, Gioconda Belli, Julio López Campos, and Carlos Tünnermann Bernheim have for years denounced the authoritarian, corrupt, and repressive character of this government. Ortega's stepdaughter, Zoilamérica Narváez, has accused him of continued sexual harassment and rape. He made a pact with the sectors most representative of the former opponents of Sandinismo, the partisan right, the Superior Council of Private Enterprise, and the hierarchy of the Catholic Church. They reached a national agreement with former President Arnoldo Alemán that allowed the government, and its former enemies on the right, control of all state institutions. The guidelines of the International Monetary Fund have been followed. With the favorable votes of the Sandinista National Liberation Front (FSLN) parliamentarians, both the Free Trade Agreement with the United States and the complementary laws required to comply with its stipulations were approved (Baltodano 2007). The rapprochement with the leadership of the Catholic Church and Cardinal Obando led to changes in legislation on abortion. Since Nicaragua's first penal code in 1837, the decriminalization of therapeutic abortion when the life of the mother was in danger, an exception that was maintained through various subsequent amendments to the code, in 2007, with the full support of the Ortega government and its parliamentary bench, a new penal code was approved in which abortion was criminalized without exception, even if the pregnancy is the result of rape or the mother's life is in danger. At that time Nicaragua became one of only four countries in the world where abortion was illegal without exception. The FSLN began to "act as a confessional party where a religiously charged message prevails, all its main party events are presided over by a hierarch of the Catholic Church" (Baltodano 2007). From Sandinista secularism, there has been a shift to religious fundamentalism and the political instrumentalization of religion.

94 *Crisis of Civilization*

The collective leadership of the FSLN has been replaced by the unipersonal control of Daniel Ortega. In 2011, in violation of the constitution prohibiting presidential re-election in continuous terms, through a fraudulent electoral process, Daniel Ortega, this time accompanied by his wife Rosario Murillo as vice-president, was re-elected as president of Nicaragua.

The levels of corruption at the top of the government are very high, much of it associated with resources coming from Venezuela.

In one of the most extreme surrenders of sovereignty in the history of the continent, and outside of any public debate, the Ortega-Murillo government, after a hasty approval by the parliament under its control, granted a strip of national territory from the Pacific to the Atlantic to a Hong Kong businessman for the construction of an inter-oceanic canal: the Grand Canal of Nicaragua. It also authorized the construction of ports, airports, hotels, and other diverse economic activities. The concession will last for 50 years, extendable for a further 50 years. The contracts are confidential and have not been made public. Whether or not the canal is built, an extraordinary level of freedom was granted to the owners of the concession to operate in that territory with limited state regulation. If the canal is built, something that already seemed rather doubtful in 2018, it would threaten to contaminate Lake Nicaragua, the most important freshwater reservoir in Central America, and displace tens of thousands of peasants. A broad national movement of opposition to the canal has been generated, led by the peasant communities that would be displaced from their territories. These struggles, as well as those of women's organizations that have demanded the decriminalization of abortion, have been systematically repressed.

Since April 2018, in the face of massive and continuous popular mobilizations against the government throughout the country, with the participation of students, peasants, and other social sectors, the government accuses the demonstrators of being terrorists and coup plotters, instruments of imperialism, criminals, drug addicts, alcoholics, and "possessed by Satan." It responds with brutal repression by police and paramilitary forces with a death toll widely documented in the hundreds.

How does the official Latin American Left respond to the chants of "Daniel and Somoza are the same thing" in the streets of Managua? The Foro de São Paulo ratifies its unconditional solidarity with the "Sandinista Revolution." In reality, more than solidarity, it is guilty complicity.

> We reject the foreign interference and interventionism of the government of the United States through its agencies in Nicaragua, organizing and directing the local ultra-right to apply once again its well-known formula of the misnamed "soft coup" to overthrow governments that do not respond to its interests, as well as the biased

Crisis of Civilization 95

actions of international organizations subordinated to the designs of imperialism, as is the case of the Inter-American Commission on Human Rights (IACHR).

We condemn the destabilizing, violent and terrorist actions of the right-wing coup plotters who, following the same strategy applied in other countries such as Venezuela, are trying to overthrow the constitutional order in Nicaragua after failing in their initial objective of overthrowing the Sandinista government headed by Comandante Daniel Ortega Saavedra, who has promoted dialogue and consensus as a way to overcome the crisis that has arisen.

We denounce the serious acts of barbarism and violation of human rights committed by the Nicaraguan right wing terrorists and coup-supporters with the denial of the right to free movement, destruction and burning of homes and public buildings, kidnappings, torture and assassinations, as well as the kidnapping of entire cities by the criminal hordes of fascist groups in the service of U.S. imperialism, imposing terror and death among its inhabitants and, in particular, among the Sandinista population.

We recognize the legitimate right to defense, exercised by the Sandinista government in the face of the aggressions perpetrated against it by the lackeys of the empire; a legitimate defense that the right-wing media has tried to present as crimes against the people, just as they try to present as political prisoners the criminal delinquents and torturers captured by the Nicaraguan authorities

(Foro de São Paulo 2018b)

Venezuela

Likewise, the current Venezuelan government has little to do with the democratic, popular, and anti-imperialist government as it is characterized by sectors of the Left. In recent years, particularly since mid-2017, the Venezuelan government has been subjected to severe destabilizing internal and external pressures. There is no doubt that the U.S. government has threatened a military invasion and that the financial blockade has as its stated purpose the overthrow of the government of Nicolás Maduro. But this is by no means enough to explain the profound political, economic, and humanitarian crisis that the country is experiencing.

When it overwhelmingly lost the December 2015 parliamentary elections and the opposition won a qualified two-thirds majority in the National Assembly, the government had to opt between respecting the constitution and the will of the people expressed in those elections or remaining in government at any cost, leaving aside the Bolivarian

96 *Crisis of Civilization*

constitutional order. It clearly chose the second option, beginning a sustained authoritarian drift.

It disregarded the electoral results of the state of Amazonas, whose representatives had already been proclaimed by the National Electoral Council, in order to prevent the opposition from having that majority in the Assembly. The National Assembly was declared in contempt and its functions were divided between the executive and the judicial branches. Openly violating the 1999 constitution, Maduro has ruled by decree of economic emergency since February 2016. Since that year in Venezuela, elections have not been held when provided for by the constitution, but when the government decides, arbitrarily disqualifying parties and candidates,[31] under the conditions and electoral rules it decides. In violation of the constitution, without a public referendum on whether or not the people wanted to change the 1999 constitution, a one-party National Constituent Assembly was elected, which upon being installed, declared itself *supra-constitutional* and *plenipotentiary*, that is, an absolute power without any check or balance.

The country is experiencing the most severe economic and humanitarian crisis in its history. Since 2014, three years before the financial blockade measures imposed by the Trump administration, the Venezuelan economy has been in a steady decline. By the end of 2018, Venezuela's GDP was 50% of its 2013 level. Oil production has collapsed.[32] The inflation of 2018 exceeded much more than a million percent, completely dissolving wages. All the main public services (health, education, transport, telecommunications, electricity, water ...) are in clear decline and, in some cases, even collapse. As a consequence of all this, there is a severe humanitarian crisis in the country. Poverty, measured in terms of income, increased from 48.4% to 87.0% between the years 2014 and 2017 (ENCOVI 2018).[33] According to UNHCR, the UN Refugee Agency, and IOM (the International Organization for Migration) in November 2018, the number of refugees and migrants from Venezuela worldwide reached three million people, almost 10% of the total population of Venezuela (PROVEA 2018). A growing proportion of those who remain in the country depend on remittances. The government systematically denies the existence of this crisis and, in properly criminal behavior, prefers that children die of malnutrition (*Sistema de Alerta, Monitoreo y Atención en Nutrición y Salud y Caritas Venezuela* 2018; *Contrapunto* 2018) or lack of medicines, rather than accept humanitarian aid, even from organizations such as Caritas, as this would be interpreted as a failure of its management.[34]

This systematic decline in the living conditions of the population, which reverses the improvements achieved during the first decade of the Bolivarian government, has generated protest actions and mobilizations in defense of wages, collective bargaining, access to food and medicine,

Crisis of Civilization 97

demanding the functioning of public services, particularly the water supply, and security. These demonstrations are blocked and often repressed. Union leaders and opposition politicians are persecuted and detained from the right as well as from the Left. There are political prisoners, often held incommunicado and tortured.[35] The political police, the Servicio Bolivariano de Inteligencia, SEBIN, decides at will whether or not to respect release orders issued by the courts. The right to collective bargaining is severely restricted and a high proportion of pay rates are defined by presidential decree. Politicians and journalists are stripped of their passports. Faced with rampant criminality, and one of the highest homicide rates in the world, the police and military have killed hundreds of people through the cynically named Operation Liberation of the People (Operación de Liberación del Pueblo/OLP) (Ávila 2017). There is a growing militarization of Venezuelan society. There is massive and widespread corruption amounting to tens of billions of dollars. With the resources that have been illicitly taken out of the country, the current humanitarian crisis could be significantly reduced. Despite the extraordinary experience of solidarity and collective organization that characterized the first phase of the Bolivarian process, the predominant action in the face of the crisis since 2014, even in the popular sectors, has been fundamentally that of individualism and competition. The *bachaqueo*, the purchase of subsidized goods to be resold speculatively or to be smuggled to Colombia, today represents an important, unrecorded proportion of the Venezuelan economy. There is a ripping of the fabric of society and a generalized ethical crisis. Surviving, however, are rich local and regional experiences of self-organization with varying degrees of autonomy that flourished under *chavismo* and seek to redefine their political action in these new and difficult circumstances.

Despite all this, the Foro de São Paulo continues to express its unconditional solidarity with the Maduro government. In its special statement on Venezuela from the meeting held in Havana in July 2018, after referring to the crisis that the country is going through and attributing it exclusively to the action of imperialism, without even considering the possibility that the government has had any responsibility, they once again conclude by giving full support to "Compañero Presidente Nicolás Maduro."

> The participants of the XXIV Meeting of the Foro de São Paulo ratify that solidarity with the homeland of Simón Bolívar and Hugo Chavez is a priority task of all the parties of Latin America and the Caribbean; of all social and workers' organizations and of all democratic institutions. At the same time, they call for the deployment of multiple activities in defense of peace, Bolivarian democracy, respect for the sovereignty of Venezuela and the demand for the lifting of the criminal blockade and the sanctions imposed on that brotherly people, denouncing in the world the serious and dangerous threats

98　*Crisis of Civilization*

of military intervention that U.S. imperialism has expressed against that nation.

Likewise, we salute the conscience, morality, courage and dignity of Venezuelan men and women who, as demonstrated by the splendid and resounding victory of President Nicolás Maduro in the elections of May 20, remain steadfast in defense of the legacy of the greatest leader of the Bolivarian Revolution; a process that took place with full normality and with the broadest guarantees for all, as the international accompaniers present in the South American country were able to confirm

(Foro de São Paulo 2018c).

This lack of a critical or even moderately problematized view of these experiences is not the exclusive fault of these organizations and parties. Recognized left-wing intellectuals with full knowledge of the realities in these countries, apart from pointing out some "errors," from both Latin America and Europe, give priority to a geopolitical perspective and choose to leave aside any substantive criticism in their solidarity-based analyses of these processes. Certain umbrella representations from Latin American social organizations, such as the ALBA Social Movements, which for years were supported with resources from the Venezuelan government, can hardly become critical when the country enters into crisis. This self-censorship is having serious consequences. The statements of the Left have lost credibility, and the case of Venezuela is used as a scarecrow in the electoral campaigns of the right across the continent.

The Crisis of the Left

The camp that has historically identified itself as the political Left is today facing a profound crisis, an existential crisis, not only in Latin America but throughout the world. The conditions that, according to the traditional perspectives of the Left, could have led to widespread anti-capitalist popular struggles and rebellions have arisen in recent decades: widespread insecurity, adjustment policies and the withdrawal of public policies for social protection, the hollowing out and delegitimization of liberal democracy, and the accelerated increase in social inequalities. However, popular responses tend to point in the opposite direction, reaffirming the most perverse features of these societies in crisis. In all parts of the world—India, the Philippines, Hungary, Poland, the United States, Argentina, Brazil, Turkey, among others—right-wing and extreme right-wing leaders with racist, patriarchal, xenophobic, and openly pro-business political orientations are gaining broad electoral support among popular sectors that were once the support base of the Left. European social democracy either tends to be increasingly

Crisis of Civilization 99

neoliberal or is on the defensive trying to slow down the advance of those policies. In recent years, the Left has lacked credible alternative projects capable of seducing the population.

Reiterating what has been stated in this text, for a few years South America seemed to walk against the tide of global trends. In particular, the political processes in Venezuela, Ecuador, and Bolivia generated new hopes for the realization of anti-capitalist horizons insofar as they subverted or profoundly renewed the conceptions and practices that had characterized most of the parties of the Left throughout the 20th century. As has been pointed out, other axes of confrontation are present (questioning patriarchy, anthropocentrism, the monoculture of colonial modernity), as well as other subjects (women, indigenous and Afro-descendant peoples and communities, subaltern, urban, and LGBT communities ...) and organizational alternatives to the parties.

However, to the extent that in each of these processes' traditional partisan, state-centric, and developmentalist logic was imposed by the governments, and pluriculturalism and the protection of Mother Earth had to take a back seat. These processes exhausted their transformative dynamics and the preservation of power ended up becoming their guiding principle. The other sectors of the anti-capitalist struggle, the other non-state plural left-wing currents, marginalized or repressed by progressivism during these years, now face the challenge of their reconstruction in the face of the aggressive return of the right.

As the declarations of the Foro de São Paulo clearly illustrate, state- and party-based official Left, far from recognizing the depth of the crisis it faces, the impotence of its forms of politics, and the historical exhaustion of state-centered and developmentalist socialism as an alternative to both capitalism and a civilization in crisis, is entrenched in the dogmatic reaffirmation of abstract principles that have ceased to account for reality. This Left closes in on itself trying, in this way, to defend the indefensible. Apart from some "errors" and "deviations," the cause of all the evils of contemporary society and the problems faced by the processes of change is on the other side: in capitalism, in imperialism, in the right.

The reflexive and genuinely self-critical inquiry into why all historical experiences of socialism—the actually existing socialism—have failed as alternatives to this society in crisis and why socialism has ceased to operate as an imaginary future both desirable and possible is fundamentally absent, not in the intellectual political debate of our times—these debates are actually more than a century old—but in this official Left.

Anti-capitalist connections and struggles today transcend, indeed, have always transcended, the traditions of what has historically been known as the Left. On the other hand, a broad spectrum of what self-identifies as left-wing does not necessarily assume anti-capitalist or anti-systemic positions. Can extractivist developmentalist governments be considered anti-capitalist? Are they left-wing despite their systematic

100 *Crisis of Civilization*

attacks on the plurality of indigenous and Afro-descendant cultures in Latin American societies? Even if they do not question patriarchal cultural patterns that, among other things, deny women sovereignty over their own bodies? Do they represent the Left if, far from contributing to an expansion of democratic practices, they tend to increase state control and place limits on the exercise of democratic rights and participation? Can economic policies that prioritize the increase of primary exports of energy, agricultural products, and minerals, products that contribute to feeding the unrelenting machinery of global capital accumulation, be characterized as anti-capitalist? Are they anti-systemic governments even if their policies lead to the destruction of nature? If despite overwhelming evidence of the consequences of hegemonic models of production and consumption that contribute to accelerating climate change, these governments have not been able to begin a transition to other ways of living in harmony with nature? Are the notions of Left and Right historically blurred or outdated? Are these distinctions relevant to some issues but not to others?

It is not surprising that, as happened in the Eastern countries that experienced the socialism of the 20th century, and in the absence of any self-criticism, socialism ends up becoming a negative reference identified with authoritarianism and corruption. What is the responsibility of that Left with its exclusionary arrogance and widespread corruption, among other things, in the development of the right in the continent, and in particular in the "anti-PTism" (in reference to Lula's Workers' Party/ PT) that led to a character like Jair Messias Bolsonaro being elected as president of Brazil?

With the failure of the experiences of the so-called progressive governments in Latin America as alternatives capable of moving beyond capitalism and offering at least some initial ways or transitions out of the civilizational crisis, we are facing the final of several historical cycles. It is not only the short historical cycle of high commodity prices or the so-called progressive governments. It is also the end of a longer historical cycle, a cycle that arguably began with the publication of the Manifesto of the Communist Party in 1848. It is the historical cycle of anti-capitalist struggles based on the idea that, through the capture or control of the state, it would be possible to carry out a process of profound transformation in society as a whole. This has been the shared belief of revolutionary uprisings like the storming of the Winter Palace; European social democracy; Third World liberation movements and guerrilla struggles; and, again, the political projects of progressive governments in South America. We are also at the end of the historical era of the Revolution, the idea that it was possible to transform the whole of society, in all its various spheres, in a short period of time. The socialism of the 21st century in Venezuela was the first attempt to build a socialist-statist society in the century. It will probably also be the last.

Crisis of Civilization   101

We are at the end of the long historical phase in which, from the most diverse political and ideological positions, in the modern colonial world system, human well-being and happiness are identified with an ever-increasing material abundance, progress, and unlimited economic growth. The limits of the planet oblige us to recognize that we have entered a new and turbulent era. The official Left seems not to have taken notice.

A Final Insistence on the Left

As has been argued in this text, the tradition of the left identified with Marxism and socialism is constituted by the specific historical, geographical, and cultural context of industrial capitalism emerging in Western Europe. As such, it is inevitabotherly marked by its epoch, with contradictory relations to the central axes of that new pattern of civilization that is taking shape. It clearly constitutes a radical critique of that society insofar as it exposes the logics of commodification, exploitation, and subjugation that characterize capital and the concentration of wealth and power to which it leads. But, at the same time, it incorporates into its perspectives, uncritically, to different degrees and levels of contradiction, the cognitive patterns and hegemonic common sense of that society, in particular the idea of progress, including its teleological dimensions; the belief in the role of the productive forces of capitalism as emancipatory forces; the subject/object and society/nature dualisms that are at the basis of modern science; as well as positivist conceptions of truth in the knowledge of social-historical reality. Likewise, it propagates predominantly Eurocentric perspectives in which European history is conceived as the standard reference for universal history (Lander 1990).

It is a program of radical thought/action that seeks to provide answers in the particular historical context from which it arises. Its limits become visible when, based on universalizing logic, it seeks to interpret the realities of other peoples and cultures, other territories, and other histories, fundamentally, through the same political and conceptual-theoretical categories that proved so acute and fruitful in characterizing the historical context from which they arose.

Since 1848, the date of publication of the *Manifesto of the Communist Party*, the world has changed extraordinarily. As has been argued throughout this text, the modern colonial pattern of civilization has entered a terminal crisis, that is, through environmental collapse, endangering the conditions that make life on planet Earth possible. It is a multidimensional crisis that transcends the central axes of class relations that constituted the core of Marxist interpretations of capitalism. As has been argued in this text, a Left exclusively focused on the relations of exploitation and their geopolitical dimensions, which does not also incorporate, in a structurally fundamental way, the dimensions of anthropocentrism,

102 *Crisis of Civilization*

patriarchy, racism, sexism, mono-cultural coloniality, eurocentrism, and a complete rejection of authoritarianism, is not only incapable of offering alternatives to a civilization in crisis but also constitutes within itself an expression of the world in crisis. The transformative projects of the Left that has opted for state-centered socialism and notions associated with the idea of progress have failed and have little to offer as an alternative to capitalism and civilization in crisis. As the experience of the various socialisms of the last century has shown and the experience of progressive governments in Latin America has confirmed, the state-centric and developmentalist Left, far from representing alternatives to the existing order, has become part of the problem and with its relative political and its relative discursive hegemony as an alternative to capitalism, has contributed to deny and obstruct the emergence and visibility of other alternatives.

There has always been an extraordinary plurality and diversity of theoretical and political positions, as well as modalities of anti-capitalist struggles and alternatives to colonial modernity, with unique vigor in the Global South. Some self-identify as "Left," others do not. In dialogues, reciprocal exchanges and learning, and common struggles within the vast range of quests for alternatives, we find today the most promising potential to put a stop to the overwhelming advance of the destructive hegemonic logic and pave the way for another civilization.

Translation: Matti Steinitz

Notes

1. The characteristics, diversities, and transformative potentialities of these other forms of politics and of the construction of non-capitalist alternatives in the here and now are not part of the objectives of this text, and are therefore only briefly addressed in terms of reference.
2. These reports have been published in 1990, 1996, 2001, 2007, and 2014.
3. These trends are comprehensively analyzed in a report prepared by UNESCO for the 2018 UN Climate Change Conference (COP24) held in Katowise, Poland, in December 2018 (UNESCO 2018).
4. The following organizations and individuals are co-responsible for this report: Climate Policy Initiative, Conservation International, International Renewable Energy Agency, The New Climate Economy, Partnership on Sustainable Low Carbon Transport Raid Detxhon (a Foundation), We Mean Business, and World Resources Institute.
5. From this reductionism, and the solutions proposed from it, there is not even an adequate account of the various sources of greenhouse gases beyond the burning of fossil fuels. Incorporating the need to drastically reduce methane emissions from cattle into the negotiations would mean confronting strong corporate interests and challenging the carnivorous food patterns that have expanded rapidly in the decades of neoliberal globalization.
6. For critical analyses of the green economy, see Lander (2011) and Moreno (2013).
7. This map is available at https://map.geoengineeringmonitor.org/.
8. On "race" as an epistemological political device of hierarchical classification of different peoples in the modern colonial world system, see Quijano (1992; 2000).

Crisis of Civilization 103

9. This part of the text is based extensively on the paper: "Renewed assault on the reproduction of life. Política energética y cambio climático en la era de Trump," presented at the meeting *Horizontes en disputa: Modernidad capitalista, nuevas derechas posdemocráticas y alternativas desde los márgenes*, Grupo de Trabajo Permanente del Alternativas al Desarrollo. Andean Regional Office of the Rosa Luxemburg Foundation based in Quito. The meeting was held in Playas on May 25–29, 2018.
10. This is the case known as Citizens United vs. Federal Election Commission. See Liptak 2010.
11. For an analysis of the enormous anti-democratic consequences of this decision, see Public Citizen (2010).
12. In November 2018, the Fourth National Climate Report was released, a study that, by congressional mandate, is jointly produced by the main federal institutions that have some competence in matters related to the environment (U. S. Global Change Research Program 2018). This report once again confirms the severity of the environmental threats facing the planet. Yet Trump continues to insist time and again that he does not believe the scientific reports on climate change.
13. This report, which provides a very detailed record of the involvement of the world's leading banks in fossil energy, is supported by numerous organizations from around the world involved in environmental protection struggles including: 350.org, Christian Aid, Foundation for Gaia, Friends of the Earth Scotland, Friends of the Earth USA, Greenpeace Japan, Greenpeace USA, Indigenous Climate Action and the Philippines Movement for Climate Justice.
14. The exploitation of Alberta's oil sands, which are located far inland is highly dependent on the construction of pipelines to transport crude oil to refineries and consumer markets in the United States. The construction of the main such pipeline, the controversial Keystone XL, which had generated widespread local and national resistance, was blocked at the end of the Obama administration and authorized by Trump in March 2017 (Nuncombe 2017).
15. This part of the text is largely based on the presentation "Latin America. Challenges in the face of the civilizational crisis after progressivism," given at a workshop organized by Médico Internacional, in Salvador de Bahia, March 2018, in the context of the World Social Forum.
16. Of the abundant political and academic production of criticism of extractivism, the following can be cited: Gudynas (2015), Svampa and Viale (2014), Svampa (2017), Acosta (2009), Machado Aráoz (2013), Roa and Navas (coordinators) (2014), and Seoane, Taddei and Algranati (2013).
17. For an important conceptual contribution to this debate, see Acosta and Brand 2017.
18. For additional information on mining activity in Ecuador and its conflicts, see Sacher and Acosta (2012) and Van Teijlingen et al. (2017).
19. These two decrees were repealed by President Lenin Moreno in October 2017
20. Internally, some of the main beneficiaries of the MAS government's mining policies and tax legislation have been the new elites of popular origin who control the so-called mining cooperatives (Díaz Cuellar 2017, 62). These cooperatives have become one of the main pressure groups capable of influencing public policies, and an important support base for the MAS government.
21. The socio-environmental impacts of mega dams have been addressed in the first part of this chapter.

104 *Crisis of Civilization*

22. This section on the Orinoco Mining Arc makes free use of the statements made on this issue by the Plataforma Ciudadana en Defensa de la Constitución (Citizens' Platform in Defence of the Constitution). Caracas, Venezuela, 2016–2017.
23. The South American Council for Infrastructure and Planning (COSIPLAN) is the political and strategic discussion body for planning and implementing the integration of infrastructure in South America, committed to social, economic, and environmental development. It is made up of the ministers of infrastructure and/or planning or their equivalents appointed by the Member States of UNASUR (COSIPLAN-UNASUR 2009).
24. I would like to thank Miriam Lang for her valuable comments on a draft version of this part of the text.
25. This is what Johannes Fabian has called "the negation of simultaneity" (1983).
26. Among a vast production, see Quijano (2014), Dussel (1994), Mignolo (1995), Walsh (2009), Coronil (2002), Castro-Gómez (2005), and Lander (2000).
27. The online journal *Climate and Capitalism* regularly publishes valuable material from this critical perspective.
28. Given the more limited objectives of this text, with emphasis on the policies of progressive governments in the face of the challenges of the civilizational crisis, it was decided not to attempt a characterization of the broad and heterogeneous diversity of movements and positions that today constitute the non-state-centric plural anti-capitalist sphere.
29. According to the website of the Foro de São Paulo, the following are the organizations that make up the Forum. Argentina: Frente Grande, Frente Transversal Nacional y Popular, Movimiento Evita, Movimiento Libres del Sur, Partido Comunista, Partido Comunista -Congreso Extraordinario, Partido Humanista, Partido Intransigente, Partido Obrero Revolucionario-Posadista, Partido Socialista, Partido Solidario, Unión de Militantes por el Socialismo. Aruba: Democratic Network Party. Barbados: People's Empowerment Party. Bolivia: Movimiento al Socialismo, Movimiento Bolivia Libre, Partido Comunista de Bolivia. Brazil: Partido Democrático Trabalhista, Partido Comunista del Brasil, Partido Comunista Brasileiro, Partido Patria Libre, Partido Popular Socialista, Partido Socialista Brasileiro, Partido de los Trabajadores (PT). Chile: Izquierda Ciudadana, Movimiento Amplio Social, Movimiento de Izquierda Revolucionaria, Partido Comunista, Partido Humanista, Partido Socialista Allendista, Partido del Socialismo Allendista, Revolución Democrática. Colombia: Marcha Patriótica, Movimiento Progresista, Partido Alianza Verde, Partido Comunista Colombiano, Polo Democrático Alternativo, Presentes por el Socialismo, Unión Patriótica, Movimiento Poder Ciudadano. Costa Rica: Partido Frente Amplio, Partido Vanguardia Popular-Partido Comunista. Cuba: Partido Comunista de Cuba. Curaçao: Sovereign People's Party. Ecuador: Movimiento de Unidad Plurinacional Pachakutik-Nuevo País, Movimiento Alianza País, Movimiento Popular Democrático, Partido Comunista del Ecuador, Partido Comunista Marxista-Leninista del Ecuador, Partido Socialista-Frente Amplio, Partido Comunista Ecuatoriano. El Salvador: Frente Farabundo Martí para la Liberación Nacional. Guatemala: Convergencia, CPO-CRD, Movimiento Político Winaq, Unidad Revolucionaria Nacional Guatemalteca. Haiti: Organization of the People in Struggle. Honduras: Partido Libertad y Refundación-libre. Martinique: Communist Party for Independence and Socialism, National Council of Popular Committees. México: Partido de la Revolución Democrática, Partido del Trabajo, Morena. Nicaragua: Frente Sandinista de Liberación Nacional.

Crisis of Civilization 105

Panama: Partido del Pueblo, Partido Revolucionario Democrático, Frente Amplio por la Democracia. Paraguay: Frente Guasú, Partido Comunista Paraguayo, Partido Convergencia Popular Socialista, Partido del Movimiento Patriótico Popular, Partido del Movimiento al Socialismo, Partido País Solidario, Partido de la Participación Ciudadana, Partido Popular Tekojoja. Peru: Ciudadanos por el Cambio, Partido Comunista del Perú-Patria Roja, Partido Comunista Peruano, Partido Nacionalista del Perú, Partido del Pueblo, Partido Socialista del Perú, Tierra y Libertad. Puerto Rico: Frente Socialista, Movimiento Independentista Nacional Hostosiano, Partido Nacionalista de Puerto Rico. Dominican Republic: Alianza por la Democracia, Fuerza de la Revolución, Movimiento Izquierda Unida, Partido Alianza País, Partido Movimiento Patria para Tod@s, Partido Comunista del Trabajo, Partido de la Liberación Dominicana, Partido de los Trabajadores Dominicanos, Partido Revolucionario Dominicano, Partido Revolucionario Moderno. Trinidad and Tobago: Movement for Social Justice. Uruguay: Asamblea Uruguay, Compromiso Frenteamplista, Frente Amplio, Movimiento 26 de Marzo, Movimiento de Liberación Nacional - Tupamaros, Movimiento de Participación Popular, Movimiento Popular Frenteamplista, Partido Comunista del Uruguay, Partido Obrero Revolucionario Troskista-Posadista, Partido por la Victoria del Pueblo, Partido Socialista de los Trabajadores, Partido Socialista del Uruguay, Vertiente Artiguista. Venezuela: Liga Socialista, Movimiento Electoral del Pueblo, Partido Comunista de Venezuela, Partido Socialista Unido de Venezuela, Patria para Todos.

30. The analysis presented below is based on the final declarations of the meetings held by the Sao Paulo Forum since the beginning of the progressive era in Latin America (2000–2018).

31. For the December 2018 council elections, most opposition political parties and organizations were disqualified. Among these: Mesa de la Unidad Democrática (MUD), Primero Justicia (PJ), Voluntad Popular (VP), Acción Democrática (AD), Un Nuevo Tiempo (UNT), La Causa R (LCR), and Alianza Bravo Pueblo (ABP). Observatorio Electoral Venezolano: Todo lo que debes saber sobre las elecciones del 9-D (2018).

32. As noted in the second part of this text, oil production at the end of the 2018 had fallen to less than 1.2 million barrels per day.

33. For several years now, no official figures have been available with which to compare these data.

34. According to the Network of Intellectuals and Artists in Defense of Humanity, this is an "alleged" humanitarian crisis: "Alleged humanitarian crisis and military intervention of the empire in Venezuela" (Red de Intelectuales y Artistas en Defensa de la Humanidad 2017). To denounce the repeated use of critical situations in other countries that the government of the United States effectively utilizes to justify military intervention in accordance with its interests, one does not need to deny the suffering that the Venezuelan people have experienced.

35. According to Amnesty International'Global Human Rights Report 2017–2018, "Venezuela remained in a state of emergency, repeatedly extended since January 2016. A National Constituent Assembly was elected without the participation of the opposition. The Attorney General was dismissed under irregular circumstances. Security forces continued to use excessive and undue force to disperse protests. Hundreds of people were arbitrarily detained. There were many reports of torture and other ill-treatment, including sexual violence against demonstrators. The judicial system continued to be used to silence dissidents, including using military jurisdiction

106 *Crisis of Civilization*

to prosecute civilians. Human rights defenders were harassed, intimidated and subject to raids. Conditions of detention were extremely harsh. The food and health crises continued to worsen, especially affecting children, people with chronic illness and pregnant women. The number of Venezuelans seeking asylum in other countries increased" (Amnesty International 2018).

Bibliography

Acción Ecológica. 2011. *Ecuador: criminalización de la protesta social en tiempos de 'revolución ciudadana.'* Quito, August 23 [https://www.accionecologica.org/ecuador-criminalizacion-de-la-protesta-social-en-tiempos-de-revolucion-ciudadana/].

Acción Ecológica. 2016a. *Alto a la criminalización de los pueblos indígenas y la militarización del territorio Shuar. Basta de violencia contra mujeres y niños*, Quito, December 24 [https://www.redlatinoamericanademujeres.org/alto-a-la-criminalizacion-de-los-pueblos-indigenas-y-la-militarizacion-del-territorio-shuar-basta-de-violencia-contra-las-mujeres-y-ninos/].

Acción Ecológica. 2016b. *Catastro minero=catástrofe ambiental*, Quito, May 30 [http://www.accionecologica.org/editoriales/1941-2016-05-30-19-22-43].

Acosta, Alberto. 2009. *La maldición de la abundancia*, Quito: Swissaid, Abya Yala and CEP.

Acosta, Alberto and Ulrich Brand. 2017. *Salidas del laberinto capitalista. Decrecimiento y postextractivismo*. Quito: Fundación Rosa Luxemburg, Oficina Regional Andina.

Agencia Venezolana de Noticias. 2016. "Gobierno nacional prevé certificar en año y medio reservas del Arco Minero Orinoco." Aporrea. Caracas, February 25 [https://www.aporrea.org/actualidad/n286400.html].

Ahmed, Saleh and Mahbubur Meenar. 2018. "Just Sustainability in the Global South: A Case Study of the Megacity of Dhaka." Journal of Developing Societies, 34 (4), 1–24.

ALBA. 2013. *Declaración del ALBA desde el Pacífico*, XII Cumbre de Jefes de Estado y de Gobierno del ALBA-TCP, Guayaquil, July 30 [https://www.urjc.es/images/ceib/revista_electronica/vol_7_2013_2/REIB_07_02_Doc04.pdf].

Alimonda, Héctor, Catalina Toro Pérez and Facundo Martín (eds.). 2017. *Ecología política latinoamericana. Pensamiento crítico, diferencia latinoamericana y rearticulación epistémica*. Vol. 1, Colección de Grupos de Trabajo. Buenos Aires: CLACSO.

Alvaredo, Facundo, Lucas Chancel, Thomas Piketty, Emmanuel Saez and Gabriel Zuman. 2018. *World Inequality Report 2018*. World Inequality Lab. [https://wir2018.wid.world/].

Amnesty International. (2018). *Amnesty International Report 2017/2018: The state of the world's human rights*. Amnesty International UK. [https://www.amnesty.org/en/documents/pol10/6700/2018/en/].

Anderson, Kevin. 2018. "Response to the IPCC, 1.5°C Special Report." Manchester Policy Blogs: All posts. [http://blog.policy.manchester.ac.uk/posts/2018/10/response-to-the-ipcc-1-5c-special-report/].

Antillano, Andrés, José Luis Fernández-Shaw and Damelys Castro. 2018. "No todo lo que mata es oro. La relación entre violencia y rentas mineras en el sur del Estado Bolívar." In: Karin Gabbert and Alexandra Martínez (Ed.):

Crisis of Civilization 107

En Venezuela desde adentro. Ocho investigaciones para un debate necesario. Quito: Fundación Rosa Luxemburgo, Oficina Región Andina. [https://www. rosalux.org.ec/producto/venezuela-desde-adentro-ocho-investigaciones-para-un-debate-necesario/].

Ávila, Keymer. 2017. "Las Operaciones de Liberación del Pueblo (OLP): entre las ausencias y los excesos del sistema penal en Venezuela." *Crítica Penal y Poder*, no. 12. Barcelona: Universidad de Barcelona. [http://revistes.ub.edu/index.php/CriticaPenalPoder/article/view/16878].

Baltodano, Mónica. 2007. "¿La izquierda gobernando en Nicaragua?." *Alai. América Latina en Movimiento.* Quito, August 31. [https://www.alainet.org/es/active/19412].

Banco Central de Venezuela. 2018. *Información Estadística. Importaciones y exportaciones de bienes y servicios según sectores.* Caracas. [https://www.bcv. org.ve/estadisticas/comercio-exterior].

Bascopé Sanjinés, Iván. 2017. "Vulneraciones al derecho de consulta previa, libre e informada en la otorgación de derechos mineros." in: *CEDLA, Reporte anual de industrias extractivas.* La Paz. [http://www.cedla.org/ieye/libro/53214].

Bennis, Phyllis. 2003. "The Day the World Said No to War." *Institute for Policy Studies.* February 15 [https://ips-dc.org/february_15_2003_the_day_the_world_said_no_to_war/].

Bidau, Claudio J. 2018. "Doomsday for Insects? The Alarming Decline of Insect Populations around the World." *Entomology, Ornithology & Herpetology: Current Research,* 7(1), 1–2. [https://www.omicsonline.org/open-access/doomsday-for-insects-the-alarming-decline-of-insect-populationsaround-the-world-2161-0983-1000e130-99176.html].

Bolivia (Plurinational State of) 2009 Constitution—Constitute. 2009. Oxford University Press, Inc. [https://www.constituteproject.org/constitution/Bolivia_2009?lang=en].

Bollier, David and Silke Helfrich. 2012. *The Wealth of the Commons. A World Beyond Market & State.* The Commons Strategy Group, Amherst: Levellers Press.

BP. 2018. "BP Energy Outlook. 2018 Edition." [https://www.bp.com/content/dam/bp/business-sites/en/global/corporate/pdfs/energy-economics/energy-outlook/bp-energy-outlook-2018.pdf].

Brand, Ulrich and Markus Wissen. 2018. *The Limits to Capitalist Nature. Theorizing and Overcoming the Imperial Mode of Living.* London, New York: Rowman & Littlefield.

Brie, Michael and Mario Candeia. 2012. *Just Mobility Postfossil Conversion and Free Public Transport.* New York: Rosa Luxemburg Foundation. [https://www.rosalux.de/fileadmin/rls_uploads/pdfs/Analysen/Analyse_Just_Mobility.pdf].

Brown, Wendy. 1995. "Finding the Man in the State." *States of Injury, Power and Freedom in Late Modernity.* Princeton, NJ: Princeton University Press.

Cabello, Joanna and Tamra Gilbertson. 2012. "A Colonial Mechanism to Enclose Lands: A Critical Review of Two Redd+-Focused Special Issues." *Ephema. Theory and politics in organization*, 12, 162–180. [http://www.ephemerajournal. org/sites/default/files/12-1cabellogilbertson.pdf].

Casey, Nicholas and Clifford Krauss. 2018. "It Doesn't Matter if Ecuador can Afford this Dam. China Still Gets Paid." *The New York Times*, December 24.

108   *Crisis of Civilization*

Castro-Gómez, Santiago. 2000. "Ciencias sociales, violencia epistémica y el problema de la 'invención del otro." In: Edgardo Lander (Ed.): *La colonialidad del saber: Eurocentrismo y ciencias sociales. Perspectivas latinoamericanas.* Buenos Aires: UNESCO/CLACSO.

Castro-Gómez, Santiago. 2005. *La hybris del punto cero. Ciencia, raza e ilustración en la nueva granada (1750–1816).* Bogotá: Pontificia Universidad Javeriana.

CEPAL. 2002, 2010, 2016, 2017. *Anuarios Estadísticos de América Latina y el Caribe, 2002, 2010, 2016, 2017.* Santiago de Chile.

CEPAL. 2016. *Relaciones económicas entre América Latina y el Caribe y China. Oportunidades y desafíos.* Santiago de Chile [https://repositorio.cepal.org/bitstream/handle/11362/40743/1/S1601155_es.pdf].

Chávez, Hugo. 2006. *Lineamientos para la construcción del socialismo del siglo XXI. Acto de reconocimiento al Comando Miranda.* Teatro Teresa Carreño. Caracas: December 15.

Chávez, Hugo. 2012. *Propuesta del Candidato de la Patria. Comandante Hugo Chávez para la Gestión Bolivariana Socialista 2013-2019.* Caracas, June 11. [http://www.mppp.gob.ve/wp-content/uploads/2018/05/Programa-Patria-2013-2019.pdf].

Chow, Lorraine. 2018. "Norway to Ban Deforestation-Linked Palm Oil Biofuels in Historic Vote." *Ecowatch*, December 7 [https://www.ecowatch.com/norway-bans-palm-oil-2622712445.html].

Climate and Capitalism. [https://climateandcapitalism.com/].

CNN. 2018. "¿El principio del fin de Unasur? 6 países suspenden su participación." April 21 [https://cnnespanol.cnn.com/2018/04/21/el-principio-del-fin-de-unasur-6-paises-suspenden-su-participacion/].

Contrapunto. 2018. "La FAO asegura que el hambre en Venezuela continuó creciendo en 2017." Caracas, March 8 [http://contrapunto.com/noticia/la-fao-asegura-que-el-hambre-en-venezuela-continuo-creciendo-en-2017-190407/].

Coraggio, José Luis. 2011. *Economía social y solidaria. El trabajo antes que el capital.* Quito: Abya Yala, Universidad Politécnica Salesiana and FLACSO Ecuador.

Coronil, Fernando. 2002. *El Estado mágico. Naturaleza, dinero y modernidad en Venezuela.* Caracas: Desarrollo Científico y Humanístico de la Universidad Central de Venezuela y Nueva Sociedad.

Correa Delgado, Rafael. 2013. *Decreto 16.* Quito, June 4 [https://faolex.fao.org/docs/pdf/ecu140190.pdf].

Cosiplan-UNASUR. 2009. Quito. [http://www.iirsa.org/Page/Detail?menuItemId=119&menuItemId=134].

Credit Suisse Research Institute. 2017. *Global Wealth Report, 2017.* [https://www.google.com/search?q=Credit+Suisse.+2017.+Global+Wealth+Report%2C+2017&source=hp&ei=KQr0Y_7kNYeFwbkP5dqZkAc&iflsig=AK50M_UAAAAAY_QYOTCvnWr-XNb_m2ao5bqX0CYh3rC8&ved=0ahUKEwi-ndaAqKX9AhWHQjABHWVtBnIQ4dUDCAg&uact=5&oq=Credit+Suisse.+2017.+Global+Wealth+Report%2C+2017&gs_lcp=Cgdnd3Mtd2l6EAMyCggAEPEEEB4QogQyBQgAEKIEUKkPWKkPYJtvaAFwAHgAgAHQAYgB0AGSAQMyLTGYAQCgAQKgAQGwAQA&sclient=gws-wiz].

D'Alisa, Giacomo, Federico Demaria and Giorgos Kallis (eds). 2015. *Decrecimiento. Vocabulario para una nueva era.* Barcelona: Icaria Editorial.

Crisis of Civilization 109

Dag Hammarskjöld Foundation. 2009. "Carbon Trading. How It Works and Why It Fails." *Critical Currents*, 7, 1–104. Stockholm.

Díaz Cuellar, Vladimir. 2017. "Ganancia y salario en el sector minero en Bolivia durante el gobierno del MAS (2006-2015)." In: *CEDLA*. *Reporte anual de industrias extractivas*. La Paz. [http://www.cedla.org/ieye/libro/53214].

Dussel, Enrique. 1994. *1492. El encubrimiento del otro*. La Paz: Ediciones Plural. Universidad Mayor de San Andrés.

El Comercio. 2018. "Informe abre la puerta a que se retome consulta popular sobre el Yasuní." Quito, November 7 [https://www.elcomercio.com/actualidad/informe-cne-firmas-consulta-yasuni.html].

El Deber. 2018. "Promulgan la Ley del Etanol en el norte de Santa Cruz." Santa Cruz, 15 de septiembre. [https://www.eldeber.com.bo/economia/Promulgan-la-Ley-del-Etanol-en-el-norte-de-Santa-Cruz-20180915-0015.html].

El País. 2007. "La ONU alerta de que 150 especies se extinguen al día por culpa del hombre." Madrid, May 22 [https://elpais.com/sociedad/2007/05/22/actualidad/1179784806_850215.html].

El Telégrafo. 2015. "Nuevo Ministerio de Minería se crea por Decreto Ejecutivo." Quito, February 15.

El Universo. 2009. "Infantilismo' tensa relación Correa-Acosta." Quito, January 21 [https://www.eluniverso.com/2009/01/21/1/1355/51D-051981FE44D54A46A-35DBEFEC9037.html].

ENCOVI. 2018. *Encuesta sobre Condiciones de Vida en Venezuela*. Caracas: Universidad Católica Andrés Bello, Universidad Simón Bolívar y Universidad Central de Venezuela. febrero. [https://www.proyectoencovi.com/encovi-2018-encuesta-nacional-de-condiciones-de-vida-copy].

Escobar, Arturo. 2007. *La invención del tercer mundo. Construcción y deconstrucción del desarrollo*. Caracas: Fundación Editorial El Perro y la Rana.

Escobar, Arturo. 2010. "Latin America at the Crossroads. Alternative Modernizations, Postliberalism or Postdevelopment?" *Cultural Studies*, 24 (1), 1–65.

Estado Plurinacional de Bolivia. 2010. "Ley de Derechos de la Madre Tierra. Ley núm. 071." La Paz, December 21. [http://www.planificacion.gob.bo/uploads/marco-legal/Ley%20N°%20071%20DERECHOS%20DE%20LA%20MADRE%20TIERRA.pdf].

Estado Plurinacional de Bolivia. La Asamblea Legislativa Plurinacional. 2011."Ley núm 180, Ley de Protección del Territorio Indígena y Parque Nacional Isiboro Sécure – Tipnis." La Paz: Gaceta Oficial, October 24. [https://www.ilo.org/dyn/natlex/docs/electronic/90573/104493/F1293369730/BOL90573.pdf].

Estado Plurinacional de Bolivia. La Asamblea Legislativa Plurinacional. 2017. "Ley núm 969. Ley de protección, desarrollo integral y sustentable del Territorio Indígena y Parque Nacional Isiboro Sécure-Tipnis." La Paz, August 13. [http://extwprlegs1.fao.org/docs/pdf/bol170307.pdf].

Exxonmobil. 2017. *Outlook for Energy: A View to 2040*. [https://corporate.exxonmobil.com/en/energy/energy-outlook/a-view-to-2040].

Fabian, Johannes. 1983. *Time and the Other. How Anthropology Makes Its Object*. New York, NY: Columbia University Press.

Fahey, Jonathan. 2012. "Climate, energy fears overblown, says ExxonMobil boss." London: *The Guardian* (June 28). [https://www.theguardian.com/environment/2012/jun/28/exxonmobil-climate-change-rex-tillerson]

110   Crisis of Civilization

Federación Internacional de derechos humanos y otros. 2018. *Examen Periódico Universal, Tercer Ciclo de Evaluación de las Obligaciones Extraterritoriales de la República Popular de China desde la Sociedad Civil: Casos de Argentina, Bolivia, Brasil, Ecuador y Perú. Octubre.* [https://www.google.com/search?q=Examen+Peri%C3%B3dico+Universal%2C+Tercer+Ciclo+de+Evaluaci%C3%B3n+de+las+Obligaciones+Extraterritoriales+de+la+Rep%C3%BAblica+Popular+de+China+desde+la+Sociedad+Civil%3A+Casos+de+Argentina%2C+Bolivia%2C+Brasil%2C+Ecuador+y+Per%C3%BA&source=hp&ei=Rwz0Y4mqJuGxkvQPgqagoAg&iflsig=AK50M_UAAAAAY_QaVxRd7G5Nw5qPUjKBi6tP9VinTn5s&ved=0ahUKEwjJ6f-CqqX9AhXhmIQIHQITCIQQ4dUDCA0&oq=Examen+Peri%C3%B3dico+Universal%2C+Tercer+Ciclo+de+Evaluaci%C3%B3n+de+las+Obligaciones+Extraterritoriales+de+la+Rep%C3%BAblica+Popular+de+China+desde+la+Sociedad+Civil%3A+Casos+de+Argentina%2C+Bolivia%2C+Brasil%2C+Ecuador+y+Per%C3%BA&gs_lcp=Cgdnd3Mtd2l6EAxQwwlYwwlgniRoAX-AAeACAAQCIAQCSAQCYAQCgAQKgAQGwAQA&sclient=gws-wiz].

Foro de São Paulo. 2000. "IX Encuentro del Foro de São Paulo, Declaración de Niquinohomo." [http://forodesaopaulo.org/wp-content/uploads/2014/07/09-Declaracion-de-Niquinohomo-2000.pdf].

Foro de São Paulo. 2001. "Declaración Final del X Encuentro del Foro de São Paulo." *Diario Granma.* La Habana: December 7.

Foro de São Paulo. 2002. "Declaración final XI Encuentro del Foro de São Paulo." Antigua. *[http://forodesaopaulo.org/declaracion-final-antigua-2002/].*

Foro de São Paulo. 2005. "Declaración final del XII Encuentro del Foro de São Paulo."SãoPaulo.[https://studylib.es/doc/960974/declaraci%C3%B3n-final-%E2%80%93-s%C3%A3o-paulo---2005].

Foro de São Paulo. 2008. "Declaración de Montevideo 2008." Montevideo.

Foro de São Paulo. 2009. "Declaración Final del XXI Encuentro del Foro de São Paulo en la Ciudad de México DF." México. [http://forodesaopaulo.org/declaracionfinal-del-xxi-encuentro-del-foro-de-sao-paulo-en-la-ciudad-de-mexico-df/].

Foro de São Paulo. 2012. "Declaración Final XVIII Encuentro del Foro de São Paulo." Caracas. [http://albaciudad.org/2012/07/declaracion-final-xviii-encuentro-del-foro-de-sao-paulo-caracas-2012/].

Foro de São Paulo. 2013. "Declaración Final xix Encuentro del Foro de São Paulo." São Paulo. [http://forodesaopaulo.org/wp-content/uploads/2014/07/19-Declaracion-de-Sao-Paulo-III-2013.pdf].

Foro de São Paulo. 2014. "Declaración Final del xx Encuentro del Foro de São Paulo." La Paz. [https://fpabramo.org.br/wp-content/uploads/2014/09/declaracion_final_-_la_paz.pdf].

Foro de São Paulo. 2015. "Declaración final del XXI Encuentro del Foro de São Paulo." Ciudad de México, August 1. [http://forodesaopaulo.org/wp-content/uploads/2014/07/19-Declaracion-de-Sao-Paulo-III-2013.pdf].

Foro de São Paulo. 2016. "Declaración Final del XXII Encuentro del Foro de São Paulo."SanSalvador.[https://forodesaopaulo.org/wp-content/uploads/2016/06/Declaraci%C3%B3n-Final-2016.pdf].

Foro de São Paulo. 2018a. "XXIV Encuentro del Foro de São Paulo 2018." La Habana. [https://forodesaopaulo.org/?p=83544].

Crisis of Civilization 111

Foro de São Paulo. 2018b. "Nicaragua. XXIV Encuentro del Foro de São Paulo." La Habana, 15 al 17 de julio.

Foro de São Paulo. 2018c. "Venezuela. XXIV Encuentro del Foro de São Paulo." La Habana, July 15–17. [https://forodesaopaulo.org/wp-content/uploads/2018/08/11-Nicaragua.pdf].

Foro Social Mundial. 2002. "Carta de Principios." Porto Alegre. [https://fsm2016.org/es/sinformer/a-propos-du-forum-social-mondial/].

Friends of the Earth International. 2014. "Yasunidos. Ecuadorian Authorities Thwart National Referendum on Yasuní-ITT Through Fraud and Militarization." [https://www.foei.org/news/yasunidos-ecuadorian-authorities-thwart-national referendum-on-yasuni-itt-through-fraud-and-militarization].

Fundación Solón. 2017a. "El caso del Chepete y El Bala." La Paz, May 10. [https://fundacionsolon.org/2017/05/10/el-caso-del-chepete-y-el-bala/].

Fundación Solón. 2017b. "Inviabilidad económica del Chepete y El Bala." La Paz, May 10. [https://fundacionsolon.org/2017/05/10/inviabilidad-economica/#more-2944].

Fundación Solón. 2018. "La carretera por el TIPNIS ¿cómo nos afecta?." La Paz, August 30. [https://fundacionsolon.org/category/pacha/tipnis/].

G20. 2019. *G20 Leaders' declaration: Building consensus for fair and sustainable development* Buenos Aires. [http://www.g20.utoronto.ca/2018/buenos_aires_leaders_declaration.pdf].

Gaceta Oficial de la República de Venezuela. 1999. *Constitución de la República Bolivariana de Venezuela*. Caracas. [http://www.mppp.gob.ve/wp-content/uploads/2018/05/GO-36860_constitucion3.pdf].

Gárate, Javier. 2016. "Represión, persecución y criminalización de las luchas sociales en Bolivia." *Red Antimilitarista de América Latina y el Caribe*. Bolivia, May 1. [https://ramalc.org/represion-persecucion-y-criminalizacion-de-las-luchas-sociales-en-bolivia/].

García Linera, Álvaro. 2007. "Fue un error no liderar el pedido autonómico." Interview in: *El Deber*. Santa Cruz de la Sierra, January 21. Cited by Eric Toussaint in: *¿Un capitalismo andino-amazónico?*, cadtm/Rebelión. [https://rebelion.org/un-capitalismo-andino-amazonico/].

García Linera, Álvaro. 2012. *Las empresas del Estado. Patrimonio colectivo del pueblo boliviano*. Vicepresidencia del Estado Plurinacional de Bolivia, La Paz.

García Linera, Álvaro. 2013. *Geopolítica de la Amazonia. Poder hacendal-patrimonial y acumulación capitalista*. Vicepresidencia del Estado Plurinacional. Presidencia de la Asamblea Legislativa Plurinacional, La Paz.

Gilbertson, Tamara. 2017. "Carbon Pricing. A Critical Perspective for Community Resistance." Indigenous Environmental Network. [http://www.ienearth.org/wp-content/uploads/2017/11/Carbon-Pricing-A-Critical-Perspective-for-Community-Resistance-Online-Version.pdf].

Global Carbon Budget. 2018. *Global Carbon Budget 2018*. [https://essd.copernicus.org/articles/10/2141/2018/].

Global Footprint Network. 2009. *Ecological Footprint Standards 2009*. Oakland, CA: Global Footprint Network. Available at www.footprintstandards.org.

Global Footprint Network. *Glossary*. Oakland, CA: Global Footprint Network. [https://www.footprintnetwork.org/resources/glossary/].

112 *Crisis of Civilization*

Global Forest Coalition. 2008. The Real Cost of Agrofuels: Impacts on food, forests, peoples and the climate, pp. 1–85. [https://globaljusticeecology.org/files/Truecostagrofuels.pdf].

Gómez Fuentes, Copitz Ahahí. 2015. "Redes y movimientos sociales en contra de la construcción de presas en México. El caso del Movimiento Mexicano de Afectados por las Presas y en Defensa de los Ríos." In: *Revista Espacio Académico*, no. 167.

Gómez, Anahí. 2014. "Resistencias sociales en contra de los megaproyectos hídricos en América Latina." in: *Revista Europea de Estudios Latinoamericanos y del Caribe*, no. 97.

Grain. 2010. "La agricultura campesina puede enfriar el planeta." *Rebelión*, October 15. [https://rebelion.org/la-agricultura-campesina-puede-enfriar-el-planeta/].

Grain. 2018. "Emissions impossible: How big meat and dairy are heating up the planet." [https://www.grain.org/article/entries/5976-emissions-impossible-how-big-meat-and-dairy-are-heating-up-the-planet].

Grupo ETC. 2010. "Geopiracy: The Case Against Geoengineering." Ottawa, Canada, November 25 [https://www.etcgroup.org/sites/www.etcgroup.org/files/publication/pdf_file/ETC_geopiracy_4web.pdf].

Grupo Intergubernamental de Expertos sobre el Cambio Climático. 2014. *Cambio climático 2014. Informe de síntesis*. Ginebra. [https://www.ipcc.ch/site/assets/uploads/2018/02/SYR_AR5_FINAL_full_es.pdf].

Gudynas, Eduardo. 2015. *Extractivismos. Ecología, economía y política de un modo de entender el desarrollo y la Naturaleza*. Cochabamba: CEDIB & CLAES.

Hanley, Steve. 2018. "US, Russia, Saudi Arabia, & Kuwait Torpedo COP 24 Conference in Poland." *Clean Technica*, December 10. [https://cleantechnica.com/2018/12/10/us-russia-saudi-arabia-kuwait-torpedo-cop-24-climate-conference-in-poland/].

Hardin, Garrett. 1968. "The Tragedy of the Commons." *Science*, 162(395), 1243–1248, Dec 13.

Idso, Craig D. et al. 2014. *Climate Change Reconsidered II. Biological Impacts*, Chicago: Nongovernmental Panel on Climate Change, Heartland Institute. [http://climatechangereconsidered.org/climate-change-reconsidered-ii-biological-impacts/].

Instituto Boliviano de Comercio Exterior (IBCE). 2018. "Cifras del comercio exterior boliviano 2017." *Comercio Exterior*, no. 259. Santa Cruz. [http://ibce.org.bo/images/publicaciones/ce-259-Cifras-del-Comercio-Exterior-Boliviano-2017.pdf].

Intergovernmental Panel on Climate Change. 2014. "Climate Change 2014 Synthesis Report." [https://www.ipcc.ch/site/assets/uploads/2018/05/SYR_AR5_FINAL_full_wcover.pdf].

Intergovernmental Panel on Climate Change. 2018. "Global Warming of 1.5°C." [https://www.ipcc.ch/sr15/].

International Energy Agency. 2017. *World Energy Outlook 2017*. [https://www.iea.org/weo2017/].

International Forum on Globalization. *Kochtopus*. [http://ifg.org/kochtopus/].

Jamail, Dahr. 2018. "As Glacier-Fed Rivers Disappear. One-Sixth of Global Population Is at Risk." *Truthout*, June 4. [https://www.dahrjamail.net/2018/06/04/as-glacier-fed-rivers-disappear-one-sixth-of-global-population-is-at-risk/].

Crisis of Civilization   113

Jamasmie, Cecilia. 2017. "Ecuador anticipates \$4 billion in mining investments by 2021." *Mining.com*, March 10 [http://www.mining.com/ecuador-anticipates-4-billion-in-mining-investments-by-2021/].

Jara Triviño, Margarita de Jesús. 2017. *Criminalización de la protesta social enel Ecuador desde la constitución del 2008.* Guayaquil. [http://repositorio.ucsg.edu.ec/bitstream/3317/8739/1/T-UCSG-POS-MDC-105.pdf].

Javis, Brooke. 2018. "The Insect Apocalypses is Here. What does it mean forthe rest of life on Earth?." *The New York Times* (November 27).

Jonas, Hans. 1984. *The Imperative of Responsibility: In Search of an Ethics for the Technological Age.* Chicago and London: The University of Chicago Press.

Klare, Michael. 2018. "The Strategy of Maximal Extraction. How Donald Trump Plans to Enlist Fossil Fuels in the Struggle for Global Dominance." *TomDispatch.com*, February 11. [http://www.tomdispatch.com/blog/176384/].

Kothari, Ashish y K. J. Joy. 2017. *Alternative Futures: India Unshackled.* India: Paranjoy Guha Thakurta for AuthorsUpFront Publishing Services Private Limited.

Lancet. 2018. "Informe del Lancet Countdown sobre la salud y el cambio climático 2018: dando forma a la salud de las naciones en siglos venideros". London. [https://www.actasanitaria.com/documentos/informe-lancet-countdown/].

Lander, Edgardo (ed.). 2000. *La colonialidad del saber: eurocentrismo y ciencias sociales. Perspectivas latinoamericanas.* Caracas: UNESCO & Universidad Central de Venezuela.

Lander, Edgardo. 1990. *Contribución a la crítica del marxismo realmente existente: Verdad, ciencia y tecnología.* Caracas: Universidad Central de Venezuela.

Lander, Edgardo. 2004. "Sujetos, saberes, emancipaciones." In: *Reforma ou Revolução?* Fundação Rosa Luxemburg y Laboratório de Políticas Públicas da UERJ. São Paulo: Editora Expressão Popular.

Lander, Edgardo. 2011. *La economía verde. El lobo se viste con piel de cordero.* Amsterdam:Transnational Institute. [https://www.tni.org/es/publicacion/la-economia-verde-el-lobo-se-viste-con-piel-de-cordero].

Lander, Edgardo. 2018. "Venezuela. The Bolivarian Experience. A Struggle to Transform Capitalism." In: Miriam Lang, Claus Dieter König and Ada-Charlotte Regelmann (Ed.): *Alternatives in a World of Crisis, Global Working Group Beyond Development.* Brussels: Rosa Luxemburg Foundation.

Lander, Edgardo. 2019. "Renovado asalto a las condiciones de reproducción de la vida. Política energética y cambio climático en la era de Trump." Text presented at "Horizontes en disputa: Modernidad capitalista, nuevas derechas posdemocráticas y alternativas desde los márgenes." organized by Grupo de Trabajo Permanente del Alternativas al Desarrollo, Oficina Regional Andina of Rosa Luxemburg Foundation, Quito.

Leff, Enrique. 2006. *Aventuras de la epistemología ambiental.* México: Siglo XXI Editores.

Levenson, Eric y Brandon Miller. 2018. "2018 is on pace to be the 4th-hottest year on record." CNN, July 28. [https://edition.cnn.com/2018/07/28/us/2018-global-heat-record-4th-wxc/index.html].

Liptak, Adam. 2010. "Justices, 5-4, Reject Corporate Spending Limit." The New York Times, January 21.

114 Crisis of Civilization

Löwy, Michael. 2012. *Ecosocialismo. La alternativa radical a la catástrofe ecológica capitalista*. Madrid: Editorial Biblioteca Nueva. [https://climateandcapitalism.com/].

Machado Aráoz, Horacio. 2013. *Potosí, el origen. Genealogía de la minería contemporánea*. Buenos Aires: Mardulce.

Madrid Lara, Emilio. 2013. Colectivo de Coordinación de Acciones Socio-Ambientales, Bolivia. "Resistencias y persistencias ante la visión fetichizada de la minería y el desarrollo." *Astrolabio*, no. 11. [https://revistas.unc.edu.ar/index.php/astrolabio/article/download/5548/7396].

Maduro Moro, Nicolás. 2016. República Bolivariana de Venezuela. "Decreto 2248 de Creación de la Zona de Desarrollo Estratégico Nacional 'Arco Minero del Orinoco'." *Gaceta Oficial de la República Bolivariana de Venezuela*, no. 40.855, Caracas, February 26. [https://www.juris-line.com.ve/data/files/3311.pdf].

Malins, Chris. 2017. *For peat's sake. Understanding the climate implications of palm oil biodiesel consumption*. Oslo: Rainforest Foundation Norway. [https://d5i6is0eze552.cloudfront.net/documents/Publikasjoner/Andre-rapporter/For-peats-sake-Climate-implications-of-palm_May2017.pdf?mtime=201705311701].

Martínez Allier, Joan. 2009. *El ecologismo de los pobres*. Barcelona: Editorial Icaria.

Martínez, Esperanza y Alberto Acosta (eds.). 2010. I*TT-Yasuní. Entre el petróleo y la vida*. Quito: Abya Yala.

Martínez, Esperanza. 2009. *Yasuní. El tortuoso camino de Kioto a Quito*. Quito: Abya Yala y Comité Ecuménico de Proyectos (CRP).

McCarthy, Michael. 2004. "Only nuclear power can now halt global warming." *The Independent*. London, May 24. [https://www.independent.co.uk/environment/only-nuclear-power-can-now-halt-global-warming-61804.html].

Mcdonald, Charlotte. 2015. "How many Earths do we need?" BBC News, June 16. [https://www.bbc.com/news/magazine-33133712].

Merchant, Carolyn. 1980. *The Death of Nature: Women, Ecology and the Scientific Revolution*. San Francisco, CA: Harper and Row.

Metiendoruido.com. 2016. "Proyecto IIRSA. Cuando la geografía es un obstáculo para el saqueo." [https://porlatierraycontraelcapital.wordpress.com/2016/09/07/proyecto-iirsa-cuando-la-geografia-es-un-obstaculo-para-el-saqueo/].

Mies, Maria. 2008. "Decolonizing the Iceberg Economy." In: *Feminist Perspectives, Social Knowledge: Heritage, challenges and perspectives*. International Sociological Association.

Mies, Maria and Shiva Vandana. 2016. *Ecofeminismo. Teoría, crítica y perspectivas*. Barcelona: Editorial Antrazyt.

Mignolo, Walter. 1995. *The Darker Side of the Renaissance. Literacy, Territoriality and Colonization*. Ann Arbor, MI: The University of Michigan Press.

Millán aria, Einstein. 2019. "PDVSA: Entre fallidos negocios y contratos." *Aporrea*. Caracas, January 10. [https://www.aporrea.org/imprime/a274047.html].

Moreno, Camila. 2013. "Las ropas verdes del rey. La economía verde: una nueva fuente de acumulación primitiva." In: Miriam Lang, Claudia López & Alejandra Santillana (Ed.): *Alternativas al capitalismo/colonialismo del siglo XXI*. Grupo Permanente de Trabajo sobre Alternativas al Desarrollo. Quito: Rosa Luxemburg Foundation.

Crisis of Civilization 115

Moreno, Camila, Daniel Speich Chassé and Lili Fuhr. 2017. *La métrica del carbono:¿el CO_2 como medida de todas las cosas? El poder de los números en la política ambiental global*. Mexico: Heinrich Böll Foundation. [https://mx.boell. org/sites/default/files/carbon_metrics-impresion.pdf].

Naciones Unidas. Departamento de Asuntos Económicos y Sociales. 2014. *Decenio Internacional para la Acción 'El Agua fuente de vida' 2005-2015*, February 2. [http://www.un.org/spanish/waterforlifedecade/human_right_to_ water.shtml].

Nuncombe, Andrew. 2017. "Donald Trump gives presidential approval to Keystone XL oil pipeline." *The Independent*. London, March 24. [https:// www.independent.co.uk/news/world/americas/donald-trump-keystone-xl-oil-pipeline-presidential-approval-environment-a7647721.html].

Observatorio Electoral Venezolano. 2018. *Todo lo que debes saber sobre las elecciones del 9-D*. Caracas, October 31 de octubre. [http://www.oevenezolano. org/2018/10/31/todo-lo-que-debes-saber-sobre-las-elecciones-del-9-d/].

OCMAL (Observatorio de Conflictos Mineros en América Latina). 2017. *Criminalización de la protesta social por oposición a la minería en América Latina*, July 21. [https://www.cedib.org/biblioteca/criminalizacion_de_la_protesta_ social_por_oposicion_a_la_mineria_en_america_latina/].

OPEC. 2018. *Monthly Oil Market Report*. Vienna: December. [https://momr. opec.org/pdf-download/index.php].

Oppenheim, Maya. 2017. "Noam Chomsky: Republican Party is the most dangerous organisation in human history." London: *The Independent*, April 27. [https://www.independent.co.uk/news/world/americas/noam-chomsky-republican-party-most-dangerous-organisation-human-history-us-politics-mit-linguist-a7706026.html].

Ortega, Espinosa and María Isabel. 2016. *Terrorismo y derechos humanos, ¿terror para quién?* Quito: Universidad Andina Simón Bolívar. [http://repositorio. uasb.edu.ec/bitstream/10644/5425/1/T2173-MDE-Espinosa-Terrorismo.pdf].

Oxfam International. 2018. *Reward Work, not Wealth*. [https://www.oxfam.org/ en/research/reward-work-not-wealth].

Pacheco, Mayra. 2018. "La Contraloría identifica 7648 fisuras en la hidroeléctrica Coca Codo Sinclair." Quito: *El Comercio*, November 15.

Padura, Leonardo. 2018. *La transparencia del tiempo*. Barcelona: Editorial Tusquets.

Palacín Quispe, Miguel. 2011. "¿Criminalización en Bolivia?". *Alai, América Latina en Movimiento*. Quito, September 13 de septiembre. [https://www. alainet.org/es/active/49412].

Pateman, Carol. 1980. "Feminist Critiques of the Public/Private Dichotomy" & "The Patriarcal Welfare State." In: Carol Pateman (Ed): *The Disorder of Women*. Chicago, IL: The University of Chicago Press.

Plataforma Ciudadana en Defensa de la Constitución. 2018. "Acuerdos de Servicios de PDVSA comprometen la soberanía, violan la Constitución y la Ley de Hidrocarburos." *Aporrea*. Caracas: December 27 de diciembre. [https:// www.aporrea.org/energia/a273526.html].

Popovich, Nadja, Livia Albeck-Ripka and Kendra Pierre-Louis. 2018. "66 Environmental Rules on the Way Out Under Trump." *The New York Times*. January 31 [https://www.nytimes.com/interactive/2017/10/05/climate/ trump-environment-rules-reversed.html].

116 Crisis of Civilization

Potsdam Institute for Climate Impact Research et al. 2017. *2020: The Climate Turning Point.* [https://www.mission2020.global/climate-turning-point/].

Prada Alcoreza, Raúl. 2017. "Los nuevos patrones, los nuevos conquistadores." Clajadep: Red de divulgación e intercambios sobre autonomía y poder popular, August 20. [https://clajadep.lahaine.org/?p=18869&print=1].

Prada Alcoreza, Raúl. 2018. "Las organizaciones paralelas apócrifas." *Red Bolivia Mundo*, January 21 [http://www.boliviamundo.net/las-organizaciones-paralelas-apocrifas/].

PROVEA. 2018. "ACNUR. La cifra de personas refugiadas y migrantes venezolanas alcanza los 3 millones." Caracas, November 9. [https://www.derechos.org.ve/actualidad/la-cifra-de-personas-refugiadas-y-migrantes-venezolanas-alcanza-los-3-millones].

PSUV. 2009. "Estatutos del Partido Socialista Unido de Venezuela." Caracas. [http://www.psuv.org.ve/psuv/estatutos/].

Public Citizen. 2007, June. "Nuclear Power and Global Warming." [https://www.citizen.org/sites/default/files/nuclearglobalwarming.pdf].

Public Citizen. 2010. "12 Months After the Effects of Citizens United on Elections and the Integrity of the Legislative Process. Washington. [http://www.citizen.org/12-months-after].

Queensland Museum. 2010–2019. *Biodiversity and the Great Barrier Reef.* [http://www.qm.qld.gov.au/Find+out+about/Environment/Great+Barrier+Reef].

Quijano, Aníbal. 1992. "Raza, etnia, nación: cuestiones abiertas." In: Roland Forgues (Ed.): *José Carlos Mariátegui y Europa. La otra cara del descubrimiento.*Lima: Amauta.

Quijano, Aníbal. 2000. "Colonialidad del poder, eurocentrismo y América Latina." In: Edgardo Lander (Ed.): *La colonialidad del saber: Eurocentrismo y ciencias sociales. Perspectivas latinoamericanas.* Buenos Aires: CLACSO.

Quijano, Aníbal. 2001. "Colonialidad del poder: Globalización y democracia." *Revista de Ciencias Sociales de la Universidad Autónoma de Nuevo León.* Nuevo León.

Quijano, Aníbal. 2014. *Cuestiones y horizontes. De la dependencia histórico estructural a la colonialidad/descolonialidad del poder. Antología esencial.* Buenos Aires: CLACSO.

Rabatel, A. et al. 2013. "Current State of Glaciers in the Tropical Andes: A Multi-Century Perspective on Glacier Evolution and Climate Change." *The Cryosphere*, 7, 81–102. [www.the-cryosphere.net/7/81/2013/].

Rainforest Action Network. 2018. *Banking on Climate Change. Fossil Fuel Finance Report Card 2018.* [https://www.banktrack.org/download/banking_on_climate_change/banking_on_climate_change_2018_web_final.pdf].

Rattani, Vijetta. 2018. "Climate wrecker' US pushes its regressive agenda at IPCC talks." *Down to Earth*, October 4. [https://www.downtoearth.org.in/news/climate-change/-climate-wrecker-us-pushes-its-regressive-agenda-at-ipcc-talks-61792].

Red de Intelectuales y Artistas en Defensa de la Humanidad. 2017. *Revista Humanidad en Red*, August 15. [http://www.humanidadenred.org.ve/?p=8617].

RED-DESC. n.d. Movimiento de Afectados por las Represas (MAB). [https://www.escr-net.org/es/miembro/movimiento-afectados-por-represas-mab].

República Bolivariana de Venezuela. Asamblea Nacional Constituyente. 2017. "Ley Constitucional de Inversiones Extranjeras Productivas". *Gaceta Oficial de la República Bolivariana de Venezuela*, no. 41.310, Caracas, December 29 [http://dctos.finanzasdigital.com/Gaceta-Oficial-41310-Ley-Inversion-Extranjera.pdf].

República de Bolivia, Asamblea Constituyente. 2009. *Constitución Política del Estado*. La Paz. [https://www.bcn.cl/procesoconstituyente/comparadordeconstituciones/constitucion/bol].

República del Ecuador. Asamblea Constituyente. 2008. *Constitución de la República del Ecuador*. Quito. [https://www.acnur.org/fileadmin/Documentos/bdl/2008/6716.pdf].

República del Ecuador. Asamblea Constituyente. 2009. *Mandato Constituyente Minero*, no. 6. Quito, April 18 [https://flacsoandes.edu.ec/web/images-FTP/10874.Mandato_Constituyente_6_Minero.pdf].

República del Ecuador. Asamblea Nacional. 2009. "Ley de minería." *Registro Oficial Suplemento 517 del 29 de enero*. [http://www.oas.org/juridico/pdfs/mesicic4_ecu_mineria.pdf].

República del Ecuador. La Corte Constitucional para el periodo de transición. 2010. *Sentencia núm. 001-10-SIN-CC*. Quito. [https://www.palermo.edu/derecho/pdf/publicaciones/Revista_DerechoAmbiental_Ano4-N1_04.pdf].

República del Ecuador. Ministerio de Justicia, Derechos Humanos y Cultos. Subsecretaría de Desarrollo Normativo. 2014. *Código Orgánico Integral Penal*. Quito. [https://oig.cepal.org/sites/default/files/2014_codigopenalart.147-150_ecuador.pdf]

República del Ecuador. Ministerio de Relaciones Exteriores y Movilidad Humana. 2015. *El caso Chevron/Texaco en Ecuador. Una lucha por la justicia ambiental y social*. Quito. [https://www.cancilleria.gob.ec/wp-content/uploads/2015/06/Expediente-Caso-Chevron-abril-2015.pdf].

República del Ecuador. Secretaría Nacional de Planificación y Desarrollo. 2009. *Plan Nacional para el Buen Vivir 2009-2013*. Quito. [http://www.planificacion.gob.ec/plan-nacional-para-el-buen-vivir-2009-2013/].

Resina de la Fuente, Jorge. 2012. *La plurinacionalidad en disputa: el pulso entre Correa y la CONAIE*. Quito: Abya Yala.

Ribeiro, Silvia. 2016. *La nueva medida de todas las cosas: el carbono*. México: Grupo ETC. [https://www.etcgroup.org/es/content/la-nueva-medida-de-todas-las-cosas-el-carbono].

Ribeiro, Silvia. 2018. "Caos climático, capitalismo y geoingeniería." *La Jornada*. México, October 13

Roa, Tatiana and Luis María Navas (eds.). 2014. *Extractivismo, conflictos y resistencias*. Bogotá: Censat Agua Viva – Amigos de la Tierra.

Rodríguez Araque, Alí. 2014. "Recursos naturales como eje dinámico de la estrategia de UNASUR." *ALAI, América Latina en Movimiento*. Quito, March 24 [http://cancilleria.gob.ec/wp-content/uploads/2013/07/declaracion-alba-guayaquil-julio-2013.pdf].

Rodríguez Rosas, Ronny. 2018. "Gobierno exonera el pago del Islr a Pdvsa, filiales y empresas mixtas." *Efecto Cocuyo*. Caracas, August 4. [http://efectococuyo.com/principales/gobierno-exonera-el-pago-del-islr-a-pdvsa-filiales-y-empresas-mixtas/].

Romero, César and Francisco Ruiz. 2018. "Dinámica de la minería en pequeña escala como sistema emergente. Dislocaciones y ramificaciones entre lo local y lo nacional." In: Karin Gabbert y Alexandra Martínez (Ed.): *Venezuela desde adentro. Ocho investigaciones para un debate necesario*. Quito: Rosa Luxemburg Foundation. [https://www.rosalux.org.ec/pdfs/VENEZUELA-DESDE-ADENTRO_12.pdf].

118 *Crisis of Civilization*

Rushkoff, Douglas. 2018. "La supervivencia de los más ricos y cómo traman abandonar el barco." *Ctxt. Revista Contexto*, August 1 [https://ctxt.es/es/20180801/Politica/21062/tecnologia-futuro-ricos-pobres-economia-Douglas-Rushkoff.htm].

Sacher, William. 2017. *Ofensiva megaminera china en Los Andes. Acumulación por desposesión en el Ecuador de la "Revolución Ciudadana."* Quito: Abya Yala.

Sacher, William and Alberto Acosta. 2012. *La minería a gran escala en el Ecuador.* Quito: Abya Yala.

Salleh, Ariel. 2007. *Ecofeminism as Politics. Nature, Marx, and the Postmodern.* London: Zed Books.

Salva la Selva. 2013. "Exigen que se detengan concesiones petroleras en la Amazonía." [https://www.salvalaselva.org/noticias/4924/indigenas-ecuatorianos-exigen-que-se-detengan-concesiones-petroleras-en-la-amazonia].

Salva la Selva. 2017. "En 2018 sigue la defensa del TIPNIS en Bolivia." December 20 [https://www.salvalaselva.org/noticias/8552/en-2018-sigue-ladefensa-del-tipnis-en-bolivia].

Scott, James C. 1998. *Seeing Like a State. How Certain Schemes to Improve the Human Condition Failed.* New Heaven and London: Yale University Press.

Segato, Rita. 2018. Presentation at the meeting of Grupo Permanente de Trabajo de Alternativas al Desarrollo, Rosa Luxemburg Foundation, Oficina Quito, "Horizontes en disputa: modernidad capitalista, nuevas derechas posdemocráticas y alternativas desde los márgenes". Playas, Ecuador.

Seoane, José, Taddei, Emilio and Algranti, Clara. 2013. *Extractivismo, despojo y crisis climática. Desafíos para los movimientos sociales y los proyectos emancipatorios de Nuestra América.* Buenos Aires: Ediciones Herramienta/El Colectivo/Grupo de Estudios sobre América Latina y El Caribe.

Servindi. 2011. "Bolivia: Violenta represión a la marcha indígena por el TIPNIS." Videos, September 26 de septiembre. [https://www.servindi.org/actualidad/52119].

Servindi. 2016. "IIRSA: la infraestructura de la devastación." October 24. [https://www.servindi.org/actualidad-noticias/23/10/2016/documental-sobre-extractivismo-iirsa-la-infraestructura-de-la].

Servindi. 2018. "Evo Morales cambia su discurso y ahora favorece a los biocombustibles." [https://www.servindi.org/opinion/12/09/2018/evo-moralesy-el-fin-de-un-discurso-en-contra-los-biocombustibles-en-bolivia].

Shell. 2018. Shell Energy Transition Report (2018). [https://www.shell.com/energy-and-innovation/the-energy-future/shell-energy-transition-report.html].

Singer, S. Fred. 2008. *Nature, Not Human Activity, Rules the Climate.* Chicago: Heartland Institute. [https://www.co2web.info/NIPCC-Final_080303.pdf]

Sistema de Alerta, Monitoreo y Atención en Nutrición y Salud & Caritas Venezuela. 2018. *Monitoreo de la situación nutricional de niños menores de cinco años.* Caracas. [https://caritasvenezuela.org/wp-content/uploads/sites/6/2022/04/6to-Boletin-SAMAN-Enero-Marzo-2018.pdf].

Somos Sur. 2014. "Un reactor nuclear en Bolivia." [https://somossur.net/index.php/economia/mega-proyectos-bajo-la-lupa/1510-planta-de-energia-nuclear-en-bolivia].

Somos Sur. 2016. "TIPNIS: infamia de una 'Consulta' manipulada. Revisión de informes sobre la "Consulta previa, libre e informada a los pueblos indígenas del Territorio Indígena y Parque Nacional Isiboro Sécure (TIPNIS)." [https://somossur.net/documentos/20170725_tipnis_consulta.pdf].

Crisis of Civilization   119

Stockholm Resilience Center. 2015. *Planetary Boundaries – an update*. Stockholm. [http://www.stockholmresilience.org/research/research-news/2015-01-15-planetary-boundaries—an-update.html].

Superville, Darlene. 2018. "Trump signs $700 billion military budget into law." PBS News Hour, December 12. [https://www.pbs.org/newshour/politics/trump-signs-700-billion-military-budget-into-law].

Svampa, Maristella and Enrique Viale. 2014. *Maldesarrollo. La Argentina del extractivismo y el despojo*. Buenos Aires: Katz Editores.

Svampa, Maristella. 2017. *Del cambio de época al fin de ciclo. Gobiernos progresistas, extractivismo y movimientos sociales en América Latina*. Buenos Aires: Edhasa.

Tejada Soruco, Alicia. 2011. *Minería en las tierras bajas de Bolivia*. Cochabamba: Centro de Documentación e Información Bolivia (CEDIB). [https://cedib.org/wp-content/uploads/2012/08/mineria_tierras_bajas.pdf].

Temple, James. 2017. "President Trump Takes Immediate Aim at Obama's Climate Action Plan." *MIT Technology Review*, January 20 de enero. [https://www.technologyreview.com/s/603418/president-trump-takes-immediate-aim-at-obamas-climate-action-plan/].

Territorios en Resistencia. 2014. "Comunarias toman la maquinaria de la cooperativa Relámpago, en la localidad de Teoponte." October 15. [https://ibce.org.bo/principales-noticias-bolivia/noticias-nacionales-detalle.php?id=47372&idPeriodico=3&fecha=2014-10-16].

The Heartland Institute. January 21, 2023 [https://www.heartland.org/].

The Nongovernmental Panel on Climate Change. 2017. Heartland Institute, Arlington Heights, Ilinois. [http://climatechangereconsidered.org/about-the-nipcc/].

The White House. 2017a. "Presidential Executive Order on Promoting Energy Independence and Economic Growth." Washington, March 28. [https://www.whitehouse.gov/briefings-statements/remarks-president-trump-unleashing-american-energy-event/].

The White House. 2017b. *National Security Strategy 2017*. Washington, December. [https://www.whitehouse.gov/wp-content/uploads/2017/12/NSS-Final-12-18-2017-0905.pdf].

Transnational Institute and Carbon Trade Watch. 2007. *El cielo no es el límite: el mercado emergente de gases efecto invernadero*. Amsterdam. [https://www.tni.org/es/publicacion/el-cielo-no-es-el-limite].

Transnational Institute. 2016. *Towards Energy Democracy*. Discussions and outcomes from an international workshop, Amsterdam. [https://www.tni.org/en/publication/towards-energy-democracy].

Trump, Donald. 2017. "Remarks by President Trump at the Unleashing American Energy Event." All News U.S. Department of Energy Washington D.C., June 29. [https://trumpwhitehouse.archives.gov/briefings-statements/remarks-president-trump-unleashing-american-energy-event/].

U.S. Global Change Research Program. 2018. *Fourth National Climate Assessment*. Washington, November. [https://www.globalchange.gov/nca4].

UNASUR. 2008. *Declaración de presidentes UNASUR por crisis en Bolivia*, Reuters, Santiago, September 15. [https://lta.reuters.com/article/domesticNews/idLTAN1533709020080916].

UNASUR. 2011. Tratado Constitutivo de la Unión de Naciones Suramericanas. Quito, March 11. [http://www.iirsa.org/admin_iirsa_web/Uploads/Documents/rp_brasilia08_cumbre_unasur_tratado_constitutivo.pdf].

120   *Crisis of Civilization*

UNESCO. 2018. *Atlas de glaciares y aguas andinos. El impacto del retroceso de los glaciares sobre los recursos hídricos.* París. [https://es.unesco.org/news/lanzamiento-atlas-retroceso-glaciares-andinos-y-reduccion-aguas-glaciares].

Union of Concerned Scientists. 2018. *The Nuelar Power Dilema*, October 9. [https://www.ucsusa.org/resources/nuclear-power-dilemma#.W-WE5NVKiUm].

United Nations Environmental Program UNEP 2011. Towards a Green Economy: Pathways to Sustainable Development and Poverty Erradication. [https://sustainabledevelopment.un.org/index.php?page=view&type=400&nr=126&menu=35].

United Nations General Assembly. 1987. *Report of the World Commission on Environment and Development: Our Common Future* (Brundtland Report). [https://sustainabledevelopment.un.org/content/documents/5987 our-common-future.pdf]

Van Teijlingen, Karolien et al. 2017. *La amazonia minada. Minería en gran escala y conflictos en el sur del Ecuador.* Quito: USFQ and Abya Yala.

Vía Campesina. 2015. "¡Juntos podemos enfriar el planeta!." [https://viacampesina.org/es/juntos-podemos-enfriar-el-planeta/].

Vitti, Minerva. 2018. "Una mirada estructural del megaproyecto Arco Minero del Orinoco." Revista SIC. Caracas, June 27. [http://revistasic.gumilla.org/2018/una-mirada-estructural-del-megaproyecto-arco-minero-del-orinoco-i/].

Wallerstein, Immanuel. 2002. "Porto Alegre 2002." México: *La Jornada*, February 10. [http://www.jornada.com.mx/2002/02/10/026a1mun.php?origen=index.html].

Walsh, Catherine. 2009. *Interculturalidad, Estado y Sociedad. Luchas (de)coloniales de nuestra época.* Quito: Universidad Andina Simón Bolívar and Abya-Yala.

Widrig, Marcel. 2018. "New visionaries and the Chinese Century. Billionaires insights 2018." USB & PWC. [https://www.pwc.ch/en/insights/fs/billionaires-insights-2018.html].

Wikipedia. 2018. *Global Climate Coalition.* March 25. [https://en.wikipedia.org/wiki/Global_Climate_Coalition]

World Economic Forum. 2016. *The number of cars worldwide is set to double by 2040*, April. [https://www.weforum.org/agenda/2016/04/the-number-of-cars-worldwide-is-set-to-double-by-2040].

WWF et al. 2016. *Planeta vivo. Informe 2016. Riesgo y resiliencia en una nueva era.* [http://awsassets.panda.org/downloads/informe_planeta_vivo_2016.pdf].

WWF et al. 2018. *Living Planet Report 2018: Aiming Higher.* Gland, Switzerland. [https://wwf.panda.org/knowledge_hub/all_publications/living_planet_report_2018/].

Zaconeta Torrico, Alfredo J. 2017. "El zinc en Bolivia: entre la negligencia y el desconocimiento." in: *CEDLA. Reporte anual de industrias extractivas.* La Paz. [http://www.cedla.org/ieye/libro/53214].

Zibechi, Raúl. 2006. *IIRSA: la integración a la medida de los mercados.* Programa de las Américas. Informe Especial, June 13. [https://alternative-regionalisms.org/wp-content/uploads/2009/07/zibechi-iirsa.pdf].

Zibechi, Raúl. 2010. "Luces y sombras de la década progresista." México: *La Jornada*, December 31. [https://www.jornada.com.mx/2010/12/31/opinion/017a2pol]

Zibechi, Raúl. 2016. "Interconexión sin integración: 15 años de IIRSA." Centro de Derechos Económicos y Sociales (CDES). [https://cdes.org.ec/web/interconexion-sin-integracion-15-anos-de-iirsa/].

Zibechi, Raúl. 2018. "Ellos" se preparan, nosotros..." *Aporrea*, Caracas, December 9. [https://www.aporrea.org/actualidad/a272863.html].

Zorrilla, Carlos. 2017. "Ecuador's extractive policies and the silencing of dissent." *Democracia abierta*, March 16. [https://www.opendemocracy.net/en/democraciaabierta/ecuador-s-extractive-policies-and-silencing-of-dissent/].

2 The Refeudalization of Society
Social Inequality and Political Culture in Latin America

Olaf Kaltmeier

Global Refeudalization or Latin American "Feudal Mania?"

The small syllable "post" has been the indispensable prefix for the diagnosis of time. The boom of "post" ranges from the post-industrial society to the end of the grand narratives of modernity in postmodernism to theoretical approaches of poststructuralism, post-feminism, and postcolonialism. Despite all differences, these "post" approaches have a shared paradoxical foundation. On the one hand, they refer to a crisis-like upheaval in contemporary social development that can no longer be understood in conventional terms and theories. This crisis is so profound that one can speak of a veritable epochal upheaval. The end of modernity has been heralded without it being possible yet to draw the precise outlines of a subsequent epoch. Despite this ambiguity, the temporal prefix "post," on the other hand, refers to a future horizon of expectations and implicitly contains a utopian promise of the future. It refers to something that comes after, still in the process of becoming.

Instead, the term refeudalization—which is the key concept of this book—calls into question the implicit optimism regarding the prospects of progress typical of previously common "post" concepts. Rather, it points out that even in periods of change, there can be conjunctures that are oriented to the past in form and content. In this sense, more recent "post" approaches have also been more skeptical. Colin Crouch argued in *Post-Democracy* that the current developments of democracy are rather to be understood as regressions to a feudal, pre-democratic period (2004, 13). In this respect, his concept of "post" is rather skeptical, as he argues not only temporally, but also qualitatively: "we are moving *beyond* democracy" (31), thus taking a qualitative step backward that projects us back to feudalism on an imaginary developmental timeline.

Nevertheless, in Latin America in the 1990s and 2000s, there was a particularly optimistic boom in "post" approaches. With the wave of democratization in the 1990s, military dictatorships and authoritarian systems were swept away. At the same time, relevant social actors arose, exemplified by indigenous movements that have advanced postcolonial

DOI: 10.4324/9781003308850-3

approaches in the direction of pluricultural recognition, decolonization, and even plurinationality.

The late 1990s and early 2000s saw a remarkable wave of leftist movements and governments in the region, putting an end to neoliberalism in its purest form through the adoption of post-neoliberal economic models. With high economic growth rates, democratically consolidated regimes and comprehensive policies of inclusion, the region, traditionally considered to be in crisis, became a remarkably stable reference point in the midst of global times of crises such as the financial crisis in the European Union (2009–2010) or the U.S. housing crisis in the 2000s.

With the end of center-left governments in Brazil (2016), Argentina (2015), Chile (2010 and 2018), Bolivia (2019), Uruguay (2020), the rightward slide in Ecuador (2017), and the political crisis in Venezuela and Nicaragua, this phase came to an end at the dawn of the 2020s. The push of the last decades for democratization has been overtaken by new authoritarianism and a significant shift to the (extreme) right. It is in the context of this turn to the right, which is not limited to Latin America, that reflections of the refeudalization of capitalism emerged. In the 2020s, a second, moderate turn to the left can be observed. The Peronist electoral success of Alberto Fernández in Argentina in 2019, the election of Andrés Manuel López Obrador in Mexico in 2018, and of Pedro Castillo in Peru in 2021, as well as the process of a new constitution as the result of massive street protests and the subsequent electoral victory of Gabriel Boric in Chile in 2021 also certainly points to a persistence of post-neoliberal political approaches. Especially significant is also the electoral victory of Gustavo Petro and Francia Márquez in Colombia, who established in 2022 the first leftwing government in a country known as a fortress of conservatism in the region. These second pink advances reveal that the takeover of the state and the society by the aristocratic elite is not uncontested. But also the turn to the right has not ended. This can be evidenced by the victory of the refusal, *rechazo,* of the proposal of the new constitution in Chile on September 4, 2022, elaborated by a truly democratic and popular constitution convent, which means that the authoritarian and neoliberal constitution of the Pinochet dictatorship remains in force. The failed assassination attempt against Argentine vice-president Cristina Fernández de Kirchner, the most prominent expression of political violence since the end of the military dictatorship in 1983, reveals the growing misogyny and anti-popular political culture. In recent decades there has been a significant transformation of societal relations in both the elite and general public, articulated as well to global dynamics of capital accumulation. In this sense, refeudalization is understood as a historical conjuncture that transcends short-term events.

It is the central concern of this book to analyze in more detail the multiple dimensions of the current refeudalization of capitalism that can be observed in a wide variety of social fields. Refeudalization is not limited

124 *The Refeudalization of Society*

to Latin America, in contrast, this process must be placed in the context of the capitalist world system. But what does the refeudalization of capitalism mean?

A key phenomenon of refeudalization is the concentration of power in the hands of a small social group that is increasingly separating itself socioeconomically and culturally from the rest of society and at the same time occupying more and more positions of power economically and politically. This group, which makes up 1%–10% of the population in Latin American societies, will be referred to in the following chapters as the moneyed aristocracy. The choice of this term from the semantic field of feudalism follows observations of the increasing refeudalization of social relations worldwide. For example, Hans Jürgen Krysmanski, a researcher of elites, noted in his book on *The Empire of the Billionaires* that "capitalism is transitioning into a transcapitalism with neo-feudal structures" (2015a, 9).

With the German sociologist Sighard Neckel, who has presented a highly inspiring draft of the tendencies of refeudalization, I would like to pursue an even broader and more analytical perspective on the refeudalization of capitalism: "As a paradoxical model of social development, the analytical perspective of a 'refeudalization' of capitalist modernity is instructive for the study of social change as a whole, whether we are dealing with the erosion of democratic institutions in post-democracy or the economic neo-feudalization in modern financial markets" (2013a, 49). Following this current debate on refeudalization—especially in the global framework of the capitalist global system—this book discusses seven dimensions of refeudalization, adapted to the specific regional context in Latin America.

The first refers to the dramatic change in the form of the social structure, which is increasingly moving away from the democratic promise of equality or at least equality of opportunities (*equidad*). Thus, Neckel notes a refeudal transformation globally of the social structure and a deepening of social inequality, "which shows clear characteristics of feudalization in its features of polarization of incomparable social situations and the status-related solidification of social background" (2013a, 49). What this means here is, above all, the setting apart of a global moneyed aristocracy—the famous 1%—from the remaining 99% of the world's population. This transformation of the social structure is particularly evident in Latin America, a region of the world characterized by extreme social inequality due to its colonial past and present.

Second, there is a worldwide tendency toward refeudalization of the economic field. This can be seen in the way economic processes are organized and in the neo-feudal status of the dominant groups leading the financial market. Beyond this global tendency, it is necessary to point out the unchanged centrality of the preindustrial extractivist economic sectors in Latin America and the imminent importance of the

The Refeudalization of Society   125

concentration of land in the hands of a few as a factor in the polarization of the social structure. These tendencies of economic refeudalization are characterized also by the necessity of accumulation through dispossession, which principally takes hold of public goods.

The third aspect of these current refeudalization tendencies to consider is the profound changes with regard to social norms, values, and identities. For Neckel, the core of the

> refeudalization of values and the justificatory order of financial market capitalism lies in the erosion of the performance principle through performance-free incomes from inherited positions, assets, and property titles as well as a refeudalization of recognition that takes place in the world of the celebrities of the media age through the effects of celebrity status
>
> (2013a, 49).

In the current consumer society, in which identity formation also takes place through consumption (Bauman 2007), luxury consumption, driven by the "invidious comparison" that Thorstein Veblen had already identified in his classic work on the "leisure class" in 1899 as the driving social force behind distinction of class, becomes a central indicator for the formation of a monetary aristocratic identity. In contrast, the lower segments of society—driven by the cultural promises of the consumer society—fall into a credit-card-driven compulsion to consume, pushing them into a new form of debt bondage.

Fourth, the most central spatial expression of the current processes of refeudalization is that of the wall. The social distinction and separation of the moneyed aristocracy find its spatially equivalent expression in segregation. Not only neighborhoods segregated but also spaces of consumption and circulation for the rich are removed from public spaces. As can be observed in processes of gentrification, these developments often go hand in hand with intense social struggles. Beyond this segregation of spatial form, a nostalgic recourse to colonial esthetics can be observed, especially regarding the use of architectural motifs.

A fifth dimension of refeudalization is expressed in the increasing colonization of the political field by a monetary aristocracy. Neckel refers here above all to billionaire initiatives such as the *Giving Pledge*, initiated by Bill Gates, which promotes a self-commitment of billionaires to more charity. Neckel sees here a "refeudalization of the welfare state that reprivatizes public social policy as endowment and donation and transforms welfare state entitlements into dependence on private charity" (2013a, 49–50). This tendency is rather marginal in Latin America and has little political impact. There is also a tendency toward post-democracy in the region (Crouch 2004), according to which economic interest groups undermine democratic will-formation and decision-making processes.

126   *The Refeudalization of Society*

Recently, there is an increased tendency for millionaires to take over political power directly. This shows a dangerous tendency toward the doubling of economic and political power, which bears the traits of a new moneyed-aristocratic despotism.

A sixth aspect of the current refeudalization of capitalism is its articulation with neoconservative right-wing identity politics that reestablish racist, misogynist, and elitist discourses and performativities based on whiteness and masculinity. The transformation of political cultures in Latin America introduced by these violent forms of identity politics, to mention the seventh and last dimension of refeudalization in the region, finds its expression in changes in the patterns of political rationalities. The neoliberal form of (ethno-)governmentality is increasingly replaced by a refeudal mode of sovereign power.

In addition to the discussion on these dimensions of the current refeudalization of capitalism, there is also a need for a conceptual discussion on feudalism, capitalism, and refeudalization. As Steve Stern makes clear in his classic overview of the feudalism debate in Latin America, "the feudal 'diagnosis' of the colonial legacy" (1988, 832) goes back as far as the 19th century (832). The persistence of feudal structural elements in modern Latin American societies is primarily connected to the agrarian regime and the persistence of forms of bonded labor until the 1960s and 1970s. Accordingly, José Carlos Mariátegui judged as early as 1928 in his "Seven Interpretive Essays on Peruvian Reality": "The land owning aristocracy of the colony, holder of power, maintained intact its feudal rights over the land and, consequently, over the Indian. All of the measures seemingly designed to protect them have not been able to do anything against the feudalism that still exists today" (2007, 35).[1]

An important strand of debate about the relationship between feudalism and capitalism can be found in the Latin American social-historical and sociological discussions on dependency theory from the 1970s onward. Its conceptualization of feudalism was shaped by Marxist theoretical approaches that focused on the exploitation of labor. The debate gained new momentum with world-systems theory, which, almost five decades after its introduction by Immanuel Wallerstein, is still relevant in Latin America today. Wallerstein argued that Europe solved the crisis of feudalism through the expansion into the Americas and the subsequent construction of a capitalist world system. Based on a broad concept of capitalism in the sense of exploitation of labor for the capitalist global market, the proponents of world systems theory then argued that it was no longer possible to speak of feudalism in Latin America during the 19th and 20th centuries since these economies were already largely integrated into the international division of labor of the capitalist global market.

Ernesto Laclau, on the other hand, argued that although there was integration into the global market, this did not change the fact that there

The Refeudalization of Society 127

were several different modes of production in Latin America at the same time, including a feudal one that has found its peak expression in the *hacienda* regime. Following Laclau, it can be stated that there can be several intertwined modes of production within the framework of a capitalist world system. This simultaneity of the non-simultaneous is not a relict, but rather essential for the functioning of the capitalist world system, as the representatives of the *Bielefeld approach of entanglement* have pointed out using the example of the articulation of subsistence production and capitalist production of goods (Evers 1987).

A closer look at the Latin American feudalism-capitalism debate is necessary to understand the current concept of refeudalization used here. As a matter of fact, feudalism is not an unmarked term in Latin America. There is a special tension between the history of the concept and social history when a term from another historical, and also spatial, context— in this case, the Western European feudalism of the early modern era— is used for a new context as in this case contemporary Latin America. Tellingly, it was precisely the concept of feudalism with which Reinhart Koselleck associated this tension: "With the extension of the use of later concepts to earlier times or, conversely, the stretching (as is common in the use of feudalism today) of earlier concepts to later phenomena, there is at least hypothetically a prerequisite of minimal commonalities in the subject matter" (1989, 128). So the question is what exactly the common grounds in the subject matter area are when terms from the semantic context of Western European feudalism currently reappear in the cultural and political debates. At this point, it will not be possible to carry out a historical investigation of the current use of the concept of (re)feudalization. But it is striking that terms from the semantic field of feudalism are used precisely to name new inequalities and concentrations of power in global capitalism. One can think of terms like cosmocracy, moneyed aristocracy, and, of course, refeudalization. These terms do not follow a rigid theoretical model, rather they have an explorative character and are able to perceive social fissures and crises in an almost seismographic manner.

It is striking, however, that the question of the exploitation of labor and the status of wage labor, a central point of discussion in the social-historical feudalism-capitalism debate, is hardly addressed in the use of terms from the semantic context of feudalism to describe contemporary society. However, it is estimated that modern forms of slavery spread worldwide. It is estimated that 40,3 million people live and work under conditions of refeudal slavery. (Rosa Luxemburg Stiftung 2021, 11) In a regional panorama, Latin America is not the prime region of refeudal slavery, although bonded forms of labor are especially present in domestic work, the sex industry, and extractivist sectors. Although slavery was abolished in Brazil in 1888, in the period between 1995 and 2021 alone— especially under the Worker' Party-government (2008–2013)—56,000

128   *The Refeudalization of Society*

persons have been freed of slave-like bonded forms of labor in coal production, deforestation, and agro-industrial plantations (Rosa Luxemburg Stiftung 2021, 34–35).

Not only modern slavery and bonded labor are aspects of the trend toward refeudalization in labor relations, but there is oversupply of non-classified labor worldwide, in fact, due to deindustrialization in several parts of the world. This finds expression in a rising informal sector as well as the emergence of "superfluous populations" (Bauman 2005), which goes far beyond the debate about the "industrial army reserve." Under these circumstances, although it might sound cynical, it becomes almost a privilege to be exploited through wage labor. In this respect, the conceptualization of refeudalization processes chosen here hardly connects to the feudalism-capitalism debate of the 1970s.

A different political-economic approach to refeudalization can be identified following approaches from dependency theory that analyze the relationship between centers and peripheries in the capitalist world system. In this sense, Alain Supiot sees a main juridical shift away from the rule of law, in which all are treated equally, to a rule of persons. He sees the latter in feudal systems and also in the refeudalizing tendencies in which power is held by person-centered (global) networks ultimately undermining the power of (nation-state) laws. In this sense, Supiot identifies a "transition from law to bond" (2013, 141) in international politics. This approach highlights important internationally effective tendencies of refeudalization.

However, this book focuses less on global tendencies and more on regional dynamics in Latin America. To this end, it makes sense to work with a less economically oriented concept of refeudalization. One suitable approach can be found in the early work of the social theorist and philosopher Jürgen Habermas on the transformation of public space in Europe. In his analysis of the structural transformation of the public sphere, he introduces the concept of refeudalization into critical theory. Habermas explores the relationship between the public sphere and the common on the one hand and the private on the Other. For Habermas, the concept of the public sphere is defined by the principle of universal access: "A public sphere from which ostensible groups would be excluded eo ipso is not only incomplete, rather it is no public sphere at all" (Habermas 1962, 156). In post-industrial societies, Habermas identifies a dynamic of weakening the public sphere due to the pressure of commercial interests and their penetration through strategies aimed at achieving political legitimacy (1962). With this approach, the changes in everyday culture, social dynamics, and political representation already indicated can be discerned.

With the five dimensions just outlined, the current process of refeudalization has a double structure that can be described with the terms form and content. Thus, various social forms of the current conjuncture of refeudalization—for example, in terms of the pyramid-like social

The Refeudalization of Society 129

polarization, the tendency of class consolidation and social segregation take on a form that resembles pre-democratic forms of feudalism on the eve of the French Revolution. Recent sociological literature on refeudalization in the modern capitalist world-system primarily from Neckel (2010, 2013a, 2013b) to Tanner (2015) and Martens (2016) to Piketty (2014) addresses this homology in social form. In this book, however, the perspective of analysis engages with the refeudalization of social forms, while at the same time expanding it to include the dimension of a refeudalization of content. The main aim of this extension is to integrally include the cultural-political forms of expression and representation in the analysis. As an example, the social form of urban segregation can be understood through various esthetic concepts. In this context, a reference back to colonial esthetics, motifs, and designs can be observed in Latin America. Refeudalization in this sense is linked to the currently detectable waves of nostalgia (Boym 2001) and retrotopia (Bauman 2017) in social forms, which in Latin America are especially expressed in new forms of retro-coloniality (Kaltmeier 2011, 2017).

Another aspect that needs to be clarified with regard to the use of the concept of refeudalization concerns historiographic categorization and, ultimately, the foundations of the philosophy of history as well. Contrary to time-diagnostic concepts, which refer to a time after, to partly undefined, partly further developed concepts of "post-," the "re-" addresses a temporal vector that refers to an era long thought to have been overcome. This is understood by many theorists of refeudalization as a thoroughly paradoxical regression. Thus, Tanner holds,

> [t]he postindustrial and post-Fordist society of postmodern post-democracy differed from the Fordist industrial system of democratic capitalism precisely in showing feudal elements to such an extent and intensity that the triad of enlightened public sphere, democracy, and capitalism drifted toward a *nouveau ancien regime*
> (Tanner 2015, 740).

This regression, however, cannot be understood as a simple return to earlier social formations, but it can, as Supiot highlights, be understood as a return of feudal elements: "The idea of a 'refeudalization of law' put forward by several authors does not mean a return to the Middle Ages, but the re-emergence of a legal structure that had become obsolete through the birth of the nation-state" (2013, 138). Sighard Neckel formulates this as follows: "'Refeudalization' is thus not to be understood as the return of a historically long-gone epoch and does not mean a return to old times. Refeudalization, in particular, does not represent a state, but a process" (2013b).

This process is accompanied by social crises and upheavals that can have an almost performative dimension. Regarding the crisis of exploitation

130 *The Refeudalization of Society*

and simultaneous explosion of the productive forces, Marx pointed out in *The Eighteenth Brumaire of Louis Bonaparte* that the upcoming proletarian revolution strips off the burden of the past and is oriented toward the future: "The social revolution of the nineteenth century cannot draw its poetry from the past, but only from the future" (1978, 115). For Marx, however, this future-oriented transformation is by no means self-evident. Rather, he assumes with Hegel that the "great world-historical facts and persons occur twice," meaning "one time as tragedy, the Other time as farce." Marx sees here the tendency to nostalgic masquerade. In social crises, the actors invoke "the ghosts of the past to their service anxiously, borrow from them name, battle slogan, costume, in order to perform the new scene of world history in this time-honored disguise and with this borrowed language." (1978, 115) Today, this tendency can be seen in the global reach of heritage and retro fashions, which are accompanied by a particular revaluation of the (esthetic) colonial heritage in Latin America. This shows that the horizon of expectations of social elites is currently not very optimistic about the future; rather, the recourse to the past serves to protect their more fortunate social position in the present.

With such an understanding of refeudalization, it is necessary to think about temporality. Colin Crouch has described a parabolic trajectory with the concept of "post-democracy." He sees the apex of development realized in Western democratic welfare states, whereas now a downward trend can be observed. When this parabola is folded over on itself, our current moment coincides with the times of absolutism. The fundamental difference between the experiential worlds of these marked points consists in the accumulated experience and memory of the formerly achieved democratic values, insofar as we carry "the inheritance of our recent past with us" (Crouch 2004, 5). This point is plausible, but Crouch's approach also has problematic aspects. First, Crouch—in the bad tradition of Eurocentric development and stage models—presents the Western European democracies of modernity as the ultimate reference points of democracy. Second, he suggests a mathematization of historical processes that leaves little room for regionally explanatory patterns or local dynamics. Third, it is an oversimplified parabola, constrained to showing the democratic quality of the timeline. Thus, spatial differences and interdependencies such as center-periphery remain unconsidered. And fourth, this model hardly allows us to elaborate any further innovative concepts since it establishes a clear point of reference. This is shown particularly in the uninspiring, almost nostalgic-sounding final chapter.

Instead, it seems to me to make more sense—analogous to the entanglement of modes of production—to think about the entanglement of temporalities. Especially in the Latin American present, the presence of different times is evident. In this context, it is above all the persistence and permanent renewal of coloniality as a longue durée phenomenon

The Refeudalization of Society   131

that should be pointed out (Mignolo 2000; Moraña, Dussel, and Jáuregui 2008; Quijano 2000). However, coloniality is also not solely to be understood as a fixed layer of time; rather, historically different conjunctures of colonization and decolonization can be demonstrated, which I have developed through the example of one specific place in the Ecuadorean highlands from the colonial period until today (Kaltmeier 2016). From this point of view, feudal and colonial elements always have been present in modern capitalism. The point is about the impact of these elements within specific historical periods. In this sense, the contemporary wave of refeudalization is not unique in the history of capitalism. A historical comparison with the period of the Gilded Age in the United States, which can be understood also as a conjuncture of refeudalization, is particularly helpful (Kaltmeier 2019, 29–42).

It is of particular importance for the argument presented in this essay that the current conjuncture of refeudalization has global dimensions and extends to the entire capitalist world system. At the same time, however, there are also regionally specific manifestations. For Latin America, the entanglement of the current conjuncture of refeudalization with deep structures of coloniality is of importance. In this region—if we may disregard local differences for once—the global conjuncture of refeudalization can also be understood as a renewed conjuncture of colonization.

Now, the debate on coloniality advanced in postcolonial studies by no means indicates a relapse into the *feudal-mania* (Grosfoguel 2008, 307) of the 1960s and 1970s. Back then, feudal structures were primarily associated with an overarching universal model of development, according to which social development has to pass through the same social stages everywhere in the world—virtually as a law of nature. Thus, the critique of Ramón Grosfoguel: "Feudal-mania was a means of 'temporal distancing' to produce knowledge that denied simultaneity between Latin America and the so-called developed European countries" (2008, 308).

With the prospect of a "catch-up" for the supposedly underdeveloped regions, a spatio-temporal distance between them was constructed. This is different now. In the current imagination of refeudalization, a utopian overcoming of "backwardness" through development is not envisioned. Instead of a catch-up, there is a cut-off, an exclusion.

At this point, there is no intention to present a strict and stringent theory of refeudalization. Instead, this political essay aims to highlight the potential of the aforementioned analytical perspective by referring to the five dimensions of refeudalization mentioned at the beginning. The concept has proven to be particularly fruitful in bringing together hitherto barely connected critical positions on contemporary tendencies of social crisis under the prism of refeudalization. Furthermore, this book invites the reader to think about historical change and the entanglement of temporalities and spaces in the overall context of the capitalist world system. And ultimately, this book also aims to provide food for thought

132   *The Refeudalization of Society*

for overcoming various phenomena associated with the processes of refeudalization, such as the exacerbation of social inequality, cultural and spatial exclusion, ecological degradation, and the tendency toward political despotism.

The 1% and the Refeudalization of the Social Structure

The hypothesis of refeudalization is based on the extreme expansion of social inequality and the associated sustained polarization of the social structure. This can be seen on different spatial scales, especially in the distribution of wealth worldwide. Occupy Wall Street, a movement critical of capitalism, deserves credit for drawing attention to the top 1% of the richest people. The non-governmental organization Oxfam highlighted these global social inequalities in the report "An Economy for the 99%" in January 2017 and brought them into the broader political debate (Oxfam 2017). Since 2015, the richest 1% of the world's population has had more wealth than the entire rest of the world's population. And to translate these bare figures to real flesh-and-blood individuals, it can be said that in 2015 the richest eight men (the gender breakdown is also meaningful)[2] have had as much wealth as 3.6 billion people, half the world's population. Just in the last two decades, the number of billionaires has increased significantly. In 2015, the number of billionaires reached 2473 (Wealth-X 2016, 2). Thereby, the average billionaire had a net wealth of 3.1 billion U.S. dollars in 2014 (Wealth-X 2016, 16). Due to the historical structures and hierarchies within the capitalist world system hyper-wealth is concentrated in economically powerful countries. 62,9% of the billionaire moneyed aristocracy come from only four countries, namely the United States, Japan, Germany, and the rising hegemonic power China (Capgemini 2021, 9).

However, the emergence of hyper-wealth is a worldwide phenomenon that is by no means limited to the capitalist centers or the geographic North—comprises North America and Western Europe. In the geographic South, the number of billionaires has increased rapidly as well. In recent decades, this has been particularly true in Central and South America, and the Caribbean. According to Wealth-X, Latin America saw the world's largest growth rate in billionaires in 2014.

Furthermore, hyper-wealth is even more pronounced in Latin America than in the rest of the world. Latin American billionaires have above-average wealth compared with their counterparts in other regions of the world. At $6.2 billion, Mexico has the world's highest average wealth for billionaires, but this is mainly due to the hyper-wealth of Carlos Slim. In second place among the countries with the world's richest billionaires is Brazil, with an average fortune of $5.2 billion—despite the dramatic loss of Eike Batista's fortune (Wealth-X 2013). The German–Brazilian billionaire, who was still considered the 7th richest man in the world at

The Refeudalization of Society 133

the end of the 2000s with an estimated 35 billion U.S. dollars, had lost 99% of his fortune due to a fall in share prices between 2012 and 2013 and now has to make ends meet with 200 million U.S. dollars (Vasella and Beutelsbacher 2013).

According to recent research by Oxfam, the social divide is intensifying during the COVID-19 pandemic. Between March and June 2020, the wealth of the Latin American moneyed aristocracy increased by 18%, and eight new individuals joined the illustrious circle of billionaires (Oxfam 2020). On the other hand, it seems that the very COVID-19 pandemic that hit Latin America hard also had an impact on HNWIs in 2020 and 2021. Thus, their number has decreased in Latin America by 4% (Capgemini 2021, 8), being the only region in the world in which a decrease was noticeable. However, this decrease is mainly due to the multiple crises and the decline of Brazil.

Worldwide, the trend toward refeudalization has been significantly intensified by the Corona pandemic and the resulting economic crisis. At the top of the social pyramid, there was a 6.3% increase in the number of super-rich people in the pandemic year 2020 alone, and this group also increased its wealth by 7.6% compared with the previous year. On the lower side of the pyramid, there is a marked increase in poverty. It is precisely the informal sector, in which the lower classes earn their living that has been massively affected by the pandemic. At the same time, lower middle class sectors have been relegated to the lower class and are affected by new poverty.

Although the billionaires' rankings give clear figures, which calculate assets down to the penny, one must be warned against the deceptive exactness of these figures, comparison tables and pie charts. The figures are based only on estimates of assets, which have their own inaccuracies (see also Piketty 2014, 544–561). In the field of wealth research, there are significant problems with measurement and data. This is especially true for Latin America and the Caribbean. Beyond the data cited in billionaire statistics, there is little robust evidence of the asset composition of the top 10%. Although there is certainly a tendency among the super-rich to ostentatiously display their wealth, the exact amount of assets often remains hidden by the use of tax oases, obscure financial transactions, and secret business shares.

The most important share of billionaires' wealth consists of their holdings in private companies and conglomerates. Beyond the economic value of income, considerable influence is exerted through these companies on the political field, above all through lobbying, sponsorship, and direct influence. An important part of this wealth is the so-called liquid assets, which the rich can access on an ad hoc basis. Wealth-X (2016, 16) estimates that this share was around 20% of total wealth in 2015, equivalent to an average of $600 million. This "petty cash" of a single cosmocrat is thus larger than the gross domestic product of Dominica,

134 *The Refeudalization of Society*

a Caribbean island nation with 72,500 inhabitants. Note that 5% of the total assets are attributable to real estate and luxury goods. Wealth-X sums up, "The typical billionaire owns four properties worth an average of US$23.5 million" (2014, 17). Luxury goods and, especially, real estate are considered safe investments, particularly in times of economic crisis. On the other hand, they are also used by billionaires themselves to indulge in a luxurious lifestyle. This also applies to prestigious collections of luxury goods, such as vintage cars, sports cars, yachts, private jets, works of art, or jewels.

Beyond the reports in the tabloids about the world of the "rich and beautiful," there are hardly any studies on the lifestyles and world views of the top 1%–10%. Yet a sociological analysis of this social group, not limited only to socio-structural classifications and statistical surveys, is highly necessary. An exception is the study by Hans-Jürgen Krysmanski, who points out that the moneyed aristocracy is not an isolated, self-sufficient group, but dependent on a complex network of other types of labor. Accordingly, Krysmanski proposed the image of a "concentric castle"—a metaphor with not entirely unintentional feudal connotations (2015, 37), according to which the actual moneyed elite is surrounded by corporate and financial elites—especially top-level executives—who are further supported and secured by political elites and administrative experts, as well as think tanks and opinion makers. In a similar recourse to feudal semantics, the Swiss sociologist and former UN Special Rapporteur on the Right to Food, Jean Ziegler, describes the group of top-level executives as new global princes supported by vassals who work for them. This model is conducive to understanding the different functions of the various factions within the top 10%. However, the possibilities of social ascent and descent, the identity-formation processes and normative ideas, as well as the everyday lifestyles of these groups are still largely unexplored in sociological theory.

Complementary to these sociological questions is the historical question of accumulation and concentration of wealth and the associated processes of group formation. The metaphors of aristocracy and refeudalization suggest that the concentration of wealth has always existed and, in this sense, does not represent a new phenomenon. This is not to be denied. Just a glance at the aristocratic palaces of the seats of the viceroyalties in Latin America or the palaces of the millionaires of the U.S. Gilded Age makes the argument plausible. But it must be countered with sober statistical figures that the concentration of wealth has increased rapidly after the crisis of Fordism and the collapse of the Soviet Union and with the worldwide rise of neoliberalism. With respect to the United States, the economist Thomas Piketty has shown that over the last 30 years, the income of the bottom 50% has not increased, while the income of the 1% of top earners has grown 300-fold (2014). A similar pattern can be observed in Latin America. In the region of the world

The Refeudalization of Society   135

where the social gap is the widest, the wealth of multimillionaires has increased by 21% per year in the last five years alone, a figure six times higher than the growth in the gross domestic product in the region.

In addition to this immense accumulation of wealth in the top 1%, another expression of the extremely unequal distribution of income and wealth has been the historic crisis of the middle class. Piketty argues that the true social innovation of the post-World War II welfare state, Fordist economy was the establishment of a middle class. This segment of a class comprised about 40% of the population in Western welfare states. But with the neoliberal shock therapies of the 1980s, whose political implementation is associated with the names of Ronald Reagan, Margaret Thatcher, and Augusto Pinochet, as well as international institutions such as the International Monetary Fund and the World Bank, the middle classes have vanished in many places. Above all, the lower middle-class segment, consisting of industrial workers in formal employment, has been massively confronted with social decline as a result of adjustment programs and relocations owed to the global capitalist logic of exploitation.

Thus, the morphology of the social structure in many countries is again approaching the historical period of the *Ancien Régime* in Western Europe in terms of social inequality. On the eve of the French Revolution, France's estate society consisted of 1%–2% nobility, 1% clergy, and about 97% of the so-called third estate. This very top 1% of the *Ancien Régime* pooled 50%–60% of the income for themselves (Piketty 2014, 313, 330). This social structure strikingly resembles the figures of today's unequal distribution in global society. With regard to this extremely polarized form of social structure alone in which the democratic and bourgeois promise of equality was abandoned, one can speak of a striking trend toward refeudalization.

Refeudalization of the Social Structure in Latin America

In Latin America, this striking trend toward the refeudalization of the social structure is deeply rooted in the colonial constitution of society and has been intensified by various historical conjunctures—such as the Second Conquest between the 1860s and the 1920s as well as the recent neoliberal turn of the 1980s and 1990s. In the 1990s, the Gini coefficient[3] of income distribution in Latin America was 0.522, while it was 0.342 in Western Europe and 0.412 in Asia. This shows that the inequality of income distribution in Latin America has been the highest, compared to other world regions. The richest tenth of households earned 48% of total income, while the lowest tenth earned just 1.6% (de Ferranti et al. 2004). Although social inequality is a constant across countries in Latin America, regional differences can be observed. At the same time that in the 1990s countries such as Brazil, Chile, and Colombia were characterized

136   *The Refeudalization of Society*

by the greatest social inequality, Uruguay, Costa Rica, and Venezuela were among the more balanced Latin American countries for household income distribution. The social scientists Alejandro Portes and Kelly Hoffman have made one of the few attempts to analyze the composition of class in selected Latin American societies in more detail. For them, the ruling class is segmented into capitalists, managers, and executives. In 2000, they conclude that the ruling class accounts for 5.2% (in Brazil) and 13.9% (in Venezuela) of the total population. The top segment of the ruling class, the capitalists, consists of 0.85% (in Panama) to 2.2% (in Colombia) of the total population. This top segment of Latin America's ruling class thus corresponds to the group that we have called the 1%, in reference to the worldwide debate on social inequality. On the other hand, the second segment, when added to the above-mentioned 1%, coincides with the top 10%. The middle class is relatively thin so Portes and Hoffman argue: "These figures imply that subordinate classes, roughly defined, make up about 80 percent of the Latin American population" (2003, 51).

The following section will provide an overview of how this trend toward refeudalization has consolidated in Latin America in the past few years. To start, a brief overview of recent economic history and the development of social inequality will be given (cf. Boris et al. 2008; Kaltmeier 2013; Thorp 1998). First, the region was shaped by the global boom of Fordist regulations in the 1940s. In Latin America, import substitution, industrialization policies, and the expansion of state bureaucracies contributed to the growth of the middle class, which included civil servants, the self-employed, and formal workers. In response to the crisis of the agro-export model in the wake of the Great Depression of 1929, national development models were implemented throughout Latin America to initiate import-substitution industrialization. These include the projects of Juan Domingo Perón in Argentina, Víctor Raúl Haya de la Torre in Peru, Getúlio Vargas in Brazil, and Lázaro Cárdenas in Mexico. This social development model lasted throughout Latin America until the 1970s, with regional variations.

Within this politics of industrialization, the growth of an urban working class can be observed. By the 1960s, a majority of the economically active population in Latin America was no longer working in agriculture. Instead, in the period between 1960 and 1980, the industrial proletariat was demographically and politically at its zenith. In politics, this was expressed in an increasing degree of organization, especially in trade unions. Nevertheless, it should be noted that the industrial proletariat remained relatively small, especially in comparison to the process of industrial development in the United States. Instead, the composition of the working class has historically been characterized by a high proportion of informal urban proletariat, living with predominantly informal labor relations (Portes 1985). In rural regions, the relations of

The Refeudalization of Society 137

quasi-feudal dependency that were determined by the *hacienda* and other forms of large-scale landownership dissolved in the course of the agrarian reforms of the 1960s and 1970s. However, these agrarian reforms had only a very limited impact on the more equal distribution of land. They led in most cases instead to the modernization of the structures of property and exploitation in the countryside, an increasing semiproletarization of peasants, and new dynamics of rural-urban migration. And for this reason, Latin America is still—since as early as the 1960s—considered the region with the greatest social inequality in the world (Deininger and Squire 1996, table 5).

These initial attempts to form a middle class were nullified by the neoliberal structural adjustments of the 1980s, thus one can speak of a true pulverization of the middle and working class (Boris et al. 2008). According to the International Labor Organization (ILO), by the end of the 1990s, half of the economically active population in Latin America was already working in the informal sector. This was due to neoliberal policies of privatization and the promotion of micro-enterprises. Social scientists Alejandro Portes and Kelly Hoffman (2003) sum it up:

> The rise of the informal proletariat is taking place in almost all countries of the region and can be interpreted as a popular counterpart to the 'forced entrepreneurship' imposed on former employees by the new economic policies. A considerable proportion of the informal working class consists of own account workers—vendors and other low-qualified workers who are forced to survive through the least remunerative forms of enterprises
>
> (50).

Mirroring the growth of the informal proletariat, the share of state-employed workers declined in the 1990s, as did the share of formally employed workers. By the end of the 1990s, the social structure had polarized to such an extent that it resembled the two-tier society of the colonial era.

A particularly striking example of the rapid social decline of the middle class is the change in the social structure of Argentina as a consequence of the 2001 crisis. The end of the convertibility of the dollar and the peso led to galloping inflation and the devaluation of savings and, roughly, a 20% decline in economic power. Small- and medium-sized enterprises fell into a profound crisis, forcing many of them to close (Svampa 2008, 53). At this moment, large parts of the middle class plunged socioeconomically into the precariat, even though they still had a high level of cultural capital. This descent of the middle class into the lower class has been described in the social science literature as "new poverty" (del Cueto and Luzzi 2010, 36). But there were not only victims in the crisis. Indeed, the oligopolies in the service and financial sectors were able to

138　*The Refeudalization of Society*

profit. While the share of traditional stores dropped from 57% to 17% in the period from 1984 to 2001, supermarkets increased their share from 27% to 53% (Svampa 2008, 55).

Significant changes in the social structure occurred around the turn of the millennium. At the beginning of the 21st century, there was an astonishing new historical conjuncture of left-leaning governments in almost all of Latin America and the Caribbean that proclaimed a departure from neoliberal economic policies. This development reached its peak in the mid-2000s with the governments of Hugo Chávez in Venezuela, Ignacio "Lula" da Silva in Brazil, Rafael Correa in Ecuador, Néstor Kirchner and Cristina Fernández de Kirchner in Argentina, Tabaré Vázquez and José "Pepe" Mujica in Uruguay, and Evo Morales in Bolivia. These governments brought about more active social policies, which were particularly successful in combating poverty. In the context of a favorable economic boom with high economic growth rates, the left-wing governments were able to increase social spending and enforce higher minimum wages. This led to enormous upward mobility into the middle class, while the poorer segments of the population benefited from special support measures. Even in Chile, which—due to the continuity of neoliberal economic policies—was considered more of a moderate representative of the so-called "pink-tide," various social programs took effect under Michelle Bachelet's government. Although social inequality continued to increase in the 1990s and poverty became entrenched among around 20% of the population, the Chilean state succeeded in significantly reducing the poverty rate in the 2000s. From 2003 to 2006, the poverty rate reduced by 5%, from 18.7% to 13.7%. By 2013, the poverty rate was only at 7.8%. (Larrañaga and Rodríguez 2015, 17), attributable to increasingly active social policies focused on redistribution.

In a study on the impact of the heterodox economic policies of leftist governments, social scientists Francesco Bogliacino and Daniel Rojas (2017) conclude the following:

> As far as causal hypotheses are concerned, the data seem to support the idea that the New Left had an indirect impact on the region as a whole, as it promoted more redistributive policies. This suggests that the *Chavez effect,* to offer a possible label, extended beyond the political orientation of the government in charge
>
> (31).

And political scientist Hans-Jürgen Burchardt (2016) sums up:

> While the global financial crisis shook the established industrial nations, Latin America experienced an economic miracle. Quite a few scholars and international organizations, who for decades had predicted the failure of commodity-led development under the

The Refeudalization of Society   139

heading of 'resource curse,' now highlighted the potentials of this democratic neo-extractivism

(7).

Despite all the successes, the sustainability of the leftist governments' social policy support programs is still under the scrutiny of history. It is clear that the reduction of social inequality is based on the reduction of poverty figures. The leftist governments were only able to achieve this because of government support programs, the financing for which was based on a favorable economic climate. However, there were hardly any significant measures to redistribute wealth in society. The state financed these programs in the framework of neo-extractivism through revenues generated from the increased export of raw materials—from oil and natural gas to copper and lithium to soy and palm oil.

In the wake of the drop in commodity prices that began in the 2010s and the accompanying economic crisis, entire social segments that had risen in recent decades seemed to fall back into the lower class.

Conversely, the top 10% were hardly affected by this social decline. Even the period of left-wing governments, which led the conservative press to paint a terrifying picture of egalitarian communism that was often used during the Cold War, did not pose a threat to the moneyed aristocracy. Paradoxically, according to a survey by the financial services company Capgemini, certainly not to be suspected of leftist bias, the number of billionaires rose sharply during the terms of the left-wing governments. From 2008 to 2016, for example, there was an increase in the number of the super-rich (or, in technocratic terms, high-net-worth individuals, HNWI) in Latin America from just under 420 to almost 560 (Capgemini 2017).

Wealth-X explains this increase in the number of billionaires in the region through demographic upheavals, i.e., by inheritance. Latin America is the region where billionaires have the highest average age, therefore wealth transfers to the next generation have already taken place in recent years. In this way, the number of billionaires has increased, but without an increase in total wealth (2014, 8–9). This transfer of wealth to the following generation points to a basic problem of many Latin American societies, which has not been effectively addressed, even during the phase of leftist governments: insufficient or even completely missing inheritance tax. Burchardt pinpoints the failures of leftist governments during the economic boom phase:

> Even during the boom-phase, no far-reaching redistributive measures were implemented. The tax system was hardly touched. The regional taxation rate is only half as high as in Europe, and most taxes are highly cyclical or even regressive, like sales tax, meaning that they are a particular burden on the low-income population.

140   *The Refeudalization of Society*

For the business elite, on the other hand, Latin America remains a tax haven: property taxation has continued to decline and contributed just 3.5 percent to total tax revenues in 2013. Overall, the tax-induced redistribution effects are less than ten percent regionally (Germany: around 40 percent). Individual tax reforms, such as those in Argentina or Ecuador, have failed

(2016, 7).

However, the explanatory model of an increase in the number of billionaires through inheritance is not sufficient to explain the contemporary developments in this segment of society. For the period from 2000 to 2008, for example, it can be seen in Latin America that not only the number of billionaires increased—which supports the inheritance-sharing thesis—but also disposable wealth. While HNWIs in Latin America still had private assets of $3.2 trillion in 2000, this figure had already risen to $5.8 trillion by 2008. Globally, Latin America, at 81%, had by far the highest rate of growth in billionaire wealth during this period (followed by the Middle East with 40%) (Beaverstock 2012, 382).

However, there are significant differences in the national distribution of billionaires in Latin America, see Table 2.1. Let's take 2014 as a reference: Brazil is the country with the most billionaires with 61, followed by Mexico with 27 and Chile with 21. However, demographics also matter when measuring the impact of the moneyed aristocracy. In 2020, Brazil had 212 million inhabitants, Colombia 49 million, and Mexico 129 million, while Chile had only 18 million inhabitants, making it the country in the Americas—if we neglect the Bermudas and the Virgin Islands because of their special situation—with the highest per capita rate of billionaires and a high degree of social inequality.

While the formation of a moneyed aristocracy in these countries is deeply rooted in history, other countries of the region were also subject to rapid historical developments. In Bermuda, for example, the number of billionaires increased from 4 to 7 from 2013 to 2014, making this island—after Liechtenstein—the second-highest spatial concentration of billionaires. However, none of these billionaires were born in Bermuda. Here, the extreme concentration of wealth is not based on endogenous dynamics, but on immigration.

Of course, the concentration of wealth is not limited to billionaires alone. More than 500,000 millionaires live in the seven countries that top one ranking of Latin American countries with the most millionaires in 2014 (Gamboa and Dextre 2016, 19).

By far the most millionaires in Latin America are to be found in Brazil, with almost 200,000 millionaires, and Mexico, followed by Chile, Colombia, Argentina, Peru, and Paraguay. Fewer millionaires live in the central Andean countries, such as Ecuador and Bolivia, the Guianas, or Uruguay, known for its exemplary social system.

Table 2.1 Number of Billionaires in Latin America and the Caribbean, 2013 and 2014

Rank	Number of Billionaires, 2014	Total Wealth US$ Billions, 2014	Number of Billionaires, 2013	Total Wealth US$ Billions, 2013	Population Change (%)	Wealth Change (%)
World	2,325	7,291	2,170	6,516	7.1	11.9
Latin America	153	511	111	496	37.8	3.0
1 Brazil	64	182	50	259	22.0	−29.7
2 Mexico	27	169	22	137	22.7	23.4
3 Chile	21	49	17	40	23.5	22.5
4 Peru	9	15	3	5	200.0	200.0
5 Bermuda	7	24	4	13	75.0	84.6
6 Argentina	7	13	7	15	0.0	−13.3
7 Venezuela	6	10	2	5	200.0	100.0
8 Colombia	5	28	2	16	150.0	75.0
9 British Virgin Islands	2	3	1	1	100.0	200.0
10 Guatemala	2	3	–	–	–	–
11 El Salvador	2	2	–	–	–	–
Other	4	10	3	5	33.3	160.0

Source: Own processing according to Wealth-X (2014, 82)

142 *The Refeudalization of Society*

At this point, it is not possible to present a sufficiently precise picture of the regional distribution of millionaires within nation-states. However, with reference to the socio-structural data of individual municipalities, a high socio-spatial polarization in metropoles, such as São Paulo, Mexico City, Rio de Janeiro, and Santiago de Chile, can be observed. On a smaller scale, it can also be argued that the super-rich is concentrated in the posh neighborhoods of Latin American metropoles, with socio-spatial polarization increasingly turning into self-segregation, not unlike the fortified castles of the European feudal regimes.

The Moneyed Aristocracy in Latin America

Many social science studies on social polarization are limited to the evaluation of statistical data on income and wealth. But here we want to give the bare figures a human face. Whereas the presentation of the personal preferences of the "rich and beautiful" ought to be reserved for the gossip press, the aim is to trace the historical dynamics of the emergence of the moneyed aristocracy in Latin America. The patterns and formations of social inequality in Latin America have deep historical roots. They can be traced back to the colonial period in which an ethnically divided society emerged as a result of the Spanish conquest in the last third of the 16th century. A "república de españoles" and a "república de indios" represented two different systems of governance in the Spanish colonial period. Racism and the exploitation of indigenous and black labor by a small white-creole elite went hand in hand (Sokoloff and Engerman 2000, 217–232).

Even after the independence of Latin American countries in the 1820s, this unequal social structure remained unchanged. Peruvian social scientist Aníbal Quijano (2008) coined the term *coloniality* for this *longue durée* phenomenon. In the colonial context, a bifurcated social structure emerges, relying on the social division of labor through racism. Stable structural elements emerged that continue to this day, while also being subject to a permanent process of change through historical conjunctures of colonization and decolonization (Kaltmeier 2016).

This paradox of "continuity in change" (Frank 1969) also applies to the formation of elites. The ruling class in Latin America is largely derived from the creole elites, except perhaps for the government of the indigenous president Evo Morales in Bolivia (Espinoza 2013). Although they broke away from the Spanish crown, these power elites were unable to overcome the colonial divisions in society. In social science theories on elites, it is made clear that, despite all continuity, they are subject to change, which can also lead to their partial replacement (Rovira Kaltwasser 2009). According to Paul Pierson (2004), however, this change is a "long-term process" that is closely linked to political and, above all, economic crises. In this respect, a historical genealogy of the top 10% is important,

The Refeudalization of Society 143

especially with regard to Latin America. Along these lines, the historical continuities from which elites derive or the crises they helped them to rise can clarify investigation. This kind of comparative work has yet to be done for all of Latin America. For this reason, I will limit myself at this point to a descriptive sketch of a historical genealogy of billionaires in Latin America.

In the spirit of the continuity of colonial elements proclaimed by the coloniality thesis, a part of today's billionaires can be traced back to the neo-feudal creole elites of the 19th century. However, there are also regional differences—due to different historical dynamics. While Mexico and Argentina were already prone to crises in the 19th century, as well as to *caudillos* and political-spatial fragmentation, Chile and Brazil have shown a high degree of stability and horizontal integration among elites (Rovira Kaltwasser 2009). Nevertheless, this elite is also subject to historical change. Thus, at the beginning of the 19th century, the old colonial dynasties intermingled with newcomers from France, England, and Spain (Fischer 2011). The bourgeois newcomers were quickly integrated into Chile, and, as Alberto Edwards (1928) writes in his classic study, a "mixed aristocracy" emerged, characterized by capitalist economic aspirations and aristocratic demarcation from the lower classes.

In the mid-19th century, Chile established a world market-oriented export model that concentrated great wealth in the hands of a small elite with access to agricultural products, saltpeter, and copper, but which became increasingly dependent on foreign intermediaries. At the same time, hardly any concessions were made by the elite to the popular masses, a reason for the perpetuation of the bifurcation of the social structure and the ensuring of the elite's close cohesion. A relatively closed marriage market reinforced the reproduction of the elite (Vicuña 2001). Fischer sums up the continuity within the Chilean economic elite as follows: "An examination of the relationships of ownership and control of Chile's 42 leading industrial enterprises shows that they were run by the same individuals, families, or groups from the entrepreneurial oligarchy between the late 19th century and the 1930s" (2011, 51).

This continuity of elites is exemplified by the family history of Sebastián Piñera, a billionaire and ex-president of Chile (2010–2014, 2018–2022). The Piñera family has a large number of influential entrepreneurs and politicians in its ranks and close ties to other neo-feudal families, such as the Chadwicks, Viera-Gallos, and Aninats. The progenitor of the family, José de Piñera y Lombera, was born in Lima, the capital of the Viceroyalty of Peru. His mother, a descendant of the Inca ruler Huayna Capac, grew up in the Lima aristocracy. In 1827, shortly after Chilean independence, he came to Chile, where he married into the local political elite. His wife Magdalena Echenique Rozas is a direct descendant of the independence hero and also related to Chilean presidents Francisco Antonio Pinto, Aníbal Pinto, and Manuel Bulnes.

144　*The Refeudalization of Society*

Another major billionaire family in Chile is the Matte family. The siblings Eliodora, Bernardo, and Patricio have more than $10 billion at their disposal, mainly through their interests in the paper and timber industries. The family's wealth has its origin in the business activities of Domingo Matte Mesías (1812–1893), a friend of President Manuel Montt, politician and founder of Banco Matte y Cía. The family fortune expanded considerably under Arturo Matte Larraín, who profited from the privatizations under the Pinochet dictatorship and the subsequent formation of oligopolies, especially in the forestry sector.

As already indicated by the Matte family, today's billionaires accumulated a large part of their wealth in the 20th century. Until the world economic crisis of 1929, the export economy ran at high speed with high profits for the elites involved. In Mexico, the revolution of 1910 and the subsequent Cristero civil war marked a striking change in the ruling elites (Smith 1979). In Argentina, on the other hand, there was little change in the elites after the Great Depression until Juan Domingo Perón readjusted the relationship between the elite and popular masses (Murmis and Portantiero 2004).

The Hochschild family is a paradigmatic example of this faction of the moneyed aristocracy that rose in the early 20th century. Moritz Hochschild, born in Germany in 1881, migrated to Bolivia and became one of the three "tin barons," note the feudal connotation, together with Simón Iturri Patiño and Carlos Victor Aramayo. These tin barons had taken over the mining sector after the silver mines were exhausted and formed an oligopoly, the so-called "rosca minera-feudal." Until the Bolivian Revolution of 1952, they determined the economic and political fate of the country. After the nationalization of the mines, Hochschild went to Peru with a significant sum in his pocket, where he continued to devote himself to the mining sector. Today, his son Eduardo Hochschild, head of the gold and silver mining group Hochschild Mining, is considered the richest person in Peru.

The Grupo Breca consortium, under the control of the Brescia-Cafferata family, rose to prominence in Peru as early as the end of the 19th century. The conglomerate is now headed by the third generation of the Brescia-Cafferata family, considered one of the richest families in Peru.

As another example of the accumulation of wealth in the agro-export sector, we can cite the Noboa family in Ecuador. Luis Adolfo Noboa Naranjo built up a banana empire in Ecuador from the 1940s onward, which he left to his wife after his death. Following a long legal dispute, his son Alvaro Noboa took over the conglomerate, now consisting of over 100 companies, including in the sectors of banking and media. In 1998, 2002, and 2006, Noboa stood as a candidate in the presidential elections and lost in the runoffs in each case.

Further segments of the ruling class were able to build large conglomerates in the 1940s. One example is Grupo Votorantim in Brazil,

The Refeudalization of Society 145

a conglomerate founded by the Portuguese migrant Antônio Pereira Inácio in 1912. Today, it has expanded its lines of business and diversified through investment funds and biotechnology, among others. Grupo Votorantim is currently controlled by Pereira's grandson, Antônio Ermírio de Moraes. Likewise, João Moreira Salles established Casa Bancária Moreira Salles in 1933, which expanded rapidly and today—still under family control—is known as Unibanco (União de Bancos Brasileiros), one of the largest banks in Brazil.

An area of the economy that expanded massively in the 20th century is that of mass media from which numerous entrepreneurs rose to the top 1% of their countries. The 20th century can be considered the century of emerging mass media. Accordingly, several of today's billionaires established the foundations of their financial rise in this sector. A striking case is Roberto Marinho who took over the Brazilian daily newspaper *O Globo* from his father in the early 1930s and expanded it into a gigantic media group. The group was able to build up a near monopoly in the media sector in Brazil, especially under the military dictatorship of the 1960s,

Another industry to which many millionaires in Latin America owe their ascent is mass consumption, which finds its expression in supermarket chains and other sales systems of consumer goods. In the 1960s, Cuban-Venezuelan entrepreneur Diego Cisneros was able to expand the conglomerate *Organización Cisneros* by investing in the TV sector in Venezuela and the United States. He started out as a small entrepreneur but was able to expand his wealth primarily through a distribution license from the U.S. Pepsi Group. Similar license agreements were also the basis for extreme wealth in other Latin American countries. In Chile, the German-born billionaire entrepreneur Horst Paulmann built his wealth on building a Latin American-wide supermarket chain with stores in Chile, Argentina, Colombia, Peru, and Brazil. Under the neoliberal turn of the 1980s and 1990s particularly, the super-rich were able to expand their corporate power on the basis of privatization and de-regulation policies. On the other hand, currently, it is above all the extractivist export sectors of agro-industry and mining, which have boomed at the turn of the millennium, producing a new rise in extreme wealth.

The question of the extent to which Latin American elites exhibit a high degree of cross-generational continuity is complex. On the one hand, a clear continuity in the reproduction of moneyed aristocracy can be identified. Over several decades, the same dynasties have shaped the economic fortunes of various Latin American countries. Only profound revolutionary upheavals, such as the Cuban Revolution of 1959, the Mexican Revolution of 1910, or the Bolivian Revolution of 1952, as well as the recent political-cultural renewal in Bolivia since 2007, seem to cause real changes in the composition of the economic elites. Economic crises and fundamental transformations of economic models also cause ruptures in the elites, non-reformable sectors are left in a state of decline,

146   *The Refeudalization of Society*

signifying the potential rise of new segments to emerge into the economic elite. In this context, changes in the world market are particularly relevant. Examples include the boom of new agricultural export products, such as bananas in the 1930s, petroleum in the 1970s, and biofuels since the 2000s. Changes in economic programs are also highly relevant. During post-World War-II industrialization efforts, which led to an economic boom in Latin America, elites built up businesses and were at that time able to massively increase their wealth, especially in the phase of neoliberal structural adjustment programs starting in the mid-1970s. For example, the Mexican billionaire Carlos Slim profited from the privatization of telecommunications in Mexico and turned the telecommunication company Telmex into a quasi-monopoly-supplier. In Chile, the Angelini Group—like the aforementioned Matte Group—expanded its conglomerate thanks to the neoliberal shock therapy of the Pinochet dictatorship. In the course of waves of neoliberal privatization, an enormous transfer of collective wealth to private individuals took place. Many of these transactions, such as the sale of the Mexican telecommunications company Telmex to the current multi-billionaire Carlos Slim, were done far below market value.

What is remarkable is the often rapid incorporation of migrants into the moneyed aristocracy. Even the colonial foundation of the moneyed aristocracy was based on the immigration of partly impoverished, lower aristocratic families from Castile, Navarre, and the Basque country. In the late colonial period, a targeted marriage policy in order to obtain titles of nobility emerged in many regions of Latin America (Büschges 1996). Also in the 19th century, the integration of foreign, economically successful migrants into the "national" elite took place largely without problems. In Chile, the French-, English-, and Spanish-born families Edwards, Cousiño, Subercaseaux, Ossa, and Urmenta were considered an integral part of the national economic elite (Fischer 2011, 34–35).

This trend of integrating migrants into the economic elite continued in the 20th century. Even today, it is first-generation migrants, i.e., former social outsiders, who have become billionaires in Latin America. The causes of migration are often causally linked to the upheavals in Europe and the Middle East. Some of the migrants fled to Latin America "in the wake of the catastrophe" of World War I (Rinke 2015). This is true, for example, of the father of Mexican multi-billionaire Carlos Slim, who fled to Mexico at the age of 14 to escape military service in the Ottoman Empire. His father built a small business in Mexico, successfully participated in land speculation, and married into a family of wealthy Lebanese immigrants, thus laying the foundations for the dramatic rise of his son. According to the Forbes list, Carlos Slim was considered the richest man in the world in 2007, 2010, and 2011. Likewise, the grandfather of Chilean billionaire Iris Fontbona, who controls the influential Luksic Group, fled from Croatia to Chile before World War I.

A similarly important period for the current composition of the top 1% of the Latin American moneyed aristocracy has been World War II, especially the immediate postwar period following the military defeat of Nazi Germany. As a result of the upheavals in Europe caused by the Shoah, the Jewish family of the Brazilian billionaire Joseph Safra moved to Brazil in 1952, where Safra later followed in the footsteps of his father and built up a banking empire.

After the collapse of fascism, people who had collaborated or done successful business with the fascist Axis powers also emigrated to Latin America where they achieved rapid socio-economic advancement. For example, the father of Chilean billionaire Anacleto Angelini emigrated as a businessman with his three sons from Italy to Ethiopia, which had been colonized by fascist Italy as early as 1936. After World War II when Ethiopia was decolonized with British support and Haile Selassie came to power, Anacleto Angelini was interned for a short period of time and then the family returned to Italy. However, Anacleto Angelini did not stay long in Italy and migrated to Chile in 1948.

Furthermore, the German-Chilean billionaire Horst Paulmann, who recently had the tallest building in Latin America—the Gran Torre Santiago in the Costanera Center—erected in the center of Santiago de Chile without a valid building permit, is worth mentioning here once again. His father was a member of the NSDAP at an early age and rose to the rank of Lieutenant Colonel of the SS. In Kassel, he was the chief judge and head of the central office of the courts of the SS and police. In 1946, like many Nazis, he migrated to Argentina, where his wife and seven sons followed him. From there, part of the family, including Horst Paulmann, moved on to Chile.

As these examples show, a migrant background does not mean that there was no capital. On the contrary, some of the migrants who placed themselves or their descendants in the top 10% relied on a remarkable stock of it. This does not only involve economic capital, but also cultural and symbolic capital in the Bourdieuian sense. It is remarkable that some of today's millionaires can readily point to careers in the finance and trade sector in their region of origin. The Brazilian billionaire Joseph Safra, considered one of the richest private bankers in the world, grew up in Syria as the youngest of nine children in a family of Oriental Jews who had been involved in trade, banking, and finance since the 19th century.

The Chilean poster-billionaire Anacleto Angelini also used the capital he had accumulated in Europe to found a paint factory together with other immigrants the same year he arrived in Chile and later proceeded to launch a construction company. Angelini then profited from the privatization wave under the Pinochet dictatorship and became one of the richest people in the country with his conglomerate (El Mercurio, 2007).

Generally speaking, however, the composition of the moneyed aristocracy in the various regions of Latin America has remained highly

148   *The Refeudalization of Society*

constant across generations. At the same time, however, there have always been spiraling processes of integration of new groups into the moneyed aristocracy. This integration is based on extreme wealth, making it that the new arrivals are particularly visible among the top 1% of billionaires.

This cursory compilation of billionaire profiles alone makes clear that the accumulation of extreme wealth in Latin America stands out from global—and especially United States—trends. Globally, entrepreneurs from the IT sector are at the top of the billionaire rankings. Bill Gates (Microsoft), Mark Zuckerberg (Facebook), Travis Kalanick (Uber), and Brian Chesky (Airbnb) are worth mentioning. In parallel, financial speculation promoted extreme wealth as well.

In Latin America, by contrast, the largest share of billionaires made their extreme wealth through industrial and trading conglomerates (Wealth-X 2013, 26). In this context, control over natural resources— agro-exports and mining—is also highly relevant. Historically, this aspect is certainly based on colonial land grabbing and the establishment of extractivist models. In this respect, an "aristocratization of the bourgeoisie" (Wallerstein 1988) can be observed. Economically, this is based on the increasing importance of feudal rentier activities, while capitalist entrepreneurship loses importance. Politically and culturally, this finds expression in aristocratic lifestyles and consumerism. Both dimensions of refeudalization will be elaborated in separate chapters in this book. At first, however, it will be important to take a conceptual look at the refeudalization of the social structure.

From Class to Estate

The change in the social structure associated with social polarization, which resembles the feudal estates-society in its quantitative and, to some extent, qualitative form, also poses new challenges for the formation of sociological concepts. The trend toward refeudalization certainly finds its most explicit expression with the formation of a moneyed aristocracy at the top of the social pyramid. As argued earlier, there has already been a rise of non-aristocratic groups into the top 10% during the late colonial period and bourgeois groups from the 19th century on in Latin America. In part, one can then speak of an "aristocratization of the bourgeoisie" in terms of the formation of lifestyles and economic forms. This tendency is also expressed in the concept of moneyed aristocracy, which refers to the rise of the *nouveau riche* industrialists in the higher nobility during the 19th century.

The cultural-identitarian aspects of the refeudalization of society will be dealt with in a separate chapter. At this point, a more in-depth look at the social processes of feudal solidification will be taken. At the center of the discussion on the persistence of the moneyed aristocracy is the question of inheritance of wealth. In the last three decades, there has been a

The Refeudalization of Society   149

worldwide accumulation of wealth in the hands of the few, unprecedented in speed and scope. As a result, a generational shift is on the horizon in the next few years, accompanied by an immense transfer of wealth. For example, UBS writes: "We estimate that fewer than 500 people will pass USD 2.1 billion to their heirs over the next 20 years. This is equivalent to India's GDP" (UBS 2016, 7).

While global wealth research tends to focus on the recent accumulation of wealth, we are largely dealing with wealth that has already been inherited over generations in Latin America. This dynastic accumulation of wealth can be traced back in part to the process of colonial land grabbing and especially to subsequent booms of colonization. This historical continuity of the moneyed aristocracy is also expressed in the genealogy of the current billionaires. In 2014, 20% of billionaires inherited their wealth, whereas 32% partially inherited their wealth. Thus, more than half of the world's billionaires have acquired their wealth due to the accumulation of previous generations. In Latin America, however, this figure is at 72%, exactly 20% higher than the global average.[4] A special feature of Latin American billionaires is the high importance of inherited wealth and the resulting continuity of aristocratic dynasties. Correspondingly, entrepreneurial investments are less pronounced in Latin America than in other regions of the world, while instead signs of estate-like solidification of social classes through inheritance are more pronounced. As early as 2013, Wealth-X pointed out: "Of all world regions, Latin America has the lowest percentage of self-made billionaires" (65). This is a clear indication that proves right Wallerstein's thesis of the aristocratization of the bourgeoisie.

Social science studies in selected Latin American countries in the 2000s have accordingly pointed to high intergenerational persistence in the top quintiles of wealth. In Brazil, 43% of the rich remain rich, in Chile 47%, and in Mexico 58% (Torche 2014). In the United States and Central European countries, these figures range from 30% to 36%. These findings have recently been approved by several quantitative analysis of the relationship between intergenerational upward mobility and inequality (Sacri et al. 2022; Song 2022). These studies utilize the Great Gatsby Curve, which depicts the positive empirical relationship between cross-sectional income inequality and persistence of income across generations. What is striking here is the extreme degree of social inequality in Latin America and, although with variations nationally, a low degree of social mobility (see Figure 2.1). Recent studies have confirmed Miles Corak's classical findings from 2012.

The dynamics described here refer to a historical process of status consolidation that has come to a head in the most recent phase of capitalist globalization. While Max Weber defined social class positions by the fact that a change of class position in the succession of generations is easily possible and even "typical" (2006, 300), this is hardly the case anymore

150 *The Refeudalization of Society*

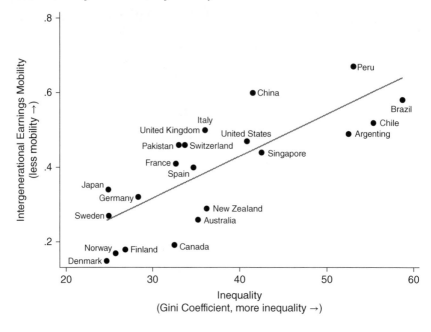

Figure 2.1 Great Gatsby Curve, Corak (2012)

with regard to the global moneyed aristocracy or its Latin American faction. The promise of modernization theory that everyone can achieve social advancement on the grounds of a market-oriented economy has not been fulfilled. Instead, contrary to the fundamentalist market ideology represented by neoliberals throughout Latin America, a market-oriented open society did not emerge, but a refeudalized society with monopolistic appropriations that strengthened the moneyed aristocracy. Wallerstein's neo-Marxist approach emphasized the aristocratization of the bourgeoisie, transforming them from capitalist to rentier. For Weber, this criterion of refeudalization would still be compatible with a society organized in social classes as the moneyed aristocracy could therefore be understood as a privileged property class (2006, 301). Central for Weber, however, is the aspect of intergenerational consolidation and the formation of distinctive lifestyles. For the status of the moneyed aristocracy, "qualification by birth" through a hereditary appropriation of privileges is particularly relevant (Weber 2019, 388). These inherited privileges go beyond the mere inheritance of wealth and economic monopoly structures. This also concerns privileges in the political field—to be elaborated on later—as well as the formation of specific neo-feudal lifestyles, especially noticeable when looking at habits of consumption and the practices of appropriating space.

The Refeudalization of Society 151

After this look at the segmentation of status in the top 10% of Latin American societies, the analysis will now focus on the lower segments of the social structure. Analogous to the metaphor of the moneyed aristocracy, which encompasses the top 1%–10%, the question arises whether one can speak of a new "third estate." The pulverization of the middle class and the formally employed working class by the 1990s was already mentioned in descriptions of the development of socio-structural dynamics in Latin America. With the privatization of state-owned enterprises, economic deregulation, de-industrialization processes, and new management and operational models (such as outsourcing), formal employment relationships in the field of industrial work came to an end, as did the related union organization processes. As a result, the specific milieus that enabled class consciousness to emerge from everyday experience also disappeared. In addition, military dictatorships and authoritarian regimes often violently dismantled labor organizations and unions. The collapse of the Soviet Union contributed further to the emergence of an ideological vacuum.

With the new precarious employment relations of neoliberalism, the boundaries between the formal and informal sectors became blurred. These processes included the increase in forms of home-based work, the practice of outsourcing, and the establishment of "one-man companies," multiple occupations, and lowered real wages. Regarding the relationship between class and gender, a feminization of labor can be observed. Especially in the formal proletariat (industrial workers) and petty bourgeoisie, the share of female employment increased, while the share of men in the informal sector increased. In this sense, the importance of women's work in the *maquila* (simple assembly companies) should be noted, as well as its importance in the agricultural export economy (cut flowers, vegetables, fruit). Accordingly, this convergence between men and women was not caused by an improvement in the position of women, but rather by men falling down the "class ladder" (Kaltmeier 2013). One of the biggest social structural changes of neoliberal reforms until the late 1990s was the widening of the social gap and the associated crisis of the middle classes, which manifested itself in tendencies of impoverishment and a "new poverty." Structurally, this polarization of the social structure is linked to the debt crisis of the 1980s, the subsequent structural adjustment programs, the reduction of the public sector, and the labor market reforms of the 1990s. The factions of the middle class associated with the export-import model, the financial services and insurance sector, and the real estate sector were mostly able to rise, while the bulk of former state employees, small and medium-sized enterprises suffered a loss of status or were relegated to the lower class (Portes and Hoffman 2003). The "new poor" therefore represents a "hybrid class" that is culturally and socially close to the middle and upper classes but approaching the "structurally poor" in terms of income, employment conditions, and social security.

152   *The Refeudalization of Society*

These processes probably expressed themselves most paradigmatically in the social crash of the middle classes in the Argentinean crisis between 1998 and 2002 (Svampa 2008). It was not until the "pink tide" of the mid-2000s that these groups were again pushed into the lower middle class due to the good economic situation and the social programs introduced by the left-wing governments.

If a look is taken at the polarization of the social structure, one can speak about the obvious tendencies of refeudalization. There are clear trends toward a consolidation of the refeudal estates, not only in regard to the 1% but also in the lower segments of the social pyramid. Poverty is inherited. And in terms of the intersectional multiplication of inequality of opportunity, the risk of poverty is particularly high for members of indigenous peoples and afrodescendant communities. At the turn of the millennium, about two-thirds of the indigenous population of Latin America was considered poor (Kaltmeier 2009). Paradoxically, even during the boom of recognizing indigenous rights from the mid-1990s onward, there was no significant reduction in poverty. In Ecuador, a pioneer state in the introduction of indigenous rights, the general poverty rate fell from 44.6% to 38.2% between 1998 and 2006. However, during the same period, relative poverty among indigenous peoples increased dramatically from 45.8% to 69.5%, while the rate of absolute poverty among the indigenous population even skyrocketed from 17.6% to 43.1% (Jijón 2013, 55). However, there have also been successes in the course of a more proactive fight against poverty by left-wing governments. In Chile, for example, the risk of poverty is higher for indigenous Chileans than for non-indigenous Chileans, but poverty rates for indigenous Chileans fell by 10% from 2009 to 2013 (UNDP 2016, 25–32).

When individuals from the lower segments of society rise socially due to proactive policies or favorable economic cycles, for example, they are nevertheless highly vulnerable to social decline. In this respect, during the phase in which left-wing governments in Latin America were economically booming, an "elevator effect" could be observed. All social segments have risen equally, without any significant redistribution between the segments. Poverty has decreased, and the moneyed aristocracy has been able to increase its wealth. In the context of lower profit margins on the world market due to the drop in commodity prices, the upward "elevator effect" is not being followed by a downward "elevator effect." Rather, a bungee effect can be observed: The moneyed aristocracy remains at the top without significant losses, while middle and lower middle class segments are crashing again socio-economically. This is expressed in a polarized social structure in which 1%–10% are at the top of a pyramid whose base is formed by the remaining 90%–99% of the population.

Here, the question of the "third estate" arises again. However, at this point, sociological caution is also required. The lower classes do not form

The Refeudalization of Society 153

their own estate in the Weberian sense, since they are hardly active as an association. Rather, the large segments of the population that are neither part of the moneyed aristocracy nor of the shrinking middle class resemble in their socially amorphous form of the Western European "Third Estate" on the eve of the French Revolution. Nevertheless, it is possible to identify tendencies of refeudalization in this social segment. It seems that the control and exploitation of simple, unskilled labor are of secondary importance in the current, post-industrial phase of capitalism. In the Industrial Revolution and the subsequent Industrial Age, there was a high demand for labor. Even the labor force that was not directly involved remained as an "industrial reserve army" within the horizon of the production process of the formal economy. This is no longer the case. Instead, entire segments of the population are completely excluded from the formal and the economically relevant informal economic cycles. In this context, sociologist Zygmunt Bauman speaks—without any euphemisms—of the social production of "wasted lives" or "people made superfluous" (2005). People who were made superfluous in the course of social modernization already existed in the industrialization processes of the 19th century. But back then there were still free "dumping grounds for the human waste of modernization" (Bauman 2005, 13). Colonization had the effect of an outflow valve, which was particularly evident in the example of Australia, a former British penal colony. But Latin America also became a preferred dumping ground for the segments of the population that had been made redundant in Western Europe. Between 1850 and 1950 alone, some 11 million Europeans migrated to Latin America, mainly to southern Brazil, northern Argentina, and southern Chile. But at the end of the 19th century, this process of colonization came to an end. Today, there is no new socially recognized place for the superfluous.

One of the most powerful battle cries of the bourgeois revolutions was that of the equality of all people. This idea finds its most striking expression in the United Nations Universal Declaration of Human Rights of 1948, the first paragraph of which states: "All human beings are born free and equal in dignity and rights. They are endowed with reason and conscience and should act towards one another in a spirit of brotherhood." This bourgeois understanding of equality of rights and dignity is being massively undermined in the current processes of refeudalization. Instead of fundamental equality, a hierarchy of individuals is increasingly produced. In this sense, philosopher Judith Butler observes that "certain lives will be highly protected, and the abrogation of their claims to sanctity will be sufficient to mobilize the forces of war. And other lives will not find such fast and furious support and will not even qualify as 'grievable'." (Butler 2003, 6).

This social production of life not worthy of mourning can be seen in many places in the Americas. During the 2016 election campaign, Donald Trump had already referred to Mexican immigrants as "rapists" and

154   *The Refeudalization of Society*

"criminals," while in 2018, he had called poorer countries in Africa and those in the Americas from which migrants come to the United States, such as Haiti, "shithole countries." But the hierarchization of societies and people does not remain merely rhetorical. The murder of migrants— and especially migrant women (keyword: *feminicidio*)—in the U.S.-Mexican borderlands, hardly prosecuted under criminal law, should be mentioned. The increasing number of murders related to drug trafficking in Mexico and Colombia, and the displacement and mistreatment of smallholder farmers and indigenous peoples in Brazil, Peru, Colombia, and Mexico are also representative of this development.

The central concept guiding this book is that of refeudalization. The anti-evolutionary aspect of a return to past historical elements was a deliberate choice. However, the prefix "re-" indicates that this return takes place in a different historical and social circumstance. In this context and in terms of social structure, the historical presence of the middle-class bourgeoisie, a social group based on class positions that did not exist in the historical period of European feudalism, should be highlighted. In the course of the industrial and bourgeois revolutions during the "Age of Revolution," the status-based criteria of honor, ethics, self-definition, and self-distinction of the aristocracy lost importance and gave way to bourgeois principles of liberty, equality, and fraternity. The twin brother of this civil *citoyen*, however, was the capitalist and benefit-oriented bourgeois, who operated on a meritocratic basis. Thus, when it came to the analytical penetration of the socio-structural dynamics of capitalist societies, class models, Marxist and non-Marxist, prevailed. As the French economist Thomas Piketty points out, the formation of a middle class as a social buffer for the stability of social formations beyond the class struggle between the bourgeoisie and the proletariat was of the greatest importance. This amorphous "intermediate class" embodied the aspiration and meritocratic promise of social advancement like no other social class. During the heyday of Fordism, sociologist Helmut Schelsky even diagnosed a "levelling middle class society" during the "economic miracle" in post-war Germany. This orientation toward the middle class allowed—at least ideologically—a permeability of class boundaries. This ideology of permeability finds perhaps its most famous expression in the U.S. dictum of "rag to riches."

The extreme polarization of the social structure mentioned at the beginning empirically refutes the approaches to the expansion of the middle class proclaimed in the mid-20th century. Instead, the social structure of contemporary societies, oriented toward the distribution of social wealth, resembles that of the feudal societies of Europe. While at the level of social consciousness, there is still emotional anchoring connected to the middle class, the extreme concentration of wealth in the top 10% has made the concept of the middle class almost absurd.

In a global comparison, a middle-class household's total income is between $6,000 and $30,000 per year. It should be noted that this does not refer to a single person, but to a household consisting of an average of at least four persons. The World Bank defines the middle class in Latin America in a similar way in their Policy Research Working Paper, "The Long-Awaited Rise of the Middle Class in Latin America is Finally Happening." Here, a daily income of 10–50 dollars, i.e., between 3,650 and 18,250 U.S. dollars annually, is sufficient to be a member of the middle class (Bussolo, Maliszewska, and Murard 2014). Based on such a minimal definition of the middle class, which in Western Europe would partly be below subsistence level, it is hardly surprising to state that "The Long-Awaited Rise of the Middle Class in Latin America is Finally Happening." But in view of the global trends of inequality in the distribution of wealth, this World Bank policy paper can be understood primarily as an ideological construct.

Here is a simple, polemical calculation. In 2015, the average gross domestic product per capita for all countries in the world was 15,800 U.S. dollars. If we relate this average annual income (which includes the income of billionaires) to the average wealth of billionaires, we can see how long it takes the average global earner to become the average billionaire. The average billionaire has a wealth of $3.1 billion. To reach this wealth, the average member of the middle class would have to save their family income for 200,000 years. Of course, all while not consuming a single cent of it.

Beyond these social quantifications, the question of group identity is key, meaning the question of whether a class in itself, i.e., the class on paper, can also form a class for itself, a social actor. With regard to the social structure, the notion of a third estate that comprises the vast majority of society may be accurate. Especially since a clearly recognizable upper segment of the moneyed aristocracy has separated itself. But, as in European feudal society, the 99% are made up of highly diverse groups, socially and culturally, so that a politically impactful union appears difficult to imagine at present. With the concept of multitude, Antonio Negri and Michael Hardt have proposed how a network for collective action could emerge from multiple singularities (2000, 123). However, before discussing the political dimension of refeudalization in more detail, the economic foundations of the current trend toward refeudalization should first be examined.

The Refeudalization of the Economy

The current debate on refeudalization focuses primarily on the "turbo-capitalism" of financial markets at the turn of the millennium. Since the 1990s, increasing value for shareholders has become the guiding principle of corporate offices, leading to the breakup and reorganization of companies, new consolidation processes, mass layoffs, and cuts in social partnership networks. Deregulation and tax cuts for companies

156   *The Refeudalization of Society*

carried out over the course of neoliberal adjustments and shock programs grew corporate profits and the wealth of investors as has hardly ever seen before in the history of global capitalism. The information technology sector boomed particularly well, with many IT entrepreneurs from Silicon Valley making it onto the Forbes list of billionaires. Equally relevant to the refeudalization thesis is a cosmocratic group that is closely tied to capitalism driven by the financial markets. Neckel argues that a new service class has emerged here, consisting of well-paid fund managers, investment bankers, brokers, and analysts who speculate with other people's property on the international financial markets for rent-seeking. With this emphasis on rents, financial market capitalism resembles—according to Neckel—the feudal economic formation of the pre-revolutionary 18th century: "For just as the landowner's rent is based on the appropriated part of the rural net product, without the need of any effort of their own, today's financialization of capitalism realizes capital accumulation without investment and guarantees returns on property titles without any entrepreneurial risk. In this, the 'proprietors without risk' resemble much more feudal landlords than bourgeois entrepreneurs" (Neckel 2013a, 51).

Despite the global dynamics of the post-Fordist financial market-driven regime, regional differences can be observed. While in the United States and Canada, over 70% of social wealth is based on monetary assets and 30% on non-financial assets, this ratio is reversed in Latin America where it sits at 28.7%–71.3% (Credit Suisse Research Institute 2016, 146). After India, Latin America is the region where non-financial assets—including land and real estate in particular—account for the highest share of the total wealth of private individuals. While in the United States one can speak of a refeudalization based on financial transactions (especially speculation), Latin America is characterized more by property. In this sense, the refeudalization of social relations in Latin America takes a different form than in Western Europe and the United States. This corresponds to the trend of an "aristocratization of the bourgeoisie" that Immanuel Wallerstein (1988) already identified in Western Europe from the 16th to the 18th century. Wallerstein argues that as economic success increases, the bourgeois seeks to hedge against market risks and falling profit rates. Tying up capital in land presents itself as a capital-securing alternative. In this process, however, a transformation from profit to rent can be observed. The capitalist becomes an aristocrat.

Landlordism and Extractivism

Colloquially, money in Latin America is often named with metaphors from the semantic field of natural resources. Probably due to the wealth of silver in the colonial era, *plata* (silver) is one of the most common expressions throughout Latin America, but also other raw

The Refeudalization of Society 157

materials—especially export products—such as *lana* (wool) in Mexico and Panama, *mango* in Argentina, *papa* (potato) in Nicaragua and El Salvador, or *cañas* (sugar cane) in Cuba are often used to denote money. This gives an indication of a particular tendency in Latin America due to its peripheral position in the world system: the importance of natural resources and land ownership. In general, it can be argued that there is a feudal-colonial continuity in Latin America that, with the exception of Cuba, was not touched by the agrarian reforms of the 1960s and 1970s. According to 2017 data from the Food and Agriculture Organization of the United Nations (FAO), the region has the most unequal land distribution in the world: The Gini coefficient—which measures inequality—for land distribution across the region is 0.79, compared to 0.57 in Europe, 0.56 in Africa, and 0.55 in Asia. In South America, i.e., Latin America minus Central America and the Caribbean, inequality is even far higher than the already high regional average with a Gini coefficient of 0.85. Correspondingly, the coefficient for Central America is still high at 0.75, slightly below the Latin American average. A recently published OXFAM report shows that 1% of production units in Latin America account for more than half of the agricultural land (FAO 2017).

This immense concentration of land suitable for agriculture is a particular facet of refeudalization in Latin America. Although the concentration of land due to coloniality and its constant renewal during different cycles of colonization is certainly historically conditioned, clear trends of land grabbing and the further concentration of land in recent years especially could be identified. This tendency to control land clearly corresponds to the basic features of the feudal mode of production, materially based on the exploitation of natural resources and, above all, agribusiness. Although the agricultural sector in Latin America has only a share of slightly more than 5% of the gross national product, this sector should not be underestimated.

Agriculture is by no means to be understood as a traditional sector that is not subject to any changes. Rather, one can observe an astonishing development in its productive forces. In his historical materialism, permeated by a philosophy of progress, Marx still assumed that the productive forces of mercantilism and the beginning industrial revolution would break the narrow chains of the feudal mode of production. Now, however, an immense development of productive forces can be seen in the agricultural sector. While the so-called "Green Revolution" in the 1970s was based solely on the development of agrochemicals and improved seeds, it is now linked to the biotechnological revolution. First and foremost, it is the widespread use of genetically modified seeds that are adapted to the certain packages of agrochemicals.[5] Thus, extractivist activities, such as mining and (export) agriculture, which are oriented toward the metropolises of the world market, continue to be core elements of the economy in Latin America. This represents a manifestation of the renewal of the

158   *The Refeudalization of Society*

colonial character of the economic structure in the region from which even the left-wing governments of the 2000s have not been spared.

In the Latin America of the 2000s, it was so tempting to follow the development path of extractivism that left-wing governments were also inclined to the simple exploitation of natural resources without industrial refinement. In recent years, environmental movements and postcolonial intellectuals have increasingly criticized the economic policies of leftist governments, primarily characterized by neo-extractivism. Eduardo Gudynas explains this critique as follows:

> This new extractivism feeds a hardly diversified framework, and as a provider of primary materials, it is very dependent on international involvement. If indeed the state plays a more active role, and gives extractivism a greater legitimacy because it redistributes some of the surplus to the population, it still repeats the negative environmental and social impacts of the old extractivism
>
> (2010, 1).

The main idea of neo-extractivism was that progressive governments continued to pursue the extractivist development path and even expanded it in a favorable global economic boom. The innovation was that the generated extra income was not privatized but used to finance social programs. Instead of an individual appropriation of capital, a state policy of redistribution took place, which could be even more effective if the state itself exercised control over natural resources or took back control through nationalization. Thus, neo-extractivism refers to a particular historical constellation of global demand for resources and progressive governments with active social policies financed through the direct or indirect revenues from extractivist economic activities. However, the concept has lost its edge with its spread through NGOs and advocacy organizations. Some use it synonymously with the centuries-old extractivism, without addressing the changed conjunctures compared to the colonial extractivism of the Spanish Crown. Recent academic discussion has also seen a softening of the concept of neo-extractivism originally related to progressive governments. For example, Ulrich Brand writes: "While the centuries-old development model in Latin America is referred to as 'extractivism,' the phase from 2000/2003 onward is considered 'neo-extractivism'- regardless of whether referring to left-wing, center-left, or conservative-neoliberal governments" (2016, 21). This approach is problematic in that conceptual elements of the original context—left-wing governments in Latin America—are carried along without corresponding to the new subject matter—the conservative governments under Temer and later Bolsonaro, Macri, or Piñera.

A major aspect that is problematic in this regard is the question of social redistribution. Under the new conservative governments, social

The Refeudalization of Society 159

redistribution—in the form of social programs, affirmative action, etc.,—is being cut back again. With that, the central element of Gudynas' definition of neo-extractivism is not applicable. Hand in hand with this shift, there has also been a general reduction of the influence of the state in the economic and sociopolitical field under conservative governments. None of the conservative, neoliberal governments are striving for a stronger role for the state; rather, private entrepreneurs are emboldened—especially those in the top 10%. However, these aspects can quickly fall under the radar if neo-extractivism is understood as a model, which above all includes the state structure. An extractivist "national competition state" that promotes agro-industry and private capital accumulation is a different social model than an extractivist redistributive state.

Moreover, the broader definition of neo-extractivism runs the risk of setting false historical anchors. Neo-extractivism refers to the historical context of Latin American leftist governments from 2000 onward, as has already been argued. For the narrow definition, this makes perfect sense. For more extensive activities of extractivism in Latin America, however, the neoliberal economic policies from the mid-1970s onward should be mentioned in addition to the leftist governments. Especially in the context of the neoliberal shock therapies, a selective integration into the world market based on the exploitation of natural resources has taken place in the sense of the neoclassical model of comparative cost advantages. At the same time, support programs based on catch-up industrialization have been scaled down.

This is illustrated by neoliberal shock therapy in Chile under the Pinochet dictatorship from the mid-1970s. Here, extensive de-industrialization took place and the economy was expanded in accordance with the classical economic doctrines of comparative cost advantages and selective world market integration in the extractivist sectors of forestry, fruit farming, and fishery. Similar structural adjustments were observed in other countries of the region, especially under the direction of the World Bank and the IMF. In all of the countries affected, the top 10% of the social pyramid was strengthened, as seen in the chapter on the refeudalization of the social structure.

In this respect, it seems sensible to actually use the concept of neo-extractivism only for progressive governments in Latin America and even limited to where there is a manifestation of social redistribution based on gains made through extractivism. Among so-called progressive governments, there are significant differences. While in some areas neo-extractivist funding for social programs is being implemented, in other regions massive processes of refeudalization particularly benefit the top 10%. The latter is certainly true for the rise of soy barons in Brazil and Argentina. However, the degree of neo-extractivist redistribution also varies. Under the Bachelet government in Chile, there were certainly successes in the fight against poverty and a stop to the further polarization

160   *The Refeudalization of Society*

of the social structure, although this was not sufficient to reverse the extreme polarization of the neoliberal shock therapy. In Ecuador, it was primarily the middle class that benefited, while in Bolivia profound redistributive programs fundamentally changed the social structure. In most cases, however, the leftist governments were unable to restructure the economy, which was based on simple resource exploitation. Doubly, the ecological consequences of the model of natural resource exploitation remained unresolved. Paradoxically, in some regions, the leftist governments even contributed to the refeudalization of society by strengthening the extractivist elites in their countries. This paradox has already been noted with regard to the increase in billionaires in the region and is also evident in the concentration of land ownership.

It has been pointed out several times that neo-extractivism peaked during a specific economic boom characterized by a high demand for resources and, from the late 2000s, by a crisis in the financial markets. In this sense, the crisis of the global financial market in 2007 and 2008 accelerated land grabbing and the concentration of land ownership extremely, as a new market for land was formed in which financial actors also invested speculatively. Mexican economist Polette Rivero Villaverde (2017) summarizes,

> Large capital funds of banks like Goldmann Sachs, powerful individuals like George Soros, former public officials, foundations like that of Harvard University, pension funds of employees from countries like the U.S. and Canada, found in the purchase of land a refuge from falling interest rates and from the fall of their profit margins caused by the crisis, which, in turn, generated high profits from speculative transactions, given the high prices of food, oil and strategic minerals.

Especially in Brazil, Argentina, and Paraguay, an immensely expanding agroindustry is displacing smallholders with huge soybean plantations. In Colombia and Honduras, the expansion of *palma africana* plantations, which are grown for oil production, has led to violent displacement and even killings. According to data collected by the non-governmental organization Global Witness in collaboration with the British daily newspaper The Guardian, in 2016 alone, approximately 200 activists advocating for land and environmental rights were murdered in Latin America, Asia, and Africa. The high number of victims specifically in Latin America stands out negatively. Just in Colombia, 49 activists have been murdered, in Brazil, 37. It is particularly noteworthy that indigenous activists are among the most frequent victims of these crimes (The Guardian 2017).

In addition, the high number of internally displaced persons due to land grabbing and other forms of violence should be mentioned. According to

The Refeudalization of Society   161

the United Nations, as of March 2018, Colombia has the highest number of internally displaced persons in the world at 7.6 million, ahead of Syria, a country at war, with 6.6 million internally displaced persons there (UNHCR 2018).

This process of expropriation of land formerly belonging to small farmers, indigenous peoples, and afrodescendant communities by agroindustrial entrepreneurs is one of the most visible and violent expressions of refeudalization in Latin America. The non-governmental organization Grain has listed farmland acquisitions by foreign investors for the period 2006–2015 worldwide, sorted by the countries concerned (Grain 2016). Rivero Villaverde (2017) has aggregated these data and shows that 3,927,450 hectares were bought by foreign investors in 59 transactions for Latin America. Brazil leads the list with 2,727,502 million hectares, followed by Argentina (513,116), Paraguay (208,549), Columbia (154,660), Uruguay (144,178), Peru (80,149), Venezuela (60,000), Bolivia (57,845), Jamaica (30,000), and Belize with 1,600 hectares. Buyers come from the United States, China, Singapore, Japan, South Korea, Saudi Arabia, India, Denmark, Luxembourg, the Netherlands, France, Germany, UK, Canada, Italy, Portugal, and other countries. But Latin America's moneyed aristocracy, especially from Brazil and Argentina, is also involved in buying up smallholder farmland.

One example is the Brazilian soy baron Blairo Maggi, who took over the Andre Maggi Group from his father and is considered the world's largest private soy producer. As in the case of feudalism, there is a dense entanglement of economic and political power. In 2002, Blairo Maggi was elected governor of the state of Mato Grosso, considered the core area for soy production. Three years later, he was awarded the Golden Chainsaw Award by the environmental organization Greenpeace for the most severe destruction of virgin forest in Brazil because of his deforestation of natural reserves in order to build soy plantations. The "award" was justified as follows: "After only two years in the governor's office, he has made Mato Grosso the leader in virgin forest destruction. 48 percent of clearcutting in the entire Amazon rainforest happens in his state" (Greenpeace 2005). Surprised by the delivery of the prize in a school auditorium, Maggi refused to accept it and instead fled, clandestinely, through the back exit. Under the conservative Temer government, Maggi was Minister of Agriculture from 2016 to the end of 2018.

Beyond its immediate economic exploitability, land is a very popular storage for capital among the rich. Economist David Harvey has conceptualized spatial elements, like agricultural land, in their function as a temporal *spatial fix* of capital (2001). Capital becomes temporally and spatially fixed by being invested in land. Under these circumstances, capital not only serves as a factor of production but can also be liquefied again—if necessary—for subsequent generations. Therefore, the high concentration of land is an essential factor for the reproduction of the

162 *The Refeudalization of Society*

elite and the progressive polarization of the social structure in Latin America.

So far, the question of refeudalization has mainly been discussed in political-economic terms. But an astonishing trend toward refeudalization can also be detected with regard to society's relations to nature and especially socioeconomic metabolism, concerning the energetic foundation of economic production. Industrial capitalism was energetically founded on the fossil revolution since the 18th century. In order to satisfy the increased energy input of industrial production, fossil fuels such as hard coal (since the 18th century), oil (since the beginning of the 20th century), and natural gas (since the second half of the 20th century) became indispensable (Altvater and Mahnkopf 1996, 510–518). Today, these limited fossil fuels are exhausted or can only be extracted with considerable effort—as in the case of fracking or offshore drilling. It is indisputable that the fossil age of industrial capitalism has been coming to an end since the end of the 20th century. The technocratic hopes for a post-fossil nuclear age, however, have been dashed after the catastrophes of Chernobyl, Harrisburg, and most recently Fukushima.

In view of the looming energy crisis, it is remarkable that we are currently witnessing a recourse to the energy sources of the age of European feudalism. Ultimately, the energy supply of feudalism was based on solar input, the power of photosynthesis, and the production of energetic organic substance. Wood, in particular, has been the most important energy source of feudalism, also as a derivative in the form of charcoal. Today, there is an astonishing return to biotic energies, finding their strongest expression perhaps in the varieties of biofuels. These are based on the oils of soy, *palma africana*, corn, coconut, and other oilseeds. Renewable fuels are not only used as biofuels for transportation, but also as pellets of grain as well as wood and coconut that are suitable for heating. The replacement of fossil fuels with renewable energy crops is one of the driving forces behind the land grabbing described above.

For the classical (neo-)Marxist discussion of feudalism and capitalism in Latin America, the question of capital accumulation is one of the most central aspects. However, much of the historical materialist debate on feudalism in Europe and Latin America has been limited primarily to the aspect of labor exploitation. As stated earlier, the issue of accumulation through the appropriation of surplus value created by labor is a core aspect of the socio-historical debate on feudalism. In contrast to the historical social formation of feudalism, the worker—formerly the vassal—is no longer linked to the "fief." Instead, land concentration and the fragmentation of mini-fundia through real estate division lead to the impoverishment of the peasant masses. In many areas of Latin America in this context, there is even talk of a process of "de-peasantization."

However, the exploitation of labor is not the only way of capital accumulation. Rosa Luxemburg particularly pointed out the importance

The Refeudalization of Society   163

of robbery and expropriation in the process of capitalist accumulation (Luxemburg 1923). This seems to me to be an essential aspect for understanding the current process of refeudalization. In this respect, the commodification of large areas of land—be it the remaining virgin forests, national parks, indigenous reserves, or areas for small-scale subsistence farming—can be understood as continued original accumulation. Currently, however, the specific expressions of accumulation through expropriation go far beyond the classical so-called original accumulation through the appropriation of land (e.g., land grabbing) (Zeller 2004, 11–15).

The first thing to mention at this point is the expansion of capitalist property and production relations. Of particular relevance is the privatization of common goods. Especially within the neoliberal turn in Latin America from the mid-1970s to the early 2000s and accompanying the structural adjustment measures, an enormous transfer of common goods to the private sector took place. Many branches of the economy have been privatized—especially in the energy and resource sectors. Likewise, extensive privatization and capitalization of the social security and education systems have been carried out. With the private-funded pension system, for example, a section of social security formerly based on solidarity and a pay-as-you-go system has been opened up to the process of capitalist exploitation. The example of the Chilean AFP, the private pension system, which is now unable to pay the intended pensions due to shrunken profits on the financial markets, reveals the social explosiveness of this situation. In 2016, there were massive protests demanding an end to this capital-funded system run by private investment funds.

Another field is the expansion of property rights allocated to goods that were previously considered common or public goods. This includes the patenting of specific animal species or plant varieties and their genetic material. In Latin America in particular, biopiracy is a such major problem that a police unit has been especially established to patrol the Brazilian Amazon region. Ecuador has also recently had several laws regulating "bioprospecting" (Heeren 2016). Appropriation through patenting in the interest of transnational corporations ignores community rights of use as well as the specific knowledge or intellectual property of indigenous peoples. All these forms are—as explained—of imminent importance for the refeudalization of the economic sphere. They are all based on a more or less conscious notion of robbery, understood as an act of expropriation.

The New Robber Barons

Accumulation through robbery is not limited to the processes already mentioned, considered legal within the framework of the capitalist economy. Rather, illegal activities are an integral part of current

164　*The Refeudalization of Society*

refeudalization trends. Take a look at the current lists of the richest people on earth, one can see that criminals stand out. As early as 1987, Forbes included Colombian drug boss Pablo Escobar Gaviria and the Ochoa brothers, Jorge Luis, Fabio, and Juan David—also Colombian— on its first list of the world's billionaires. The following year, Gonzalo Rodriguez Gacha, another person connected to the Medellín cartel, made the Forbes list, as well. The leader of the Mexican Sinaloa cartel, Joaquín Guzmán aka "El Chapo," held a spot on the list of the richest men in the world. In 2019, he was sentenced to life imprisonment in the United States. Forbes estimated his wealth in 2008 as follows: "Thirty-five billion people in the United States use drugs or abuse prescription drugs, spending more than $64 billion annually. The Drug Enforcement Agency and other industry experts believe Guzmán has controlled one-third to one-half of Mexico's drug wholesale market over the past eight years. According to the U.S. government, Mexican and Colombian drug traffickers transferred between $18 and $39 billion in revenues from wholesale deliveries to the United States in 2008 alone. Guzmán and his company probably took 20% of the profit, enough to accumulate $1 billion throughout his career and earn a place on the billionaires' list for the first time" (Bogan 2009).

As early as the mid-1980s, revenues in global drug trafficking had approached that of petroleum, at an estimated 300–500 billion U.S. dollars (Wichmann 1992, 17). Thus, illegal drugs took a leading position in the world economy. The importance of illegal drug trafficking for the capitalist world economy can perhaps be highlighted most forcefully through the example of the global financial crisis of 2007/8. Looking back at the crisis, the director of the United Nations Office on Drugs and Crime, Antonio Maria Costa, speculated that the money originating from the illegal drug trade saved the banking world from collapse, as it represented the only relevant liquid capital at that time. Accordingly, Costa argued that most of the estimated $352 billion from drug money was transferred into the formal economic system:

> In many instances, the money from drugs was the only liquid invest-ment capital. In the second half of 2008, liquidity was the banking system's main problem and hence liquid capital became an impor-tant factor. [...] Inter-bank loans were funded by money that origi-nated from the drugs trade and other illegal activities ... There were signs that some banks were rescued that way
>
> (Rajeev 2009).

This point makes clear that while the drug economy is illegalized— and because illegalization maintains a high-profit margin—it is by no means separate from the cycles of the formal economy. Rather, they are like communicating vessels with pipes between chemical corporations

The Refeudalization of Society 165

involved in production, and the banks, real estate companies, and auction houses, involved in money laundering.

The cartels have increasingly expanded their businesses beyond drug trafficking into other fields such as prostitution and human trafficking as well as the organ trade. Protection racketeering has also been a highly lucrative business. Here, the modern monopoly of the state is being dismantled, as is the human right to inviolability of the person. The simplest form of accumulation is that of robbery and extortion. Like robber barons who resisted urban trade capital and landlord authority, individual armed groups attack residents and migrants. But beyond this banditry, cartels in Mexico and Colombia are already behaving like new feudal lords, demanding tributes from those in the territories they control in exchange for security guarantees. In the suspension of civil-democratic rights, the feudal principle of paying protection money to local rulers introduces itself. In Colombia, in 2009 alone, it was assumed that "vacunas" (vaccinations), as protection payments to the mafia are euphemistically called, paid to various organized crime groups numbered in the amount of 1 billion U.S. dollars (Wallace 2013).

For the journalistic description of the moneyed aristocracy of the criminal underworld, it is common to use terms from the semantic environment of feudalism, such as drug barons or drug lords. In the sociological debate, the "warlord" type has emerged. Especially in the context of the "new wars" (Kaldor), which are no longer intrastate conflicts but those between different actors for the purpose of control over resources. Here, the "warlord" becomes a key figure. Since the late 1990s, the concept has been used, especially in African contexts, to refer to regional actors armed with weapons who spread out in the realm of progressing state collapse (failed states) and exercising territorial control for their own enrichment. Especially after 9/11 and the wars in Afghanistan, media attention turned to the new "archetypes of the warlords" (Schetter 2004). It was not until the 2000s that the rise of militant Islamism, especially in the form of Al Qaeda and the Islamic State, displaced the concept of the warlord. In Latin America, the concept has primarily been used in the context of drug gangs and paramilitary groups, especially in Colombia and Mexico. It is, however, important to note, that warlords do not simply undermine statehood; rather, they colonize state structures while ignoring the rule of law. In African contexts, anthropologist Gero Erdmann (2002) speaks of "neopatrimonial systems of power." In Colombia, this is most evident in the close cooperation between military and paramilitary forces in the 1990s, as well as—to use a Habermasian term—the subsequent colonization of the Colombian state by paramilitaries. The economic side of this refeudalization of violence is expressed in concepts, such as an "economy of violence" (Ruf 2003) and a "market of violence" (Elwert 1999). Development sociologist Georg Elwert argues that the emergence of violent entrepreneurs is shifting the ideal-typical market-based system

166   *The Refeudalization of Society*

to illegalized markets, where a lot of money can be made with little effort with threat of violence. Of particular relevance are the activities already mentioned, such as trafficking of drugs and arms, extractivist activities (precious metals and gems), but also robbery, extortion, piracy, kidnapping, and the collection of protection money and customs duties. These activities usually do not require major investments, as monitoring can be ensured with simple handguns. The proliferation of *maras* in El Salvador, armed youth gangs that emerge as violent entrepreneurs, is an apt example. It becomes clear that the spread of violent neo-feudal entrepreneurs cannot be explained by rational, purpose-driven models alone but also displays an identitarian dimension related to the lack of integration offered by existing nation-states. With the economic and violence-based refeudalization comes an identitary segmentation or even tribalization of society.

Robbery by Omission: From Panama to Paradise

So far, the debate on accumulation by expropriation has focused primarily on predatory activities aimed at incorporating new areas into the capitalist accumulation process. Furthermore, however, theft by omission should also be mentioned. Looking at this phenomenon, we are primarily concerned with avoidance strategies that attempt to overrule the legally and ethically established rules and norms of the social redistribution of wealth. What must be mentioned above all else in this context are the strategies of massive organized criminal tax evasion.

Tax evasion cannot be considered a mere individual misstep. Rather, it is key to recognize that a highly complex organized network of law firms, financial advisors, banks, and offshore tax havens stands behind the tax offenses of the moneyed aristocracy. Since the issue here is tax avoidance, anonymity is of high value in a system whose complexity and scope have not yet been sufficiently explored. An insight that resembles fine drilling into the deep swamp of corruption was recently provided by the Panama and Paradise Papers. Both are based on data leaks that were passed on to critical journalists. Within the framework of the International Consortium of Investigative Journalists (ICIJ), Bastian Obermayer and Frederik Obermaier of *Süddeutsche Zeitung* were leading the investigative work that in 2016 finally resulted in the disclosure of the so-called Panama Papers that drew on data from the Panama-based law firm Mossack Fonseca (SZ 2017). The firm had more than 14,000 clients whom it helped set up 214,488 shell companies in 21 international tax havens. Its business model was based on secrecy and anonymity, and clients were sometimes addressed only by their aliases. The law firm opened shell companies for the clients, some of which operated with specially appointed mock directors who disguised the true owners of the company. Through these shadow men, the true owners were then able to carry out financial transactions and, above all, increase their wealth through speculative financial activities. On February 10, 2017, the heads of the law firm, Ramón Fonseca and Jürgen Mossack, were arrested due to their involvement in the corruption network surrounding the Brazilian construction group Odebrecht.[6] The Panamanian public prosecutor's office has described the law firm as a criminal organization. Only a year later, in November 2017, ICIJ leaked the Paradise Papers that included data dating back to the 1950s. They are based on more than 13 million documents from the law firm Appleby and the trust company Asiaciti Trust (ICIJ 2017).

The exposure of the Panama Papers has caused a worldwide scandal with drastic consequences that are only dealt with in part here. In Iceland, the prime minister, Sigmundur Davíð Gunnlaugsson had to resign over secret investments in offshore tax havens. Gunnlaugsson's government finance minister and interior minister were also involved. Political leaders from across the globe, Russian oligarchs, oil sheikhs, European banks, and international corporations, such as Apple, Nike, and Facebook, were also involved. The investigations targeted offshore tax havens in the Cayman Islands, the Bahamas, and Malta—countries that are considered hubs of financial transactions. The leaked Paradise Papers contain data on more than 120 politicians, including many heads of state and government and even the British Queen Elizabeth II and the U.S. Secretary of Commerce of the Trump administration and multimillionaire, Wilbur Ross.

The entertainment industry has also been heavily involved. Bribe payments for broadcasting rights led the Uruguayan vice president of FIFA, Eugenio Figueredo, to resign and be arrested. The dubious agencies also list many prominent figures as their clients. The Paradise Papers include the Irish lead singer of the band U2, Bono, Madonna, and the Colombian singer Shakira as clients. According to the documents, Argentinean soccer star Lionel Messi founded the shell company Mega Star Enterprises with the support of Mossack-Fonseca. He had already concealed income from his image rights from the Spanish tax authorities between 2007 and 2009 using a complex offshore network. At that time, he was supported by a Uruguayan law firm, which later became active in Panama. He allegedly evaded 4.1 million euros in taxes for which he was sentenced to 21 months in prison in Barcelona in 2016; a sentence he finally did not have to serve (panamapapers.sueddeutsche 2017). Many top politicians are to be found among the names in the Panama Papers. A look at the politicians involved makes it clear that this is not an exclusively Latin American problem—yet it cannot be denied that the phenomenon there is very pronounced. In Panama itself, Ramón Fonseca, co-founder of the law firm Mossack Fonseca, was closely connected to the political class as an advisor to the president and vice chairman of the ruling party Partido Panameñista.

168 *The Refeudalization of Society*

Brazil was particularly affected by the corruption scandal. Here, the investigations into the Panama and Paradise Papers were combined with the corruption cases surrounding the state-owned oil company Petrobras and the construction group Odebrecht. Through "Operation *Lavo Jato*," Brazilian judiciary investigated money laundering, bribery, and tax evasion. Particularly noteworthy is that among the Mossack-Fonseca clients were more than 100 persons who were also investigated during the *Lava Jato* Operation. Significantly, no direct link could be established to the presidents belonging to the Labor Party, Dilma Rousseff and Ignacio Lula da Silva. Instead, many links could be established with Michel Temer's Brazilian Democratic Movement (PMDB) party. Temer had overthrown Rousseff in 2016 in a so-called "cold coup": Paradoxically, corruption allegations had been one of the main justifications previously for overthrowing president Rousseff.

One of the agitators for the coup, Eduardo Cunha, the radical evangelical preacher and president of the Chamber of Deputies of the Brazilian National Congress, has since been removed from office because of his involvement in the crimes disclosed by the Panama Papers. In the Paradise Papers, on the other hand, Blairo Maggi, already mentioned several times in this text, occupies a prominent position. The current Brazilian Minister of Agriculture is involved through his company Amaggi and LD Commodities. Maggi himself, however, states that he has not received any financial benefits from the company. The exact clarification is still pending (ICIJ 2017).

Brazilian Finance Minister Henrique de Campos Meirelles is also involved in obscure financial transactions. He set up the Sabedoria Foundation in Bermuda, which, according to his own information, is for the benefit of the Brazilian health system after his death. Critics and investigators, however, suspect tax evasion and corruption. A similar charity model is being pursued by Colombian President Juan Manuel Santos, who has set up companies, allegedly for promoting educational activities, in Barbados such as the Global Tuition & Education Insurance Corp., a shareholder of Global Education Group Colombia SA (Chavkin and Díaz-Struck 2017).

The ex-president of Costa Rica, José María Figueres Olsen, is active in a different sector. Figueres Olson is the son of three-time president José Figueres Ferrer. While Figueres Ferrer founded the Instituto Costarricense de Electricidad (ICE), his sons José María and Mariano have been operating through an offshore company in the private energy sector since the 1990s, with operations in Chile and Guatemala.

In Argentina, the conservative government led by Mauricio Macri from 2015 to 2019 was also affected by the revelations of the Paradise Papers. Macri's finance minister, Luis Caputo, had concealed at least two offshore investments in his mandatory financial disclosure. The Cayman Islands-based Altob Global Fund and the Miami-based Noctua Partners

The Refeudalization of Society 169

LLC had been "forgotten" by Caputo in his financial disclosures. Caputo is a cousin of Nicolás Caputo, who owns one of the largest construction groups in Argentina, and is considered a good friend of the former Argentinian president.

Secrecy and covering-up of the origin of assets and investments in tax havens and shell companies is not only key for tax evaders. These mechanisms are also highly relevant for money laundering the profits of illegal activities, such as drug trafficking. Mossack-Fonseca had direct links to the Mexican *capo* Rafael Caro Quintero, who in the 1980s set up the now-dismantled Guadalajara cartel. In the wake of the Paradise Papers, the German private bank Berenberg has come under criticism. Among its various clients was Austrian-born Martin Lustgarten, who—according to the U.S. Justice Department—laundered up to $100 million for Mexican and Colombian drug cartels and paramilitary groups.

Through such operations, drug money and income from other criminal activities flow back into the formal economy. The informal criminal economy is linked to the formal economy through a system of communicating vessels. However, the so-called shadow economy has reached such a large scale globally that classical national economics with a focus on the gross domestic product (in which the shadow economy is only indirectly included) has reached its explanatory limits. In order to be able to quantitatively and qualitatively grasp the refeudalization of the economic field through shadow economies, the broad informal economic field together with the "dark economic web" would have to be integrally included in economic indicators.

As already underlined, this also applies to the formal political economy of the cosmocrats. In this context, it would also be important to name the central actors involved in financial transactions. As mentioned earlier, Krysmanski invoked the image of the "concentric castle" to refer to the broad network of supporting institutions aligned to the needs of the global moneyed aristocracy. In that sense, Beaverstock notes, "we have seen a transformation in which the super-rich are being served by banking and financial services. The millionaires, multi-millionaires, and billionaires find themselves classified as an HNW market by a new private asset management industry, reflecting the changing social composition of the super-rich from 'old' to 'new' money" (Beaverstock 2012, 388). Relevant information is provided by think tanks specifically focused on the moneyed aristocracy, such as Merrill Lynch Capgemini. Parts of this documentation on the super-rich are publicly available and form an essential part of the sources used for this work.

While some of these consultant agencies appear with the claim of scientific accuracy, other advisors, such as the law firm Mossack-Fonseca, stand at the interface between formal and shadow economy. There is an astonishing criminal potential among the 1% with the aim of increasing private profit and preventing redistribution. Apart from the main

170 *The Refeudalization of Society*

argument here that accumulation is inextricably linked to robbery, this points to specific cultural attitudes. The consistency with which Thorstein Veblen, a leading expert on the so-called "leisure class," linked the accumulation of private wealth to the basic principle of robbery is remarkable. For Veblen, robbery is one of the preferred mechanisms of the aristocratic "leisure class" to accumulate wealth and ensure a luxurious lifestyle. For him, this is especially true in the rising financial capitalism of the Gilded Age: "The relation of the leisure (i.e., propertied non-industrial) class to the economic process is a pecuniary relation—a relation of acquisition, not of production; of exploitation, not of serviceability" (2007, 108). This observation now leads us to explore the cultural attitudes and the processes of identity formation in the context of the processes of refeudalization.

Consumer Identities: Between Luxury and Debt Bondage

If, as has become clear, the available socio-structural data and analyses of the upper class, especially in Latin America, are already insufficient. This applies all the more in a discussion of the culture or the identity politics of the richest 10%. In sociological theory, one might refer at first to Thorstein Veblen's now classic work on the "leisure class," which he wrote at the turn of the 19th and 20th centuries in view of the "Gilded Age" in the United States. In an unorthodox mixture of social Darwinist, evolutionist, and cultural anthropological approaches, Veblen identifies "invidious comparison" as the driving principle behind social differentiation and distinction. Veblen determines this basic principle in diverse developmental stages of human societies, in different forms of expression in each case. In this context, honor and prestige gained with the defeat of another group through predation (especially the kidnapping of women) is the foundation for the "invidious distinction attaching to wealth" (2007, 23). Robbery in this context also includes non-productive activities such as hunting and war, but also sports. The prestigious practices of appropriation that are predominant then change over time, from simple robbery to the appropriation of labor to money profits through speculation and the dynamics of accumulation through robbery, which were analyzed earlier. Yet the underlying motive of the invidious comparison between individuals persists, it even intensifies with the establishment of private property and the emergence of capitalism.

Even in today's society, the admiration of the heroic act is very present. Regarding the shadow economy, reference can be made to the *narcocorridos*, considerably popular songs in Mexico praising the heroic deeds of the drug barons. The heroic deed has not disappeared from the formal economy either. A look at today's business magazines and blogs makes it clear that this admiration of the heroic economic deed is still highly relevant and that self-made millionaires or successful top managers represent the heroes of our times. Busy start-up entrepreneurs and innovators of the IT sector are not only making millions with a brilliant idea or a merchandisable app but are also stylized by the culture industry as heroes of the 21st century. One may think of the Hollywood production about Facebook founder Mark Zuckerberg. The imagination of the heroic deed or stroke of genius is also reproduced in the countless "Who Wants to Be a Millionaire" shows on television. Here, the permanent invidious comparison takes place out of the TV chairs, combined with the illusion that anyone could make it to becoming a millionaire. This idea also permeates today's everyday culture. The board game developer Brent Beck brought out "Big Deal" in 2014 with the renowned German game distributor Schmidt. The game idea consists of barely disguised robber-capitalist practices paired with an ostentatious display of wealth: "Make a fortune by collecting the most valuable luxury goods and money possible—always in pairs. But why make an effort yourself? Just grab the collections of your fellow players! But watch out—suddenly you yourself may be short of matching cards and the hard-earned fortune is gone sooner than you thought ... If you collect wisely and serve yourself from your fellow players at the right time, you will come closer to your goal of winning the game as a dollar millionaire." And the publisher adds "A fun game in which you should never be too sure of your cause(s)." This idea of the "Big Deal" in the economic field permeates everyday culture and penetrates other social fields. With Donald Trump, the idea of the "Big Deal" and the associated humiliation of competitors has now also been carried into the political field in the United States and elsewhere.

Hinting at the persistence of archaic and patriarchal ideas of the warrior and hunter as markers for masculinity, Veblen elaborated how prestige is first of all acquired through heroic "exploit." In Latin American history, the *conquistador*es, mostly impoverished noblemen (*hidalgos*), could easily be identified as the prototype of the prestigious warrior. Ultimately, the heroic deed is connected to robbery as can be seen in the case of the *Conquista*. Despite all the acclaimed and hoped for the progress of civilization, this circumstance is still highly relevant in the previously elaborated processes of today's accumulation through dispossession. Veblen points at a historical transformation of the invidious comparison: "Gradually, as industrial activity further displaces predatory activity in the community's everyday life and in men's habits of thought, accumulated property more and more replaces trophies of predatory exploit as the conventional exponent of prepotence and success." (2007, 24).

While currently, the heroic deed is above all economically over determined, ostentatious consumption, especially in the luxury segment, is a distinctive feature of the (global) "leisure class." Veblen denies this ruling class any productive abilities; rather, it bases its lifestyle on predatory appropriation and cultivates displaying its idleness. That is, the distinction of this group is based on the demonstrative avoidance of any useful

172 *The Refeudalization of Society*

activity. Similar to the gift-giving feast potlatch of the First Nations of the American Northwest Coast, this ostentatious demonstration of wealth takes on the dynamics of a "race for honor and prestige," driven by "discriminating" or "invidious comparison." One's own honor—expressed in the greatest possible avoidance of productive work—is reflected in the distinction, and even despise, of the common classes. This can be achieved through the display of wealth and the ostentatious waste of time in pursuing non-useful hobbies, buying clothes, and home furnishing. It is not enough anymore to simply be rich, but wealth must be displayed. According to Veblen, there are two possibilities for this social display of wealth in (post-)modern capitalist societies: ostentatiously doing nothing or idleness and demonstrative consumption (93).

Both aspects are closely linked to feudal lifestyles. In the feudal system, the contempt for physical labor goes back, among others, to the ideas of the influential theologian Thomas Aquinas. Aquinas considered physical labor of little value, but intellectual labor as noble. With this division, Aquinas also became an ideologue and apologist for the estate society. Ultimately, each person was given their position in feudal society and through birth their position of labor. Non-work was an expression of a divinely given superiority, which ultimately was intended to be admired. It is only with Protestantism, if we want to follow Max Weber's considerations, that there was a change in the ethical meaning of work. Weber postulated a close connection, an elective relationship, between ascetic Protestantism and capitalist striving for capital accumulation. Put simply, the protestant pursuit of salvation was now secularized. Economic success thus became an indicator of an ethical lifestyle. The key element to achieve this was rational work: "What God demands is not labour in itself, but rational labour in a calling" (Weber 1958, 168–169). In this sense, the successful working entrepreneur in modern capitalism also became an ethical instance with social exemplary character. While the capitalist class was legitimized meritocratically in this way, it was conversely possible to demand diligence and obedience from the workers by justifying this ethically.

Since the 19th century, a meritocratic system based on performance was established in western capitalist societies. Social position was not to be predetermined by status as in estate society but instead depended entirely on the individual performance of each member of society. This is the foundation of the ideology of free entrepreneurship, in line with the motto that performance pays off. Especially in neoliberal writings, the entrepreneurial self was repeatedly placed at the center of governmental programs that were oriented toward the guiding principle of the maximizer of economic benefit, *homo economicus*. This ethical-religious transformation from the class division of labor to the performance-oriented work ethic was hardly expressed in the societal division of labor, as could be observed in the proletarianization processes of the industrial

The Refeudalization of Society 173

revolution in Western Europe, but it remained a basic moral principle of Western capitalist societies until the end of the 20th century.

For the sociologist Sighard Neckel, it is precisely the recent transition from industrial capitalism to financial market-driven capitalism that is the driving force of refeudalization, since it undermines the capitalist entrepreneurial ethic in the sense of Weber's capitalist protestant work ethic. The exorbitant and lightning-fast "deals" of the financial markets in the globalized capitalism of the 21st century have carried the merito-cratic system to absurdity. Profit is now no longer based on diligence, industriousness, or rational planning, but on a gambler's risk-taking nature. Similarly, potential profits became exorbitantly high allowing quantum leaps up the class ladder. Accordingly, billionaire-friendly reports like to refer to the success stories of self-made millionaires. This is hardly referring to the successful entrepreneur, but to the smart specu-lator or the ingenious inventor of the information age.

Beyond these newcomers to the moneyed aristocracy, there are also those millionaires who have not only reproduced but multiplied their wealth over generations. This applies in particular to Latin America as has already been elaborated in the chapter on the refeudalization of the social structure. Here, too, the ascetic protestant spirit of capitalism has evaporated, and we are dealing with a new global moneyed aristocracy instead. Contrary to the purely ostentatious moneyed aristocracy that Thorstein Veblen had been able to identify still in the 19th century, the new global moneyed aristocracy is, on the contrary, also being imbued with capitalist values.

Despite their ostentatious consumption of luxury, the further accu-mulation of capital in the production process continues to be a social imperative: "Despite transfer of wealth, most of today's billionaires have created some or all of their wealth themselves. In other words, entrepre-neurship is still an essential prerequisite for most people to reach billion-aire status" (Wealth-X 2014, 25).

But as already argued in the chapter on the refeudalization of the economy, this accumulation of capital via mostly industrial production is increasingly being replaced by rent-seeking forms of accumulation:

> In the past year, the number of billionaires with partially inherited wealth has increased the most, both in relative and absolute terms. These billionaires, classified as 'heirs/self-made', have attained bil-lionaire status only through a combination of inheritance and hard work, either by starting their own business or by taking an active role in their family business
>
> (Wealth-X 2014, 25).

In this way, there is a trend that monetary income depends less and less on entrepreneurship and more on the inheritance of property and investments.

174 *The Refeudalization of Society*

Even though Latin America can certainly be included in this global tendency of capitalist change in values, special features must be taken into account. These are primarily rooted in the colonial origins of contemporary Latin American societies and the particular processes of elite formation. Compared to Western Europe, Latin America is much less characterized by a meritocratic value system. In the region, the division of labor has historically been overdetermined by the racial division of society. After violent conquest, the indigenous and Afrodescendant populations were assigned the social position of simple (forced) labor in the mines, *haciendas,* and plantations. In contrast, the white conquerors took over the more highly valued work, and especially in the late colonial period new tendencies of feudalization came across in parts of the white elite, finding expression in new titles of nobility. To this day, an "aristocratic spirit" has been maintained among Latin American elites and has met with the current dynamics of refeudalization.

Consumption, Luxury, and Prestige

A key aspect of the social performance of the "leisure class" highlighted by Thorstein Veblen is ostentatious consumption, and it is still of particular importance today. Basically, not only an extreme polarization of the social structure can be observed globally but also a similar polarization in consumption. The German weekly newspaper *Die Zeit* noted:

> The real consumers are small in number but have a disproportionate share in the pie of income and consumption. There are calculations from the U.S. according to which the richest 22 percent of households there make 60 percent of consumption—but the poorest 20 percent make only three percent
>
> (Fischermann 2008).

While the multitude of the excluded must limit themselves to a "taste of necessity" (Bourdieu), luxury consumption is booming among the top 10%.

The importance of consumption for social differentiation cannot be underestimated. Already in the period after World War II, a global consumer society had spread from Western Europe and North America. In apologetic writings, the integrative character of mass consumption was emphasized. In recent years, however, striking processes of distinction have also become apparent in consumer society. Sociologist Zygmunt Bauman concludes accordingly:

> The places won or assigned on the axis of excellence/unability of consumption performance become the primary stratification factor and the main criterion of inclusion and exclusion as well as a guideline

for the distribution of social appreciation and stigmatization and for participation in public attention

(2007, 53).

Consumption in the global postmodern society is, thus, not only an expedient practice of satisfying needs but a *conditio sine qua non* of social life. Identity is no longer determined only by belonging but is produced as a permanent project through consumption. However, this process of identity "self-fabrication" is highly vulnerable. For those who do not have access to consumption, not only is the formation of identity hindered, but they are also "superfluous" as individuals in the consumer society. In this sense, identity formation through consumption is not a factor of self-realization, but a social imperative that is indispensable to one's position in society. For the hyper-rich, however, it is consumption that provides the opportunity to express their status in the global moneyed aristocracy and to mark neo-feudal distinction through ostentatious and, above all, exclusive lifestyles and the goods that go with them.

A look at the history of consumption in Latin America makes it clear that even after the end of the colonial period at the beginning of the 19th century, the tastes of the elites were oriented toward Europe. France with Paris as its cultural center became the undisputed point of reference for luxury consumption among Latin America's upper classes, in particular. Even the economic and political ascent of the United States could hardly displace France from its central cultural position. During the accelerated processes of globalization in the middle of the 20th century, luxury consumption in Latin America also became more cosmopolitan.

Just recently, Latin America also experienced a boom in the sector of exclusive fashion, design, and other luxury goods. According to Euromonitor Internacional (EI), Latin America had the highest growth rate in this sector worldwide

> with a 24% increase in the number of stores opened and a 22% increase in registered sales. Therefore, both, the number of stores and the associated sales increased. Countries such as Chile, Colombia, Brazil or Mexico are good examples of this trend. The data shows that sales in this sector in Chile increased by 14% in 2013. In Brazil, demand increased between 10% and 12% in the same year and is expected to even reach a higher level. The most significant case is Mexico where the market grew by almost 29% between 2008 and 2013 and growth of another 34% is expected by 2018
>
> (Stecchi 2015).

In the process, some Latin American cities have developed into central locations for luxury consumption and places where the main international high-end and luxury brands of the fashion industry, watch

176 *The Refeudalization of Society*

manufacturers, jewelers, and perfume products are located, as Costa da Silva said of São Paolo:

> Brands such as Louis Vuitton, Giorgio Armani, Ermenegildo Zegna, Diesel, Hermes, Chanel, Prada, Gucci, Versace, Montblanc, Rolex, Tiffany & Co, Dior Fendi, Balenciaga, Lanvin, Coach, and others have at least two to three stores in São Paulo, located in shopping malls no more than 2 km away
>
> (2015).

French philosopher Gilles Lipovetsky has identified a tendency for exploding luxury consumption around the world in recent decades, especially during the holidays like the Christmas season. Aggressive advertising strategies of the large retail chains address the middle and lower class segments specifically and fuel their desire for luxury consumption.

In contrast to this "massification" of the desire for luxury consumption (Zitzmann 2015), the top 10% focus on a "neo-individualism" in which luxury consumption becomes part of the lifestyle. Lipovetsky, who himself advises luxury brands, wants to create aristocratic distinction again, contrary to this trend. In this context, Luc Boltanski and Arnard Esquierre have pointed to collector's passion for luxury items—watches, vintage cars, and objects of art. Also the pursuit of other exquisite hobbies, such as yachts, falls within this normative of distinction, since these recreational activities are so cost-intensive that they cannot be financed by the majority of the 90%.

A more profound value-theoretical consideration of this segment of the economy is still largely pending. In this context, the French duo Boltanski and Esquerre deserve credit for having presented the first conceptual reflections on the "enrichment economy" (2016, 2017) that includes the booming sectors of luxury goods, heritage, art, and culture. The enrichment economy differs from industrial production in that "[t]he valorization of an object is based on a story—usually rooted in the past—and promises that the price of the object enriched by this narrative will rise over time" (Boltanski and Esquerre 2017, 69).

Boltanski and Esquerre see the historical origin of this form of value in the systematically built collections of the first third of the 19th century in Western Europe, although precursors can also be found in the so-called curiosity cabinets of the 17th century. Fully in line with an analysis of time in which the past becomes increasingly determinant of the present and the future, the authors see the origins of the boom in this form of value based on narratives of enrichment in the "heritage effect," creating entirely new "heritage brands" and a nostalgic fever resembling a "heritage mania" (Boltanski and Esquerre 2017, 34). The main merit of the concept of the enrichment economy lies primarily in its materialist, political-economic anchoring. Boltanski and Esquerre are less interested in the political-cultural dynamics of the "Retrotopia" (Bauman 2017), but more in the importance of (heritage) narratives for the theory of value. In doing so, they extend the normal value form of capitalist industrial mass production highlighted by Marx to include the aforementioned form of collection: the trend—in which the enriching narrative is based on brand new references, such as the lifestyle of celebrities, and ultimately the "asset form," in which goods are acquired speculatively as a monetary investment in view of expected future profits (Boltanski and Esquerre 2017, 69–70).

From a postcolonial perspective, it should be pointed out that the form of the collection is just as connected to colonial questions as heritage. The very question of which cultural heritage is worth preserving and which can be allowed to decay and be forgotten is a highly political one (Kaltmeier 2017). In Latin America and the Caribbean, it stands out that much of the material cultural heritage recognized by UNESCO relates to colonial artifacts and architectural ensembles. As can be observed by looking at gentrification processes in colonial city centers, the narrative of colonial cultural heritage contributes to the "enrichment" of artifacts, especially of the upper classes' real estate. Something similar can be observed with regard to colonial art.

Beyond considerations of theoretical value, which contribute to a further concentration of wealth in the top 10%, the cultural-political dimension of the colonial heritage boom is worth emphasizing. I have introduced the concept of retro-coloniality in other contexts (Kaltmeier 2011, 2014, 2017). For retro-coloniality, it is crucial to remove the references to violence associated with colonial heritage in order to banish the colonial shame that might prevent consumers from consumption. For this reason, retro-coloniality avoids the representation of colonial historical dynamics and establishes an ahistorical discourse. Retro-coloniality does not pretend to represent the historical colonial phase, but rather facilitates articulation with consumer culture. In this context, retro-colonial narratives refine a valuable object by giving it authenticity and singularity. At the same time, these aspects also create even further distinction from popular cultures established through their exclusivity and the fantasies of superiority based on colonial history. In Latin America, a region in which indigenous rights and identities have started to become officially recognized in the 1990s for the first time since the colonial era, the retro-colonial revaluation of colonial imaginaries and the associated prioritization of mostly white mestizos from the upper and middle classes holds the potential of social explosiveness. The narrative refinement of retro-colonial artifacts leads to an economy of enrichment that increases the social distance of the top 1% from the 99%, while also creating the narrative framework for the formation and consolidation of retro-colonial and status-based cultural identities.

178   *The Refeudalization of Society*

A New Debt Bondage

A widespread stereotypical image of Latin America is of indebtedness. This image dates back to the debt crisis of the late 1970s and early 1980s, when Latin American countries—advised by international organizations and the United States—had indebted themselves so heavily with cheap petro-dollars that they were no longer able to pay the debts or the resulting interest when the dollar exchange rate subsequently rose. This was a classic case of external public debt. Today, the panorama of indebtedness in Latin America is more differentiated. For example, the share of public debt in GDP is relatively low in Latin America compared with the rest of the world. At the beginning of 2018, Brazil ranked 40th among the most indebted countries globally at 78.4% of GDP, followed by the United States in 42nd place (CIA 2018). But public debt is only one side of the coin. From 2007 onward, 21 countries in Latin America experienced such a rapid increase in private debt that it reached the level of external debt as early as 2011.

In relation to their GDP, Brazil, Guatemala, Nicaragua, Paraguay, and Peru have the highest rates of private external debt. In Paraguay, private debt is even three times higher than public debt. These high rates are partly due to public-private partnerships, but private household debt is also increasing as a result of consumer loans. Latin America is considered to be the region with the highest rates of credit card debt worldwide. For example, Euromonitor International notes that "three Latin American countries (Colombia, Argentina, and Chile) ranked in the top 10 for the fastest growth in card lending debt since 2008. In addition, out of the top 15 markets with the greatest reliance on card lending as of 2013, four are located in Latin America (Venezuela, Colombia, Argentina and Brazil)" (Evans 2014).

In Chile, private household debt has reached historic highs, partly due to easy access to credit cards. According to Euromonitor International, Chile ranks at the top of Latin America in terms of credit card debt:

> As of 2013, Chileans had amassed the greatest amount of total card lending debt as a proportion of the country's GDP compared with every other market in the world. In fact, the average Chilean has as much credit card debt as would typically be found among developed market consumers. As of 2013, the average Chilean had credit debt valued at over US$2,100, which puts Chile ahead of markets such as Norway, Australia and the UK
>
> (Evans 2014).

It should be noted, however, that the average income in Chile is far below that of the Western countries just mentioned.

The Chilean consumer protection organization CONADECUS estimates that more than three million Chileans have been unable to pay

The Refeudalization of Society   179

a credit installment. This is mainly due to over-indebtedness with bank loans. Sociologist Tomás Moulian has attributed this to a neoliberal political culture fueled by everyday advertising: "Advertising seduces, glorifies products, praises possibilities. Ideology declares the morality of consumption and portrays consumption as the perfect act of modernity because it means access to happiness, comfort, and entertainment" (1998, 21). In this context, credit card has the immense advantage of enabling immediate consumption. Without long-term savings and without checking the financial possibilities. At the same time, the credit market has diversified: 48% say they are in debt to banks and 20% to supermarkets, but the majority (79%) are in debt to large retail chains. The desire here to fulfill (small) luxury needs seems to be at the center. Thus, having multiple debts and debt rescheduling are widespread, meaning that a large part of income has to be used to pay off credit. The poorer segments of society are particularly affected. According to surveys, the lowest fifth of income earners in Chile spend 67% of their income on loan repayments. More than 80% of those indebted assume that they are not able to repay their loans (Conadecus 2011).

Due to the relationships of dependency that develop here, Conadecus readily speaks of a modern form of slavery. It seems to me more accurate to speak of a new form of debt bondage. Known as *peonaje* (or *concertaje,* or *huasipungaje* in Ecuador), debt bondage was widespread in Latin America from the 17th century until the middle of the 20th century. It was based on the indebtedness of mostly indigenous smallholders, who were then permanently tied to the *hacienda* and whose labor was exploited without them ever being able to free themselves from their dependency. Only in the course of the agrarian reforms of the 1960s and 1970s was *peonaje* reprimanded as a "feudal relic," and subsequently abolished. Indebtedness through consumer credit also results in a form of debt bondage. Large shares of income, and thus of labor, are expended paying off the debt and the interest. At the same time, a considerable proportion of the poorer debtors hardly ever have the opportunity to pay off their debts and free themselves from their dependency. As this form of indebtedness is a relatively new phenomenon in Latin America, it is still largely the first generation that has gotten itself into debt that has been affected. According to current law, however, the descendants are liable and thus inherit debts from the previous generation. At this point, a tendency to consolidate status is emerging, which will lead to social relations in the 21st century based on a new form of debt bondage.

To an extent not yet explored the refeudalization of socio-economic relations is underway here, and the banks are emerging as the new feudal lords. The "enrichment economy" diagnosed by Boltanski and Esquerre is countered by a poverty economy perpetuated by private indebtedness. Refeudalization is characterized by the fact that it operates on the basis of capitalist and concrete neoliberal values, but then introduces

180   *The Refeudalization of Society*

mechanisms of distinction that lead to a consolidation of status. This status-based consolidation of the top one to 10% can be seen above all in the separation of living spaces from the other 90%–99%. There are hardly any more shared spaces.

Of Citadels, Fortresses, and Walls

The first spatial image that the concept of feudalization brings to mind is certainly that of a fortress. Equipped with defensive walls and high towers, this type of castle was designed to protect the inhabitants from the possible attacks of the enemies and barbarians surrounding them. A similar recurrence of protective walls and surveillance devices can be observed at the current crossroads of the refeudalization of social relations and spaces. This applies to a wide range of geographical scales, from vast empires and nation-states to neighborhoods and individual homes.

Great empires deployed walls around the world to provide material and structural protection, and to enforce both functional and symbolic spatial divisions. The Roman Empire marked its territorial expansion with the Limes: border roads, some of which were developed into guarded border fortifications, as in the example of Hadrian's Wall in Scotland. The Chinese empires began to build a protective wall against the invasions and raids of the nomadic inhabitants of the Eurasian steppe as early as the 7th century BC. Especially during the Ming Dynasty (1368–1644), the Great Wall of China, which is considered to be the largest construction project of humankind, was extended and expanded. In the 20th century, too, the marking of borders by means of walls is still in use—the Berlin Wall (1961–1989) or the separation of the Palestinian sector from Jerusalem are just two examples.

At the end of the 20th century, the "fall of the Berlin Wall" in 1989 was not only seen as the beginning of the end of Soviet-style communism but also fueled imaginaries of a borderless, globalized world. This found expression in concepts such as the "global village" or a "world civil society." The idea of the possibility of worldwide cosmopolitan integration, to be promoted primarily through free trade, became widespread. Contrary to this optimistic notion of progressive global integration and the expansion of democracy in global capitalism, new geopolitical boundaries are currently emerging. In view of the growing debate about African, Asian, and Latin American migration, Europe, the European Union, or the member countries of the Schengen Agreement are increasingly referred to as "Fortress Europe." Piquantly, the term "Fortress Europe" comes from Nazi propaganda and referred to the measures of occupied territories of Nazi Germany established for protection against the Allies. Initially, the organizations critical of migrants and refugees invoked the image of the new Fortress Europe in opposition to the often self-formulated

The Refeudalization of Society   181

imagination of a Europe open to the world. At this point, the concept has been adopted by far-right activists, including from the Identitarian Movement, to propagate "defense" against refugees. Thermal imaging cameras, police and military patrols, the private border protection agency Frontex, barbed-wire barriers, the construction of walls and fences at the external borders in Greece and Spain, the establishment of reception camps, all these are the already real aspects of an intensified policy of sealing off from the outside. Contemporary historians and sociologists have proposed to understand the 20th century as the "century of camps." Some, such as Zygmunt Bauman, refer to the ominous conflation of modernity and violence, while other authors, such as Kotek and Rigoulot, equate the National Socialist system of extermination with communist systems in a historically simplified manner and focus on the totalitarianism inherent in them. Today, this second approach loses its explanatory power to the same extent that democratic systems continue to produce new camps as well. In this respect, the thesis of the political philosopher Giorgio Agamben is confirmed, according to which the camp is the biopolitical paradigm of Western modernity. This is characterized precisely by the fact that the formal law is suspended and inmates are not treated as citizens but as "persons" and reduced to "bare life." It is against this background that the detention camps for arriving refugees at the EU's external borders, and the arbitrary controls at every other public place, are to be understood.

An analogous tendency toward isolation can be seen at the U.S.-Mexican border. The militarization of the border region and the expansion of the border wall have been part of U.S. migration policy not only since Donald Trump's grandiose announcements. The wall is not an invention of Trump. Wall construction began in 1994 under the Democratic administration of Clinton with Operation Gatekeeper and continued with the Illegal Immigration Reform and Immigration Responsibility Act of 1996. Ten years later, Republican President George W. Bush expanded the wall with the Secure Fence Act. This policy was continued by Barack Obama as well. These continuities make it clear that the U.S. border politics of delimitation toward the South have been steadily expanded since the mid-1990s—regardless of the political party of the respective presidents.

Castles in the City

The refeudal return of walls and fortresses is not only reflected along national borders but can also be observed in small spatial units. In Peru's capital Lima, a wall more than 10 km long and 3 m high, on which rolls of barbed wire are enthroned, separates the rich district of San Juan de Miraflores from the poor district of Surco. Out of fear of theft and robbery, the residents of the rich neighborhoods built the so-called "wall of shame" for social demarcation (Boano and Desmaison 2016).

182   *The Refeudalization of Society*

Given the persistence of coloniality, it is hardly surprising that such a wall was built in Lima. Lima was the capital of the Viceroyalty of Peru during the colonial period and saw itself as the "City of Kings," a name it still bears today. Subsequently, urban imaginaries were characterized by a division of the city into Spanish-born patricians and indigenous plebeians. A notion that, as colonial nostalgia, still has an impact today (Kaltmeier 2015a; Nugent 1992). The urbanist Maaria Seppänen describes the high social ethnic segregation as follows: "The plebeians should stay where they belong"; they must "know their place" in the social hierarchy and "behave accordingly" (2003, 115). If the colonized do not conform to this idea, as is the case with street vendors in the historical center, they become objects upon which fear, violence, and racial hatred are directed.

This is just one example, albeit a very striking one, of the continuing tendencies toward the isolation of the rich population within the urban space, which at the same time privatizes urban space and closes public passageways. In his analysis of contemporary trends of refeudalization, Sighard Neckel affirms that the dichotomization of social structure is a key aspect. The social distance between the cosmocratic elites and the excluded, also described as "urban outcasts" by sociologist Loïc Wacquant (2007), is growing in social and economic terms. This distance in social space also has implications for the appropriated physical space—a term introduced by Bourdieu. On the one hand, we see forced segregation with the growth of slums, favelas, and other poor neighborhoods (Wacquant 2007). On the other, we see new forms of self-segregation of elites such as gated communities or bunker architecture. Urbanist Peter Marcuse (1997) used the term *citadel* to characterize this self-segregation of the elite, alluding to the urban forms of defense of the European feudal period.

This citadel form finds its first expression in the centrally planned and developed, closed residential complexes of gated communities. While this type of housing was first developed in the United States in the 1970s in connection with urban sprawl and the model of the car-friendly city, it became established in Latin America primarily in the 1990s. A 2009 United Nations report noted that "Latin American and Caribbean cities such as Buenos Aires, Mexico City, Havana, Kingston, Lima, Naussau, Port-au-Prince, São Paulo, and Santiago have seen a dramatic increase in the number of gated communities built. In Buenos Aires alone, some 450 *barrios cerrados* were built in the 1990s for about half a million residents" (Irázabal 2009, 33).

For the population segments sealing themselves off in this way, protection against crime and the desire for socio-spatial demarcation from population groups considered "inferior" are important motives. Accordingly, the urban sociologist Peter Marcuse defines the refeudal citadel as a "spatially concentrated area in which the members of a certain group defined by its position of superiority in power, wealth, or status over its neighbors congregate to protect or strengthen that position" (1997, 247). Analogous to the geopolitical enclosure of "Fortress Europe," Blakely and Snyder

The Refeudalization of Society   183

(1999), in their classic work on gated communities in the United States, speak of the geopolitical imagination of 'Fortress America.'

For Brazil, urban sociologists have argued that gated communities function entirely on the principle of the fortifications of colonial rule. The point is to "make the entry of the undesirables impossible; to conceal the existence of strategic wealth and to facilitate the surveillance of the enemy" (Dunker 2015). In this sense, gated communities in Brazil are more than just a residential preference; rather, they express a lifestyle based on the production of separate worlds. The basic principle of gated communities is precisely to prevent the use of public spaces that are frequented jointly by different social groups. In this way, they form an enclave-like structure inside which social homogeneity prevails, while public life is restricted (Estrada Mejía and Guerrón Montero 2016).

A tendency toward refeudalization is not only expressed in the spatial structure of gated communities protected by walls and private security services. In their external form, too, gated communities often revert to feudal-colonial elements. For example, Raquel Clement and Jill Grant summarize their findings regarding the appearance of gated communities on the Caribbean island of Barbados as follows, "Gating in Barbados reflects a developmental process that is transforming traditional urban forms into globalized neo-colonial city design" (Clement and Grant 2012). Similarly, in the *cotos*, as gated communities are called in the Mexican metropolis of Guadalajara, Ulises Zarazúa has noted a consistent use of motifs that positively reference the Iberian colonial-feudal heritage.

In order to make coloniality and feudality marketable, they must be separated from their historical meaning associated with violence, forced labor, exploitation, and racism. I have defined the emptying of the signifier "coloniality" of its contents in the context of postmodern retrofashions elsewhere as retro-coloniality (Kaltmeier 2011, 2014, 2015a, 2015b).

Such a signifier, which has lost its original meaning, can now be used as a thematic term in urban planning, among others. A central aspect in the design of projects driven by professional developers is the "imagineering" borrowed from the Disney corporation, i.e., the connection of a thematic narrative (theming) with associated image worlds (image) and their material realization (engineering) (Gottdiener 1995, 2001). This is also evident in other construction projects, such as shopping centers. Here, the San Luis Shopping Center in Valle de los Chillos in Quito, Ecuador is of particular interest (Kaltmeier 2011). The entire shopping center was designed along a colonial-rural narrative like a *hacienda*. The jury of the 32nd Design and International Development Award 2008 of the International Council of Shopping Centers (ICSC) praised it for that reason:

> Architecturally, the shopping center preserves the facades of Andean haciendas with wide walls, soaring ceilings, hand-forged iron and

184   *The Refeudalization of Society*

thousands of details that belong to the Spanish colonial period. [...] It will be the first project in South America to combine history, business, and lifestyle. Two hundred years ago, the Los Chillos Valley was the heart of a thriving area with beautiful haciendas. [...] Nowadays, this part of our history is preserved through the construction of an amazing shopping center, considered by the community as the heart of the valley: San Luis Shopping

(2008).

Another outstanding example of consistent colonial theming in contemporary mega-construction projects is the development of Ciudad Cayalá in the outskirts of Guatemala City.[7] Construction activities began after the Cayalá Group was founded in 1982. After the construction of several interconnected gated communities, the development plan of an independent, integral city—the Ciudad Cayalá—was started in 2003. The centerpiece of the new urbanism is the construction of a shopping center in 2011, as well as additional housing, office space, and even a large-scale colonial-style church. In addition, there are basic health services and numerous opportunities for leisure activities (Ciudad Cayalá 2018). The entire project covers an area of 352 hectares, making it larger than New York's Central Park. With apartments starting at $260,000, this residential area targets the upper middle class. In the final construction phase, luxury apartments were also created for the top 10%. The entire planning is characterized by a colonial style, seen in the whitewashed walls, stucco ornamentation, archways, etc. Thus, the entire building project is permeated by a deep retro-colonial nostalgia. The colonial references are obvious, but in its self-representation, such as on the website or the Facebook page of the developers, the explicit mention of the colonial past is avoided in a retro-colonial manner. However, the order of the past is nostalgically evoked and cultural dominance is expressed through architecture: "The church Santa María Reina de la Familia aims to achieve the greatest possible beauty in construction and to restore the order of a now lost language of architecture. In doing so, it continues the history of a millennia-old tradition in the art of architecture" (Ciudad Cayalá 2018).

Ciudad Cayalá was designed by the Luxembourgish architect Léon Kriers, whose neoconservative, nostalgic, and historicist architecture is based on the ideas of New Urbanism (see Image 2.1). In Germany, he is known for his controversial debate with Hitler's personal architect, Albert Sperr, and more recently for publications in the neoconservative and protofacist publications *Neue Freiheit* and *Cicero*. Kriers argues, "Traditional architecture and traditional urbanism are first and foremost technologies for creating lasting beauty, both material and spiritual, with local materials and resources." And—according to Kriers—"beauty is not political" (Schwarz 2020). Thus he speaks from

The Refeudalization of Society 185

Image 2.1 Santa María Reina de la Familia Church in the town of Cayalá, Guatemala.

Source: Ciudad Cayalá (2018)

the soul of the nostalgic zeitgeist but ignores the fact that precisely the "spiritual" recourse to traditions is highly problematic in terms of historical politics and that beauty can be political and even retraumatizing after all.

The choice of a colonial narrative is by no means random, rather it is dependent on the acceptance of the theming by the targeted group of clients. In Ecuador, the political-cultural context is determined by the multi-cultural recognition policies of the mid-1990s, which initially defined the country as pluriethnic and, since 2006, even as plurinational. The revaluation of indigenous peoples, as well as the narrative

Image 2.2 San Luís Shopping Center, Quito.
Photo: Olaf Kaltmeier, 2007.

of the nation, was paralleled by a crisis of white middle and upper class identities. In this respect, the nostalgic recourse to feudal and colonial narratives proves to be a successful marketing strategy that conveys security, authenticity, and social distinction. However, the retro-colonial leitmotif cannot completely whitewash the injustice of colonial rule. Until the second agrarian reform of 1973, there were still *haciendas* in Ecuador that were based on the principle of serfdom and whose indigenous farm workers were subject to the racist arbitrariness of the *hacendados* (Kaltmeier 2011). This means that even in 2008—when San Luis Shopping Center was established—there were still contemporary witnesses who suffered under the *hacienda* regime and experienced traumatization (see Image 2.2).

Similar references to (post-) colonial violence, which has inscribed itself in spaces, can also be found in Guatemala. Stefanie Kron argues on the relationship between space and colonial violence:

> The historical significance of space in Guatemala is quickly outlined: Guatemala is one of the few countries in Latin America with an indigenous-rural majority of about 70 percent of the population. In addition, there is the large material, social and symbolic dimension

The Refeudalization of Society 187

of land ownership. Linked to both factors is a strong ethno-spatial hierarchical fragmentation of society, associated with sharp social demarcation lines

(2004, 102).

This has resulted in a postcolonial "apartheid regime" (Le Bot 1995, 309) in Guatemalan political culture that culminated in racially motivated genocide, especially in the context of the counterinsurgency programs of the Guatemalan military governments of the early 1980s. For the conflict phase between 1960 and 1996, international agencies estimate 160,000 murdered and 40,000 disappeared people—mainly Mayans. After the formal end of the conflict and a truth commission supervised by the United Nations, a change in political culture took place in the 1990s, which has been described as the "Mayanization of society" (Bastos 2014, 78). In the wake of recognition politics, indigeneity—particularly recourse to Mayan culture—became increasingly important for national identity formation. Against this background, parts of the white *ladino* upper class—similar to their counterparts in Ecuador—turned again to nostalgical, conservative, and retro-colonial imaginaries.

Retro-coloniality and post-rural feudality are—as the examples from Ecuador and Guatemala make clear—closely linked to the upper and middle classes, which are composed primarily of former landowners, the state bureaucracy of the 1970s and, since the 1990s, the emerging financial sector. As in other Latin American countries, such as Argentina, allusions to rural, aristocratic imaginaries serve as a distinguishing feature from other emerging social classes and as a form of "cultural mimesis" of the lifestyles of traditional rural elites (Svampa 2008). In the context of the identity politics of white and *mestizo* middle- and upper-class groupings in Ecuador and Guatemala, this retro-coloniality becomes a mode of social, cultural, and spatial distinction from the indigenous population. This also makes clear that even the retro-colonial emptying of meaning does not take place completely, but that a trace of the original historical meaning still remains present. Last but not least, conservative religious positioning—also contrary to liberation or intercultural theology—plays an essential role. A larger-than-life statue of John Paul II was placed in front of the church in Ciudad Cayalá. Like no other high church father, this pope stands for an anti-communist, arch-conservative bias in the Catholic Church, which was expressed in the rejection of liberation theology and the appointment of numerous bishops in Latin America associated with Opus Dei.

This retro-colonization is not only due to the political dynamics of identity in the region. Rather, these dynamics are linked to the global debates about cultural heritage and its cultural-industrial expressions as heritage tourism. In this sense, local constructions of retro-colonial identity are favored and recognized by transnational agents in the heritage

188 *The Refeudalization of Society*

field from ICOMOS to tourist agencies. This latter aspect is of paramount importance, as the colonial construction of nostalgic identity does not solely correspond now to a backward-looking traditional creole elite but is in line with recent processes of cultural globalization. Nostalgic identity receives cosmopolitan recognition from heritage institutions and international tourists in search of the past and authenticity. In this sense, these identities do not look back to the past but rather link nostalgic inventions with cultural industry and global postmodern processes.

The crisis-ridden nature of current transnationalization does not only manifest itself in the form of socio-economic marginalization but is also associated with the dissolution, liquefaction, and hybridization of identities (Bauman 2000, 2007, Sennett 2000). In this context, nostalgia can be understood as a counter-dynamic of self-reflexive identity stabilization in space and time, which has so far hardly been captured in its identity-political effect. As a specific form of past politics, the use of nostalgia as a resource in the heritage field is not about remembering and historical reappraisal, but about a harmonization of history in which conflicts and antagonisms are not named. In historical urban centers in the Americas, coloniality is thus paradoxically hidden through the staging of colonial heritage.

From Gentrification to Retro-Colonial Archipelago

The tendencies toward refeudalization in urban space are not limited to the act of foreclosure. Rather, re-feudalizing practices that aim at a proactive appropriation of urban space are also evident. In order to describe the appropriation processes of central urban areas, urbanists have deliberately chosen gentrification as a concept to allude to feudalism. The term is derived from the "gentry," an English social class between high and lower nobility. Gentrification describes processes of urban transformation in which the original population of a decaying and impoverished urban area is gradually displaced by the higher purchasing power of the upper middle class. In Europe, artists, bohemians, and alternative sectors are considered "first-stage gentrifiers." After their intervention in run-down historic districts, these sectors gain attractiveness, which is then reflected in increased income in real estate. This dynamic promotes speculation and usually leads to the displacement of the poorer original residents of the neighborhood.

In cities with colonial historical centers, such as Quito or Lima, the strategic use of cultural heritage was key to initiating the restoration or "recapture" of the historical center, where rural-indigenous migrants had settled since the 1960s. In contrast to Western European and U.S. urban gentrification processes, we cannot identify the bohemian as the first-stage gentrifier here. Rather, my argument is that the state or city government, in cooperation with governmental and non-governmental heritage organizations, has taken on the role of first-stage gentrifier.

The historic center of Quito was the first urban complex to be declared a "World Heritage Site" by UNESCO in 1978. After the damage caused by the 1987 earthquake, a massive process of restoration began, initially focusing on the rehabilitation of outstanding monuments, especially churches and convents.

In the process, the city aimed at the development of tourism. In particular, they wanted to attract foreign tourists with high purchasing power. In the brochure, "Invest in Quito," the Quito Municipal Government writes, "In general terms, and given the potential of the restored historic center of Quito, one can see in this city an important niche market for luxury tourism of the highest order" (MDMQ 2010, 30). The clientele, in the context of neo-feudal analysis, would correspond to the cosmocratic elite, the winners of neoliberal capitalism. The city government as a first-stage gentrifier—advised by expert groups from the Inter-American Development Bank (IDB) and USAID—creates favorable conditions for big capital to invest in the old city, and as the main funder of the first phase of restoration, the city bears the greatest risk.

A key operation for the revaluation of the historic center was the eviction of informal commerce in 2001. More than 10,000 informal vendors and retailers who had sold their goods in the streets and alleys of 6.4 hectares of the historic center were evicted.

As a result, nostalgic Quito residents have also jumped on the wave of gentrification, as Modesto Ponce Maldonado describes in his novel "The Devil's Palace":

> Houses that the old upper classes had left the old town fifty years ago to live in the north are now occupied by nostalgics and book lovers to help the now almost five times hundred years old city to its former glory. This is to help tourism to triumph and to plug the holes in the sack of the gross national product
>
> (2005, 280).

This process of gentrification is, as the historian Eduardo Kingman describes, "accompanied by a veritable governmentalization and biopolitics of urban populations concerned with the control of 'dangerous' sectors such as itinerant traders, street vendors, beggars, and prostitutes" (Kingman 2004, 27). Through direct coercion, negotiation, and the structural constraint of land rent, the subaltern sectors are displaced. In 1974, the historic center of Quito still had 90,000 inhabitants. In 2001, the population dropped to 51,000. In addition, the living standards of the remaining subaltern population have not improved. In a study by the International Development Bank, Pedro Jaramillo points out that—despite all the investments in urban renewal—84.4% of the total population of the historic center still lives below the poverty line (2010, 34). Nevertheless, the rehabilitation of Quito's historic center is considered a *best-practice example*.

190 *The Refeudalization of Society*

The resettlement of street vendors in the emblematic Plaza San Francisco in particular is praised as a positive example of resettlement measures, since—in contrast to Lima, for example—there was only limited use of force. But the city does not limit itself to the recovery of insular monumental heritage sites alone; rather, heritage presents itself as a dispositive for a dynamic and progressive modernization and gentrification of the city.

An emblematic example of this is the "reconquest" of La Ronda street in 2006. La Ronda was previously considered a hotbed of prostitution and petty crime. In the 1990s, it was a "no-go area" for tourists flocking to the old town as well as for Quito's middle and upper classes. Today, it is a much-praised attraction, attracting hundreds of tourists every day offering typical local food, cultural events, and souvenir stores. The city administration has placed information boards in the street highlighting the history and cultural uniqueness of La Ronda as a street of Quito's *bohème*. However, there is no reference to its past as the city's brothel. In this way, a retro-colonial cityscape is produced that presents a restricted and regulated narrative and stages the colonial legacy. In the process, the contribution of popular culture, especially that of the lower class, to urban history is suppressed and ultimately urban polyphony is replaced by a retro-colonial discourse of unity. The paradox arises that the recovery of cultural heritage through restoration ultimately puts an end to living urban culture. The street becomes a theme park.

When mayor Paco Moncayo ended his term in 2009, a large part of the urban area with historic monuments had been recovered and restored. La Ronda became the southern limit of the restoration of the historic center. Now, Quito's downtown is subject to such strict surveillance by police forces and private security services (Martínez 2009, 103) that it resembles a private mall or amusement park more than a public space.

In summary, it can be said that the various forms of citadels in the city are not to be understood simply as insular spaces. Rather, the various "islands"—from the gated community to the shopping center and the international museum to the gentrified city center—are connected to each other via well-developed traffic routes. In this respect, one can speak of a cityscape structured like a fractal archipelago. In self-similar repetition, the retro-colonial formal language of the various spatial nodes resembles each other. There are also fractal reproductions on the level of functional forms in that shopping centers, airports, and other places of the cosmopolitan moneyed aristocracy are constructed in the same way worldwide. For orientation, the chosen architectural leitmotif is secondary. When entering a shopping center, the cosmopolitan consumer knows what to expect and where—the same luxury stores and food courts in which the same transnational chains are represented.

Beyond the use of colonial motifs for architectural design, the real core of the refeudalization of space lies in this new global archipelago, which encompasses a divisive and connective restructuring of space.

The connecting character lies in the fact that the new central places of the cosmocrats are connected with each other worldwide in an exclusive network. Information technology makes real-time communication between distant points in the network possible. Money, goods, and people can circulate in this worldwide network at a rapid speed. The so-called "global cities" represent the central nodes through which the global network society is controlled (Castells).

But parallel to these globally interconnected or interwoven spaces, new spatial divisions can be observed. This socially disintegrating separation process is also particularly evident in the metropolises of the global network society. According to Manuel Castells, "the most important thing about mega-cities is that they are externally connected to global networks and to segments in their own countries, while internally they disconnect local people who are either functionally unnecessary or socially explosive" (2001, 459–460). Just as the archipelago of the super-rich extends globally to every local corner, so too does the disconnection of local groups. The archipelago, which covers the globe like a grid, is contrasted by the disconnected places, which are largely excluded from the global network.

The socio-spatial fissures and fractures are particularly striking in urban metropolises. In 2003, UN-Habitat presented a report entitled "The Challenge of Slum," according to which human history is at a turning point. More people now live in cities than in the countryside. And the vast majority of the city dwellers live in slums (Davis 2007). The spatial segregation by the "wall of shame" shows—just like the spatial coexistence of *favelas* and gated communities in Brazilian metropolises—the small-scale patterns socio-spatial segregation can assume in hyper-fragmented urban spaces.

There may well be limited social relations between these spatial segments and their inhabitants. For example, some of the urban poor work as cleaners, housekeepers, gardeners, etc., in the rich neighborhoods. But this does not result in a more solid social relationship. However, in feudal times a hierarchical relationship was established between feudal lords and the serfs, which could also result in redistributive relationships as a social form, today cross-class social relations are minimized. In comparing marginalized and socially (often also ethnically) segregated neighborhoods, the sociologist Loïc Wacquant introduced the concepts of "urban outcasts" and their spatial location in the "hyper-ghetto." Unlike the ghetto of the 1950s and 1960s, where communitarian social relations still existed, the hyper-ghetto is characterized by the ubiquitous spread of violence and the dissolution of socially collective relations even within the ghettos.

Conversely, the production of urban imaginaries of fear—fueled by the *crónicas rojas* of the mass media—also promotes the social construction of no-go areas in the city on the one hand and the self-isolation of the rich in secure citadels on the other (Zarazúa 2011).

192   *The Refeudalization of Society*

The social fragmentation of the city gives a spatial expression to the end of the modern notion of a cross-class socially integrated society. There is a homology between the habitat based on multiple segregations, the lifestyles crystallizing in the habitus, and the extreme polarization of social space. The dynamics of refeudalization bury the idea of a cross-class society. Instead of public spaces that make cross-class encounters possible, the different estates move into their own separated and controlled spaces. Instead of an integrated society based on the division of labor, we are increasingly dealing with a refeudalized and extremely hierarchized segmentary form of society

This process is far from complete. On the contrary, it is being fueled by the idea of smart cities, which will be closely networked via information technology and have rapid access to global transportation hubs. Following the massive proliferation of gated communities, planned mini-cities set up exclusively for the elites are now becoming increasingly important. Imagined in the urban planning references of New Urbanism as small towns based on the European model, in reality, however, they will lack precisely what has historically constituted a city: public life. This trend toward the privatization of urban space and the end of the urban public sphere is currently being advanced in various projects. The San Luis Shopping Center already planned the establishment of a private clinic and a private citizens' office. Further still, there are plans for Free Private Cities such as Próspera in Honduras. This project, driven by the liberal businessman and CEO Titus Gebel, is based on the idea of the special economic zone and plans for an extraterritorial city—including political administration without a state—for the 1% of the upper social class. In this new city, which is completely disconnected from any democratic regulation, the city acts as the principality of the moneyed aristocracy.

Millionaires in Power

In the global, highly segregated network society, patterns of political affiliation are changing. While citizenship linked to national states—in its variants of *ius sanguinis* (as in Germany) and *ius solis* (as in the Americas)—is certainly still the determining factor for political affiliation for the majority of the world's population, tendencies toward the dissolution of this principle are becoming apparent among cosmocrats. Among the top 1%, a separate, exclusive understanding of *global citizenship* seems to be emerging that is no longer linked to classical civic values and a sense of national belonging. Instead, it is first and foremost about the individual or dynastic security of tenure. This finds expression in the current programs of "citizenship by investment." In essence, tax havens offer citizenship for sale to billionaires through special financial service providers. Citizenship is offered at the lowest tax rates for the entire family

The Refeudalization of Society   193

and future descendants. In most cases, there is no income or inheritance tax and no taxation of wealth. Residency is often not required, but with the new passports most relevant countries in the world, including the Schengen countries of the EU can be traveled to visa-free.

Many island states of the eastern Caribbean, such as Antigua and Barbados, Grenada, St. Kitts and Nevis, or Dominica—but also some European countries—offer their citizenship for sale. Often, a one-time payment of 100,000 U.S. dollars is enough to acquire citizenship. These programs explain the rise of billionaires in the British Virgin Islands, the Cayman Islands, and Barbados, already discussed in the chapter on the refeudalization of the social structure. This trend is highly problematic in two respects. First, it undermines the fate principle of the so-called "birthright lottery" for the benefit of the moneyed aristocracy. The 1% sets itself apart from the established and internationally recognized political communities by being able to buy citizenship. This detachment has, second, quite material implications. The accumulated wealth is based to a considerable extent on public services provided by the countries of origin: think of the education system, which benefits not only the moneyed aristocracy but also above all its functional elite, other social and health systems, infrastructure, and the maintenance of public and also international security. By acquiring another, tax-free citizenship, parts of the cosmocracy withdraw from the solidarity-based distributive systems and privatize the proceeds. In this sense, the discussion about citizenship—beyond the mass-media view of migrants from the Global South and the question of "the right of blood" or "the right of land"—must urgently be expanded to include the problem of the "right of money."

While this part of the global moneyed aristocracy is primarily focused on the preservation of private property, there is another faction of this privileged class that actively intervenes in the politics of the home countries. Accordingly, the intertwining of economic power with the political sphere is a characteristic feature of current refeudalization tendencies. In Habermasian terms, massive colonization of political space by economic interests can be assumed. This political trend of refeudalization undermines the guiding principles of democratic systems, according to which political power emanates from the people who exercise this power either directly or through representative procedures. All citizens, provided they have reached the legal age of majority, are considered equal. Currently, however, as Colin Crouch argues in *Post-Democracy*, there is not only a simple reversion to feudalism to be observed. Rather, the existing formal democratic structures are being colonized:

> While the forms of democracy remain fully in place [...], politics and government are increasingly slipping back into the control of privileged elites in the manner characteristic of pre-democratic times;

194   *The Refeudalization of Society*

and that one major consequence of this process is the growing impotence of egalitarian causes

(2004, 6).

Above all, Crouch sees a change in political communication, which is determined by advertising strategies, spin doctors, and lobby groups. In his first sketch of global tendencies toward refeudalization, Sighard Neckel points to the refeudalization of the welfare state. This is expressed in the fact that public social policy is increasingly replaced by donations and the services of private foundations. Social rights that were previously fulfilled by state welfare systems are now privatized. The needy are deprived of their rights and become dependent on private charity.

This charity wave, which is particularly pronounced in the Anglo-Saxon world, is of much less significance in Latin America. Instead, another, far more direct form of refeudalization has recently become apparent here: the moneyed aristocracy itself taking over political power. With the waning of the phase in Latin America of left-wing governments, a massive rightward shift manifested itself in the region in the 2010s, in the course of which representatives of the moneyed aristocracy entered governments and in some cases—as in Argentina with Mauricio Macri, in Chile with Sebastián Piñera, and in Ecuador with Guillermo Lasso— directly took over the highest political office. As with the refeudalization processes analyzed in the previous chapters, this is by no means a genuinely Latin American dynamic. The presidency of billionaire Donald Trump in the United States points to the global character of this trend toward refeudalization. And this case also highlights the political impact of class interests on state policies—formally committed to the common good. One need only to mention the redistribution from "bottom" to "top" in the tax reform passed at the end of 2017, which provided Trump and his family with lavish tax rebates.

Just as Trump's rise can be understood primarily as an ultra-conservative reaction to the liberal and, above all, the multicultural presidency of Obama, so too the political rise of conservative millionaires in Latin America can be understood as a reaction to left-wing governments. For the moneyed aristocracy, permanent occupation of political power by representatives of the "lower estates" bearing the ethnic markers of being Afrodescendant or indigenous will not be tolerated.

Sebastián Piñera in Chile is considered to be one of the first millionaire presidents to buck the regional leftist trend in Latin America. In 2010, he became the first conservative president in Chile after the formal end of the military dictatorship in 1990. When he took office, his total assets were estimated at $2.2 billion. Among these, he held high stakes in the LAN-Chile airline, was the owner of a TV channel, and held shares in private pension funds and real estate companies. He was also the Chilean representative for Visa, Master Card, and Apple. However, he was unable

The Refeudalization of Society 195

to make a major impact during his time in office, and he rapidly lost political legitimacy in the wake of the student protests of 2011, which were directed primarily against the privatized and classist education system. Piñera was voted out of office, and in 2014 the social democratic Michelle Bachelet took over the presidency again. After the rapid loss of legitimacy for the Bachelet government, in particular, and the political class in general, Piñera then won the presidency again in 2017 and began his second term in March 2018. Despite this rightward shift in Chile, fundamental changes, especially in economic policy, are hard to be expected. In Chile, the neoliberal economic system has maintained permanency even under social-democratic governments. Accordingly, Bachelet had hardly been able to make any drastic changes even during her first term in office.

In Argentina, the election of billionaire Maurico Macri as president in 2015 led to a profound break with a twelve-year era of *kirchnerismo*. Under Néstor Kirchner, who was Argentina's president from 2005 to 2007, Argentina became a cornerstone of the leftist turn in Latin America. Under his wife Cristina Fernández de Kirchner, post-neoliberal policies continued for two terms of government, 2007–2011 and 2011–2015. With Maurico Macri, there has now been a rapid turnback toward neoliberal policies that also promote (transnational) corporations and especially benefit the top 10%. As the son of millionaire Franco Macri, who built his fortune primarily in the construction industry, Maurico Macri was born into Argentina's moneyed aristocracy. The Macri Group is one of the most important consortiums in Argentina. In addition to the construction industry, the conglomerate includes companies in the automobile industry, postal services (which were privatized under Carlos Menem), mining, waste management, and food industry, which are located beyond Argentina in Brazil, Panama, and Uruguay.

In Paraguay, the billionaire Horacio Cartes replaced the leftist government of the liberation-theology-influenced President Fernando Lugo in 2013. In retrospect, the ouster of Fernando Lugo in a political process, confirmed by the Chamber of Deputies of the Parliament, can be seen as a blueprint for the "cold coup" against Dilma Rousseff in Brazil. The Chamber of Deputies, in which Lugo did not have a majority, deposed the elected president in a process not recognized internationally. As a sanction, Paraguay was expelled from Mercosur and Unasur. The new conservative president, Federico Franco, practiced nepotism by freely granting offices to family members. In 2013, he had to hand over the presidency to Horacio Cartes due to increasing political pressure. While Lugo had strengthened the role of the state in the economy, especially against lobby groups from agribusiness, Cartes has pursued a neoliberal-inspired transformation of the state apparatus. Neoliberal technocrats with education from the United States and a basically conservative orientation pushed their way into the state apparatus, which was reshaped along corporate lines. Cartes can draw on the experience

196   *The Refeudalization of Society*

of his industrial conglomerate, the Cartes Group. It consists of the tobacco industry, agro-industry, banks, companies in the transportation sector, and breweries and is considered one of Paraguay's largest industrial conglomerates.

As in Paraguay, the refeudalization of the political field in Brazil took place through a so-called "cold coup." In 2016, the PMDB broke the existing governing coalition with the Labor Party (PT). In cooperation with PMDB-affiliated Vice President Michel Temer, the opposition put forward a vote of no confidence against President Dilma Rousseff, which won a majority first in the Chamber of Deputies and then in the Senate. Rousseff was accused of corruption and manipulation of the state budget—but to date, there has been no legal conviction. On the contrary, secret agreements that have been made public suggest that the ouster of Rousseff was intended to stop the anti-corruption programs initiated by her, since they heavily incriminated PMDB deputies, including Temer himself, as well as the top managers of the state-owned oil company, which was involved in the corruption scandals.

In Bolivia, Evo Morales had the judiciary and the Organization of American States confirm a 4th presidential candidacy, overriding a referendum that denied his attempt to change the constitution to allow him another candidacy. In the November 2019 presidential election, Morales garnered well over 47.07% of the vote, while in second place, Carlos Mesa got 36.51% of the vote. Since Bolivian law requires the winner to have more than 50% of the vote or more than 40% of the vote with at least a ten percentage point lead to win in the first round of voting, Morales won the elections in the first round, although it was extremely close. Nevertheless, accusations of election manipulation spread rapidly on social media, and the OAS pointed to irregularities as well. Meanwhile, several international studies, including one from the prestigious MIT, found no evidence of systematic manipulation and OAS could not prove their accusation. However, history took a different path. Encouraged by the accusation of election manipulation there were mass protests in Bolivia, during which the military sided with the government critics, and the military chief called on the president to resign on November 10. One day later, Morales, who had just announced new elections, went into exile in Mexico. Rejected by the MAS majority in Parliament, conservative Jeanine Áñez Chávez took office as interim president. Influenced by the far-right politician and millionaire Luis Camacho, among others, her cabinet was composed primarily of representatives of the white business elite from the Department of Santa Cruz. In October 2020, new presidential elections were held in Bolivia, which the MAS candidate Luis Arce won with a clear and uncontested majority of 55.1%. This electoral result stopped the turn toward refeudalization in Bolivia.

In Ecuador, by contrast, the right wing with its most popular candidate, multi-millionaire Guillermo Lasso, was unable to prevail several

The Refeudalization of Society   197

times at the ballot box (or via coup) against the socially democratic government of Alianza País led by President Rafael Correa. In 2013, Lasso suffered a resounding defeat to incumbent President Rafael Correa, who received twice Lasso's vote. And in 2017, Lasso was defeated by Lenín Moreno, handpicked to succeed Correa, who was not allowed to run for another term. But Moreno increasingly turned his back on his patron to the point that a veritable male hostility developed. At the same time, Moreno moved politically closer and closer to the conservative right-wing positions of the business elite. In 2019, he responded to the popular protest against the rise of petrol prices with brutal military repression. Finally, in his third attempt, he won the presidential election in 2021. With Lasso, the moneyed aristocracy finally holds power in Ecuador.

Although Donald Trump is certainly a paradigmatic expression of the trend toward the colonization of the political field by economic interests, he is not the pioneer of this phenomenon. In an international context, the presidency of Silvio Berlusconi in Italy should be mentioned, who also massively changed political communication through his media empire. Trump and Berlusconi made it clear that the recent developments in the political field in Latin America have not been an expression of supposedly backward, authoritarian political cultures but part of a global process of refeudalization.

The tendencies toward refeudalization of the political field have been clearly evident in Central and South America since the late 1990s, during the heyday of neoliberal policies. The following are some particularly emblematic cases. Vicente Fox, an entrepreneur and manager for Coca-Cola and other multinationals, was Mexican president for the conservative PAN from 2000 to 2006. His presidency was initially welcomed by large sections of society as a departure from the one-party rule of the PRI. However, he provoked protests by increasing taxes on basic food and everyday goods. In Panama, big businessman Ricardo Martinelli was president from 2009 to 2014. He is best known as the owner of the country's largest supermarket chain, Súper 99. He is also a shareholder in various Panamanian companies, including the daily newspaper *Diario por la Democracia S.A.* and Televisora Nacional de Panamá. Thus, Martinelli had a Berlusconian potential for political communication.

So far, it has been argued here that this rise of the moneyed aristocracy to the highest political offices of the state must be seen in the context of the recent global conjuncture of refeudalization. At this point, this argument shall be supported with an additional historical hypothesis. For Latin America, the diagnosed global boom of refeudalization in the field of politics is intertwined with a structural dominance of the elite in the political culture, which can ultimately be traced back to the process of colonization.

Thus, although the Latin American revolutions of the 1820s led to a breakaway from the European colonial powers and to the establishment

198   *The Refeudalization of Society*

of formal democratic republics in Hispano-America, there was no social revolution—with the exception of the so-called slave revolution in Haiti—that resulted in a change in the composition of the elite. In this respect, the close interconnections between economic and social elites and political power shape the history of the 19th and 20th centuries in Latin America. But it is precisely in the late 20th and early 21st century that personalities with a popular background have risen to the presidency: the metalworker Lula da Silva, the indigenous coca farmer Evo Morales, the bus driver Nicolás Maduro, the soldier of color Hugo Chávez, the student leader Gabriel Boric, and the feminist Afro-Columbian domestic worker Francia Márquez as vice-president in Colombia. After the legitimizing reference back to the ordinary population that emerged in the burgeoning populism of the 1940s, actors from the lower population groups now pushed their way to political power and embodied the hope for real democratization. In this sense, the massive return of the moneyed aristocracy to the direct levers of political power represents a striking step backward in terms of democratization efforts.

The Body of Money

An excursion into the history of political philosophy illustrates the far-reaching implications of this trend toward refeudalization for political representation. In his now classic study of political theology, the historian Ernst Kantorowicz put forward the theory of the "two bodies of the king" about the Middle Ages in Western Europe, starting in the 11th century and continuing into the 17th century. According to this theory, the figure of the king consists of a corporeal, mortal body and an immortal political body. This double figure of the royal body is exemplified in the ritualized words at the change of throne: *Le roi est mort, vive le roi* (The king is dead, long live the king). In the European Middle Ages, the idea of an immortal political body of the king is closely connected with religious ideas that the king is also appointed as an earthly governor by the grace of God. This double body of the king was then provided with attributes of totality, such as omnipresence, omniscience, and immortality. Thus, the body of the king was regarded as the political representation of the political community. A fitting visualization of this total representation of community can be found in the copperplate that adorns the original edition of Thomas Hobbes' *Leviathan*.

In the course of the French Revolution, a profound change in the models of political representation took place. With the end of the monarchy, the political body is decapitated. The totality of society is now difficult to represent through a single person. The political philosopher, Claude Lefort, emphasizes how knowledge, law, and power are now contestable and must be negotiated between different interests in civil society. In order to be able to meet the need for political representability for the political

The Refeudalization of Society 199

community, however, Lefort—alluding to Kantorowicz—refers to the principle of the "body of nobody." According to this principle, political power in democratic societies can no longer be fixed in a supra-historical way, since it is subject to permanent processes of negotiation in civil society. There can only ever be a temporary fixation of political power, which is symbolically fixed in the body of a natural person that, according to the democratic formula, could be everybody.

With the described tendencies toward refeudalization of the social structure and the political field, however, we see today a shift and a tendency toward solidification within this open model of democratic political representation. For now, it is not the body of an everyman that can fill the symbolic place of political power. Rather, taking over political power is reserved for the group of the moneyed aristocracy. This is a process of the colonization of the public sphere and ultimately also of the political field by economic interests, whose dangers have already been pointed out by Habermas. Unlike what Lefort had described for Western democratic societies, political negotiation now takes place less and less in the sphere of civil society. Instead, economic interests determine the broader social field. For political representation, this means that the "body of nobody" is being replaced by the "body of money."

Lefort identifies a tendency toward totalitarianism inherent in democracy, based on the fact that whoever temporarily occupies political power often attempts to establish a fixation on a supra-individual ideology. In the 20th century, Lefort sees the examples of fascism and Stalinism as particularly relevant. Here, the attempt to fixate political representation takes place by recourse to political ideologies. This is different in the current trends of refeudalization. The fixation of political power of the moneyed aristocracy takes place by referring back to an outside, namely, economic power. The latter is hardly understood as a political ideology anymore, but as a quasi-natural ontology anchored in the "nature of man" as homo economicus. Thus, the model of the "body of money" is not only an expression of a change in the personal composition of political functionaries but it is embedded in a comprehensive tendency toward the economic colonization of the political. The essentialization of the capitalist economy has become hegemonic, especially during the course of the neoliberal conjuncture. With the elaborate governmental techniques of neoliberal governmentality, economic and functional logics have colonized political institutions as well. Increasingly, state institutions are under pressure to reorganize themselves according to private sector criteria. The corporation serves as a blueprint for the public authority.

With the reference to a quasi-natural outside—i.e., the economic, purposive, and utility-maximizing anthropological constants and the economic logics resulting from them—political representation experiences a fixation similar to that of the European Middle Ages. There is a danger of the sacralization of the political power of money. Accordingly,

200 *The Refeudalization of Society*

the political philosopher Giorgio Agamben synthesized the anti-Enlightenment regress as follows: "God didn't die, he was transformed into money!" (Agamben 2014). Or, to quote Friedrich Engels. "Money is the god of this world." (Engels 1845, 343). Liberation theologian Franz Hinkelammert has deeply criticized this sacralization of the market as a false God: "The market is the supreme being for the human being. With that it has a renewed God of the Middle Ages, who has the perfectly arbitrary decision on life and death" (2021, 84). The capitalist market that is above human beings is transformed into a secular religion.

However, the doubling of economic power into political power through the sacralization of the market has a certain self-evident nature, accompanying measures are still necessary to establish political legitimacy. For this purpose, Crouch argues, post-democratic elements are used, primarily evidenced in social groups becoming objects of mass media manipulation and no longer constituting themselves as political subjects (2008, 79). With the expansion of information technology and the techniques of the culture industry to all areas of societal life (Mato 2008), political legitimacy is increasingly simulated—in Guy Debord's sense—by media spectacles. In this sense, the control of mass media by moneyed aristocrats who intrude into the political field is central. Berlusconi's rise is based precisely on his media empire. And accordingly, as already mentioned, Latin American presidents also have large stakes in the mass media.

In addition, populist traits are simulated primarily through links to other popular social fields, especially football. Mauricio Macri is closely associated with the popular Argentine top club Boca Juniors, where he was president from 1995 to 2007. Sebastián Piñera is a shareholder in the Chilean club Colo-Colo, and in Paraguay, Horacio Cortes was president of Club Libertad during his presidency.

In addition to these post-democratic strategies of establishing political legitimacy and social hegemony, recent years have seen a worrying return to pre-democratic mechanisms of coercion and political violence. While military dictatorships and authoritarian regimes in the region came to an end after the "wave of democratization" of the early 1990s and gave way to democratic governments, four dubious regime changes have been observed in recent years alone.

In Honduras, for example, the military staged a coup with U.S. support against the elected president José Manuel Zelaya in 2009. In Paraguay and Brazil, as described above, the so-called "cold coups" took place under international protest, in which elected presidents were deposed by their political opponents under dubious pretexts. In Bolivia, the resignation of Evo Morales, who was accused of electoral fraud, occurred in 2019 under direct pressure from the military and a false accusation of the OAS. The silent coup against Dilma Rousseff also marks a regional turning point here, as it manifests the beginning of the end of the cycle of leftist governments in Latin America.

Identity Politics and Political Rationalities:
Racism and the Right to Kill

Since the 1990s, Latin America has been characterized by an astonishing democratic opening of the political field for formerly highly marginalized or even excluded groups. Indigenous movements in particular, having been almost completely pushed out of the political arena since the 19th century, were able to establish themselves with heterodox political programs. They advanced anti-neoliberal economic positions and were able to implement far-reaching multicultural recognition policies. With multicultural recognition policies, the Afrodescendant communities, discriminated against racially and socioeconomically disadvantaged, were also able to increase their political visibility and presence. In parallel, parts of the remaining working class came to occupy central positions of political power historically held by traditional elites. At the same time, a remarkable step toward gender equality in the political arena was noted in the region with women reaching even the highest offices. The heads of state of Argentina (Cristina Fernández de Kirchner), Chile (Michelle Bachelet), and Brazil (Dilma Rousseff) were popularly referred to simply as *las presidentas* (the women presidents). While these *presidentas* can be attributed to the boom of left-wing governments, there were also conservative women who became presidents, for example, Laura Chinchilla Miranda (2010–2014) and Mireya Moscoso (1999–2004) in Panama. The increasing political participation of women is also evident in parliaments. (Htun and Piscopo 2014) In Bolivia, for example, the proportion of female deputies was over 50%. While in 1990 the proportion of women in parliament in South America was still only 6%, in 2013 it was at 25%, turning Latin America into the world region with the highest presence of women in parliament.

This boom in the democratic opening of the political field, which began in the 1990s and peaked under the left-wing governments in the first decade of the 2000s, is now threatening to fall apart with new right-wing governments headed by moneyed aristocrats. A return of the "white man" who nostalgically insists on old privileges can be seen. As the Tea Party movement in the United States put it: "I want my country back!" This return means above all the abolition of inclusion measures such as affirmative action and gender mainstreaming and is directed against Afrodescendant and indigenous groups as well as against feminist causes or LGBT rights.

In the United States, Donald Trump won the 2016 presidential election with a program based on these very concerns. In Latin America, the government of Michel Temer, who brought himself to power in a cold coup in 2016, is particularly noteworthy in this context. Among the members of his first cabinet, there were no Afro-Brazilian or indigenous people and, for the first time since the end of the military dictatorship,

202 *The Refeudalization of Society*

no women. The Inter-American Commission on Human Rights sharply criticized this composition: "The naming of a cabinet of ministers that does not include women or persons of African descent leaves more than half of the population excluded from the highest offices of government" (Planas 2016). And in this, the ICHR has significantly understated the case. For in 2015, only 43,709,136 out of a total of 204,855,655 Brazilians were white men. This means that the cabinet represents only 21.3% of the population, and class positioning is not included here (IPEA). Under Jair Bolsonaro, this policy was continued and deepened.

The return of whiteness manifests itself in other forms as well. In Bolivia, the separatist *Nación Camba,* made up of right-wing extremists, primarily white youth militants from the *Union Juvenil Cruceñista,* demanded the independence of the province of Santa Cruz from the Plurinational Republic of Bolivia. The ideological basis of the movement was a regionalist discourse anchored in political culture, based also on the racist attitudes of the white regional elite against the indigenous majority of the Andean highlands. After the coup in Bolivia, Luis Fernando Camacho, formerly head of the *Union Juvenil Cruceñista,* became one of the spokesmen for the transitional government. Camacho comes from an oligarchic millionaire family in Santa Cruz that suffered heavy losses in the energy sector as a result of the Morales government's nationalization policy. After the decolonial turn under the MAS government, Camacho advocated for a white, Catholic, homophobic, and extremely conservative. The transitional government even discussed a general ban on indigenous clothing in parliament. Not a single representative of an indigenous organization was represented in Jeannine Áñez's transitional cabinet. With a view to the elections scheduled for May 3, 2020, the self-proclaimed interim president Áñez had warned with undisguised racism of the "return of the savages." Fortunately, she lost these elections.

But even left-wing governments were not immune to the rhetoric of whiteness and the sense of racial superiority based on it. In Ecuador, the leftist social democrat, President Rafael Correa, referred to the country's indigenous movement as "barbarians" and an "obstacle to the progress of the nation," (Kaltmeier 2016) harkening back to mid-19th century concepts of progress, civilization, and whitening. Similarly, the Chilean government refers to Mapuche communities fighting forestry corporations for land rights as internal enemies and "terrorists" against whom the anti-terror law dating back to the Pinochet dictatorship has been used.

These examples make clear how much whiteness is anchored in coloniality. It is a concept that itself often remains unclear—"unmarked"—in order to distinguish itself all the more clearly from a colonial Other that is marked by color. This marked difference is then given moral and cultural criteria of inferiority in relation to one's own assumed superiority. Whiteness is closely linked to the class position. In Ecuador, as in other Latin American countries with a high proportion of indigenous people,

The Refeudalization of Society 203

whiteness is an indicator of social status. Describing oneself as "white" often means at the same time assigning oneself to the middle class or elite and distinguishing oneself from a lower class marked as colored or indigenous. This operation also works in Brazil. Thus, Michel Temer, son of Lebanese migrants, who is phenotypically of color, is considered "white" and treated in the same way as a "white" Brazilian of European descent. In this vein, Cynthia Levine-Rasky states,

> 'Money whitens.' If any single phrase encapsulates the association of whiteness and the modern in Latin America, this is it. It is a cliché formulated and reformulated throughout the region, a truism dependent upon the social experience that wealth is associated with whiteness, and that in obtaining the former one may become aligned to the latter (and vice versa)
>
> (2002, 73).

In this sense, the rhetorical use of whiteness has a highly strategic character, as it can improve one's position in the identity-political field. In this context, whiteness is capital that can also be invested into education, dress, naming, place of residence, etc., and the improvement of inter-generational mobility. For centuries, investing in whiteness in Latin America can be seen as a safe capital investment with high returns. Due to the colonial character of Latin American societies, white identities were hardly questioned until the boom in multicultural recognition policies and the associated redefinition of many Latin American states as pluricultural or even plurinational.

Only with the multicultural turn in the mid-1990s did the threat of devaluation of the identity-political capital of whiteness arise for the white elites. Since whiteness itself was unmarked and based primarily on distinction from the colonial Other, no simple return to whiteness was possible during this phase. Instead, a nostalgic discourse of the search for identity emerged that was deeply marked by anxiety, as shown in the example of retro-coloniality. Charles M. Blow analyzed Donald Trump's political discourse in the New York Times in this same vein: "He appeals to something deeper, something meaner: fear. His whole campaign slogan, 'Make America Great Again,' is in fact a reverse admission of loss—lost primacy, lost privilege, lost prestige" (Blow 2016).

In this context, we are dealing with a paradoxically contradictory situation. As discussed in the chapter on the refeudalization of social structure, white elites have been able to strengthen their socioeconomic position to the point of status consolidation. And also the white middle class in Latin America—unlike in the United States—has benefited from the cycle of left-wing governments. On the other hand, they have lost their previously unchallenged privileged position in the political field and political culture in general. It is precisely this loss of power that gives rise

204   *The Refeudalization of Society*

to fears of a loss of privilege, which can at the same time lead to fantasies of violence and political aggression.

At the same time, whiteness, precisely because of its undefinedness as an "empty signifier," can serve as a node for articulating fear, insecurity, and loss of identity directed against others—indigenous people, Afrodescendants, communists, feminists, and so on. In this sense, a discursive chain of equivalence is constructed according to which the male, heterosexual, white person embodies conservative values such as patriarchy—nation—superiority—security—order. This chain of equivalence is thereby diametrically opposed to other signifiers such as multiculturalism—gender—queerness—political correctness—communism—chaos. Whiteness leaves a purely defensive position through this operation and begins to articulate a discourse of reconquest and revenge. In doing so, it is astonishing and frightening how fear can lead to fantasies of revenge and violence. In this sense, Gonzalo Portocarrero (2007) analyzed the dreams of white middle- and upper-class children in Lima in the 1990s, at the time of the conflict between guerrillas and the state. He found that children dreamed of bloody revenge and violence against perceived terrorists, who were almost always imagined as indigenous.

These imaginations of violence by the white middle and upper classes have often been enacted historically as well. The use of violence, such as rape and lynching practices, is deeply rooted in colonial legacies. Furthermore, the motif of revenge can certainly be found in the orgies of violence of military dictatorships that oppose the participation of popular classes in the political field.

The forms and expressions of violence in everyday political culture are linked to prejudice, "alternative facts," and communities that increasingly segregate themselves from the public sphere of communication, with a growing tendency toward re-sacralization. More and more segments of the population are turning to—often evangelical—faith communities and their promises of salvation. In terms of identity politics, parts of these religious groups correspond precisely with the trend toward refeudalization. In particular, the ideas of a spiritual war against "diabolical powers" that were already projected during the Cold War have been renewed and, via the traditional enemy of "communism," have also been directed at ethnic groups and, above all, the so-called "gender ideology." All of this promotes a new modern authoritarianism (Schäfer 2021, 147).

In this sense, elements of discursive and non-discursive violence can be found in the current refeudal conservative backlash in Latin America, directed against three target groups that can only be roughly outlined here.

The first—almost historical—target group of "angry white man's" revenge is the ethnically constructed Other. This includes the xenophobic rejection of migrants, seen as racially inferior. Yet these racial-ethnic criteria are in flux. While the United States uses racist justifications to

The Refeudalization of Society 205

close itself off to migrants from Central and South America, in Latin Americarecently in the case of Brazil—black migrants from Haiti are being targeted. Moreover, the rights of the indigenous population, expanded under recognition policies, are now being curtailed again.

The most striking example of the refeudal turn toward exclusion is Brazilian President Jair Bolsonaro, who was named "Racist of the Year" by the NGO Survival International in 2019. He had already lamented in 1998 that the Brazilian cavalry had not been as successful as the U.S. cavalry in the genocide against the indigenous population. In 2016, he advocated arming large-scale farmers to prevent even one more millimeter of land from being given to indigenous reserves or quilombos. Bolsonaro's aim is to remove the protections for indigenous territories and protected areas in order to make the land accessible to the agro-industry.

A second target group of the "angry white men" are women or groups aimed at gender mainstreaming and the recognition of sexual rights. In Brazil, the silent coup against President-elect Rousseff was also accompanied by the dissolution of the Ministry of Women, Racial Equality, and Human Rights. And in the first five months of Temer's term alone, four projects have been launched to abolish the right to abortion and to criminalize abortion (Biroli 2016, 565). In coordinated actions, conservative groups, often supported by radical Protestant churches, pushed for the abolition of "gender ideology" in school curricula. In this context, "gender ideology"—according to Flávia Biroli (2016)—is understood as the opposite of the "natural family" and "natural gender roles."

These identity-political positionings go hand in hand with a rapid fall of political-ethical taboos, expressed in, among other things, publicly expressed fantasies of violence and hate-speech against women. In 2014, for example, Jair Bolsonaro, a conservative member of parliament, at the time, and current president of Brazil, expressed rape fantasies and ideas of male superiority over women to the deputy Maria Do Rosário. Then-president Dilma Rousseff became a particular target of hate-speech. Posters equating her with a rabid dog, for example, read: "Beware of the beast! She was in the guerrillas, planned terrorist actions, enforced communism in Brazil with weapons and was sentenced to 3 years in prison. She defends abortion and wants to be the 'mother of Brazil'. Do you believe that?" This was compounded by vulgar sexist depictions of Rousseff on posters, stickers, and flyers of the right-wing movement.[8] The Brazilian anti-gender movement has had far-reaching effects on the academic field as well. In addition to the aforementioned cutbacks and programmatic changes in education, individual academics are also being directly defamed. A conference co-organized by Judith Butler in São Paulo in November 2017 (relevantly on "The Ends of Democracy") provoked vigorous protest. The protesters demanded, among other things: "Burn the witch!" Butler herself rationalized the incident this way: "The people who are against me believe that gender is a 'devilish ideology.'

206 *The Refeudalization of Society*

[...] Much of the support on the right is based on strong traditionalist, anti-feminist, anti-(LGBTQ+) values" (Johnson 2017). In this respect, it is in the field of gender politics that the cultural-political dimension of the current trends toward refeudalization, which undermine democratic and academic debates and create the climate of a new "witch hunt," becomes apparent.

A third target is the popular sectors. In this sense, it is difficult to speak of populism on the part of the new right-wing governments. Instead, it is precisely the popular sectors that had supported the left-wing governments that are being punished. The Universidad Católica Argentina estimates that the number of poor people in the country increased by 1.4 million in the first quarter of 2016 after Mauricio Macri took office. More and more small and medium-sized enterprises are running into difficulties because prices are rising and purchasing power of Argentines has fallen by 10%, even according to the most conservative estimates. The poor have also been affected by massive the price increases for basic necessities, while organized labor has been hit by mass layoffs, especially in the public sector. The latter is also to be expected in other Latin American countries as the rightward shift is associated with a return to neoliberal policies.

So far, this analysis has focused on the positioning of the moneyed aristocracy in the political field. But in terms of social structure, it has been argued that only the richest 1%–10% of the total population are involved here. In this respect, the question arises: Who supports this ruling class of the 1%–10% and why?

The historical economic crisis of left-wing governments in Latin America is often explained by the drop in commodity prices. The leftist governments had financed social integration and programs of poverty reduction with the direct and indirect revenues generated by extractivist economic models. For this reason, an economic explanation for the political crisis of the left-wing governments is preferred in most current discussions: Falling commodity prices meant that social programs could no longer be financed. As plausible as this explanation may seem at first glance, the economic situation is far more complex. Although the drop in the price of raw materials, especially oil, cannot be dismissed out of hand, a look at the economic growth rates creates a more differentiated perspective. From 2010 to 2014, the gross domestic product (GDP) in South America increased. It was not until 2015 that GDP shrank by 0.8%. Here, the −3.5% of Brazil, the largest economy in the region and the 7th largest in the world, depressed the balance especially (Cepal 2016). Without the contraction of the Brazilian economy, South America would still have been able to show slightly positive economic growth in 2015. Accordingly, Cepal projected a 4.5% increase in GDP for Bolivia and 3.9% for Peru in 2016. Even better were the economic prospects in Central America, where high GDP growth rates were expected in Nicaragua

The Refeudalization of Society 207

(4.5), Guatemala (3.5), and Honduras (3.4). Thus, these countries were well above the expected global growth rate of 2.4% (Cepal 2016). In order to explore the link between economic stagnation and the loss of political legitimacy, a differentiated view at specific country studies is necessary, which cannot be provided in this chapter.

A similarly differentiated argument can be made for the thesis of the special relevance of conflicts involving identity politics for the crisis of political legitimacy of left-wing governments put forward in this chapter. A more far-reaching explanatory model in this direction is emerging in Brazil. The Fundação Perseu Abramo, a foundation close to the Workers' Party (PT), conducted a study to explain the loss of acceptance among the working population in the periphery of São Paulo. One finding was that it is precisely the "newer lower middle class" who benefited most from social programs and inclusion that is now turning away from the PT (Nozaki and Souza 2017). These new lower middle-class members seek individual recognition and, in doing so, are susceptible to the achievement and competition-based thinking of the neoliberal right as well as conservative evangelical churches. This analytical approach can be taken further with recourse to the considerations of the sociologist Zygmunt Bauman. Bauman identifies a new narcissism in the current global consumer society, which, ultimately, is fear-driven and on the permanent search for meaning in life in a de-ideologized society. Along with Christopher Lasch, Bauman argues that this new narcissist is quite detached from ideological dogma, which also means that he "loses the security of group loyalties and perceives everyone as a rival for the favors that a paternalistic state has to bestow" (Bauman 2017, 153). Here it becomes clear how the principle of invidious comparison aimed at distinction, which Veblen diagnosed in the leisure class, has now permeated the everyday world of all social segments.

This is accompanied by social amnesia, especially among the segments of the population that have risen to the middle class in the short term. They "forget" their class origins, or those of their parents, and see their own social advancement, which they owe to the integrative social policy of center-left governments, as individual advancement. According to their self-perception, it was not a social policy that was decisive, but—in narcissistic terms—their own abilities. Therefore, the social climber is neither obliged to society, embodied in the state nor does he have to practice solidarity with the lower classes. For the latter have been less successful in comparison to their own "performance" and are therefore to blame for their own misery. And—to return to the study—the new narcissistic middle class no longer feels addressed in the focus on poverty from the PT. Even more, they feel repelled by stigmatizing terms that link them to poverty, the working class, simple labor, etc., and seek a social distance from these segments. They now want to translate their just-won economic capital into identity-political capital—whiteness—in order to break free

208   *The Refeudalization of Society*

from racism and stigmatization. In doing so, they paradoxically reproduce the social logic of stigmatization. The children eat their revolution.

While this model certainly has a certain plausibility for parts of the new middle classes beyond Brazil, which would still have to be proven in further empirical studies, it can already be stated that it does not have an exclusive explanatory character. A look at Ecuador reveals this. Here, parts of the left-wing indigenous movement allied with the right-wing candidate, millionaire banker Guillermo Lasso, in order to prevent a new presidency of Rafael Correa's party. Accordingly, the indigenous organization Ecuarunari justified not supporting the Alianza País candidate as follows: "Better a banker than a dictator!" In the Ecuadorian case, the fault lines in the politics of identity cannot be defined by simple left-right positions alone. At an early stage, Rafael Correa had proclaimed a *revolución ciudadana*, a civic revolution, which primarily represented the interests of the mestizo middle class and had broken with the indigenous movement early on. Paradoxically, in 2019, ten years later, Correistas and the indigenous movement were reunited in the streets in protest against the structural adjustment program negotiated with the IMF by Lenín Moreno, the successor to the presidency who is now at odds with Correa. It is questionable, —, whether the wheel of history can be turned back to the beginning of the Revolución Ciudadana when both actors had worked out an innovative project of social and cultural change under the banner of *Buen Vivir* (Good Living).

The crude, racist, misogyny, and often post-factual rhetoric is only the tip of the iceberg in the transformation of political culture. Far more worrisome are the emerging techniques of government in the Foucauldian sense. Regarding indigenous people and Afrodescendant communities, there has been an end to neoliberal multicultural recognition politics. The new instances of ethno-governmentality, according to which indigenous people are supposed to govern themselves in order to establish themselves as market subjects and citizens, are being abolished or disempowered. Instead of relying on techniques of self-government, there is currently a return to sovereign power, which Foucault characterizes as the right to kill. A core aspect of the governmental techniques of the various right-wing governments is punishment—precisely in order to secure the now authoritarian-neoliberal project. For example, the Chilean government describes the Mapuche communities fighting for land rights against the forestry corporations as the enemy within and "terrorists" and applies the anti-terror laws stemming from the Pinochet dictatorship against them. A virtual state of emergency has been imposed against the Mapuche, and liberal liberties are suspended (Kaltmeier 2022, 303–333). Police and military action against indigenous peoples is also increasing in other regions, especially when they oppose extractivist projects (mining, soy, palm oil, etc.) or mega-projects (dam construction, transportation infrastructure).

The Refeudalization of Society   209

This state exercise of sovereign power is accompanied by para-state violent actors, some of whom are tolerated by the state and others who are intertwined with state authorities. According to the NGO Global Witness, Brazil, Colombia, Nicaragua, and Honduras are among the countries in which the most "defenders of the earth"—often indigenous people—are murdered worldwide. African-descendant and/or feminist activists are also targeted, as evidenced by the murder of Maristelle Franco in Brazil. Most recently, there have been pogrom-like racist outrages against Mapuche in Chile. The same can be observed in Bolivia during the period of the reactionary transitional government. While the feminist movement has been able to articulate broad protest with movements such as #NiUnaMenos or #NiUnaMás (Roth 2020), indigenous movements are limited primarily to discourses of defense.

But women are also especially affected by refeudal forms of violence. Feminist Rita Segato has analyzed the violence against women, especially with respect to femicide in Ciudad Juarez, as a "regressive trend between postmodernity and feudalism" (2016, 48). She states,

> The crimes, thus, would seem to speak of a true bestial 'right of pernada', of a feudal and postmodern baron with his group of acolytes, as an expression par excellence of his absolutist dominion over a territory, where the right over the woman's body is an extension of the lord's right over his glebe
>
> (2016, 48).

Parallel to these active techniques of punishment, the sovereign biopolitical power to decide who is designated to die is central. Instead of an active politics of empowerment, help is omitted and lives are wasted. Perhaps the most emblematic example of this is Bolsonaro's biopolitics of the pandemic, which in part even prohibited aid organizations from assisting indigenous and Afro-Brazilian communities in the fight against the COVID-19 pandemic.

From Refeudalization to a New Communism?

The feudalism-capitalism debate of the 1970s in Latin America was not conducted solely in and for the academic ivory tower. Rather, it had far-reaching implications for the elaboration of political positions and strategies. Traditional proponents of the feudalism thesis argued primarily in the intellectual universe of Western development theories, including Marxist stage models. According to them, feudalism could only be replaced by a bourgeois revolution. A socialist alternative could then only be realized after this initial stage. The problem, however, according to many dependency theorists, was that the Latin American bourgeoisie had been penetrated by the imperialist interests of North America and

210   *The Refeudalization of Society*

Western Europe and thus had not fulfilled its historical task, that of a national bourgeois revolution. In their critical appraisal of the political role of the bourgeoisie, world-system theorists such as André Gunder Frank went even further. According to them, a bourgeois or even social-ist revolution in one country, especially one from the periphery, is hardly possible due to the interdependencies in the capitalist world system.

Latin American societies are facing a very similar starting position as well as in the context of the current trend of refeudalization. There are doubts both with regard to national special paths in view of the deep embedding in a global capitalist system and with regard to a pos-sible emancipative role of the remaining factions of the bourgeoisie in Latin America. The difficulty of national special paths can be seen in Venezuela's 21st-century oil-funded socialism, still highly dependent on the price fluctuations on the world market. The most far-reaching attempt to fulfill the supposed historical role of the bourgeoisie in the process of nation-building has certainly taken place in the context of the Revolución Ciudadana in Ecuador. Here, a new bourgeois faction was temporarily built up through inclusion in the state apparatus, but this faction has become increasingly disconnected from the needs of the rural, indige-nous lower classes. A final assessment of the projects, which are currently in multiple deep crises, has yet to be made, while in many other places in Latin America, the conjuncture of refeudalization is booming.

And despite these insights from the world-systems approach, the view of the French Revolution, which repeatedly shines through as a beacon in the work of Piketty and Crouch, still has a considerable appeal. With recourse to the lessons of history, it could easily be argued that we now need a new bourgeois revolution in the face of the new refeudalization. While historical analogies always have limited explanatory depth, it is worth pointing out the problematic aspects of the transition from feudal-ism to capitalism in Western Europe. Ultimately, social polarization was hardly overcome during the bourgeois revolution. Political and social betterment did not exist for all segments of the Third Estate. In this respect, it should be said that the "citoyen," the democratic citizen, can-not have been here without the "bourgeois," the capitalist. And the latter, in a process of "aristocratization of the bourgeoisie" (Wallerstein 1988), has given rise to today's moneyed aristocracy. In this respect—especially in view of the role of the Latin American bourgeoisie in the 19th and 20th centuries—a historical skepticism with regard to a possible renewal of a bourgeois revolution is appropriate.

Instead of betting on a new bourgeois revolution, it seems stimulating to me to turn to other historical situations of feudal conflict. Thus, beyond the exploitation of unfree labor and the lack of freedom, another major field of conflict can be identified. One can think of the feudalization and colonization of common goods. Although the commons were at times integrated into the feudal system, the various forms of the commons are

The Refeudalization of Society   211

mostly indigenous legal systems of resource use that preceded feudalism. In Germany, the commons are of old Germanic origin, while in Latin America, it is mostly based on the practices of communitarian use by indigenous cultures.

In the early modern period, increasing pressure on the commons can be observed. Already in the early 16th century, the robbery of the commons was a major reason for the outbreak of the German Peasants' War. In the 18th century, the Enclosure Acts in England were directed against the commons and led to a pauperization of large parts of the population. And during European expansion, the so-called advanced primitive accumulation in the colonial territories led to land grabbing of, among other things, communally used lands.

Today, the concept of the commons is used not only for the legally regulated use of common property (pasture, water, forest) but also for all forms of use of public goods in general, especially information technology. At the same time, forms of common use beyond the regulation of the market and the state have once again become the focus of economic work. Elinor Ostrom was awarded the 2009 Nobel Prize in Economics for her work on "governing the commons," while Antonio Negri and Michael Hardt cite "commonwealth" (2009) as an alternative in *Empire*. Over the processes of refeudalization discussed here, the question of the commons is of central importance, as it is able to oppose "the further privatization and commercialization of natural knowledge, [and] public space in favor of another form of institutional organization" (Unmüßig 2012, 13). In Latin America, approaches for such alternative forms of use, embedded also in various indigenous cosmovisions, can be found above all in the current debate around Buen Vivir.

Beyond the question of use, another philosophical concept that decisively shaped the short 20th century is also at stake with the commons. Namely, communism. This is not a return to the teachings of Marx, Engels, and Lenin, but rather a movement of thought that, closely interwoven with specific historical contexts, opposes the current tendencies of refeudalizing private appropriation to focus on the question of the commons. In this conception, communism would not only be determined by the class struggle, which is today forced "from above," but also by already existing, expandable anti-hegemonic spaces and practices. For such a reorientation of communism, reference should be made to the debates between, among others, Alain Badiou, Jean-Luc Nancy, Slavoy Žižek, as well as Michael Hardt and Toni Negri, as they were conducted in London in 2009 and in the following year at the Berlin Volksbühne (Douzinas and Žižek 2012).

Following on from these debates and based on the analysis of refeudalization, this long political chapter will now conclude by outlining possible horizons for containing or overcoming the current conjuncture of refeudalization. In terms of social structure, many Latin American

212 *The Refeudalization of Society*

countries are experiencing a deepening of an already historically pronounced social polarization, which, especially in view of the latest developments in inheritance within the moneyed aristocracy, is showing clear signs of class consolidation with low intergenerational mobility. While the ruling moneyed aristocracy has managed to assert its interests politically since the 1980s, the multitude remains fragmented. Here, there is a clear discrepancy between the theoretically constructed "classes on paper" (Bourdieu), based on social-structural data, and class consciousness. A social polarization between the 1% and the 99% may be statistically ascertainable, but this does not automatically translate into a generalized awareness of this fact. In this respect, possible state or suprastate measures of redistribution are paradoxically made more expensive precisely by those segments of the middle and upper lower classes that are willing to move up and who would hardly be affected by them in real terms. One could think of such redistribution mechanisms as inheritance tax, higher wealth tax, and national and international taxation of financial transactions (Tobin tax) or the profits made from them.

Considering the extreme inequality in the distribution of agricultural land since colonial times, refeudalization tendencies can hardly be stopped without agrarian reform in Latin America. In this sense, it is desirable to re-create a social climate in which the project of agrarian reform becomes hegemonic. Just as the *hacienda* was described as a "feudal remnant" that had to be overcome in 1970s Ecuador, the extreme large-scale land ownership of the agro-barons should also be seen as amoral and a danger to social cohesion. But steps toward agrarian reform are by no means easy. Historically, every successful agrarian reform in Latin America has been accompanied by a social revolution, as in Mexico in 1910, Bolivia in 1952, Cuba in 1959, and Chile in 1970. In addition, the various forms of communitarization of land should be considered. One should think here of the allocation or restitution of land titles to indigenous and Afrodescendant peoples, but also of state nature reserves, which—sometimes in conflict with small farmers—withdraw land from extractivist use and protect it across generations.

In the economic field, a fundamental contradiction seems to be that current refeudalization is based on extensive accumulation through dispossession. Whether through neoliberal policies of privatization and the rules of the market or direct violence and displacement, communal goods have been expropriated and transferred into the private property of the moneyed aristocracy. Besides this direct expropriation, there is a hidden expropriation through tax evasion or the use or consumption of public goods without reciprocal payments. Against these tendencies of cost externalization and accumulation by robbery, it seems to be a reasonable perspective to expand public goods. Especially in the areas of social services, free, tax-financed models for health care and infrastructure for all citizens are conceivable.

The expansion of knowledge communities, as ensured by software projects such as Ubuntu or Open/Libre Office, or licenses through Creative Commons, represents a special area in this respect. It is precisely through the expansion of the knowledge commons in the IT sector that the Silicon Valley billionaires, who have made their wealth on companies such as Microsoft, Facebook, or Google, are deprived of a material basis.

In general, the current conjuncture of refeudalization has been determined in its economic dimensions by the neoliberal wave of deregulation, which, à la *Jurassic World*, lets the T-Rex and the small herbivores clash in free competition. But in some sectors of the economy, today's monetary aristocracy benefits precisely from legal restrictions. This applies above all to the dark web of capitalism. For example, the legalization and controlled distribution of drugs would dry up an illegal branch of business that not only provokes the formation of criminal associations but also represents a not negligible current in the general tendency toward refeudalization.

One of the main cultural-political problems for pushing back refeudalization processes is the deep entrenchment of consumer (un)culture in large parts of the population that are deeply divided, as is the entirety of refeudalized society. Thus, the distinctive ostentatious luxury consumption of the moneyed aristocracy is contrasted with a mass consumerism that increasingly relies on exclusivity and target group specificity, driving large parts of the population into a new debt bondage through private indebtedness. A true cultural revolution is necessary to counteract this tendency. One alternative perspective would be to replace consumption with care. This follows from feminist debates about *decent work* and often unpaid care work as well as from the demands for sustainable care (e.g., stewardship) of our planet coming from the environmental movement. More profound philosophical concepts of care can be derived from Heidegger's interpretation of care for being, which goes far beyond individualistic maximization of utility and refers to the ontological fact of a common being in the world.

Paradoxically, a seed of an implementable care economy is definitely contained in the current value creation debate of refeudalization. Thus, Boltanski and Esquerre, in their diagnosis of the "enrichment economy," also emphasized that value creation, especially with regard to heritage products, takes place through enrichment when high-quality products are cared for and refined by invested labor. In this respect, care—through repairs, restorations, or mending—can certainly also increase the value of objects, conserve resources and provide an alternative leitmotif to the current instant-to-go consumer culture.

Class boundaries, intrinsically linked to ethnic markers, were relevant for participation in public space in Latin America until well into the 20th century. This tendency has—paradoxically—regained de facto importance in a historical period that, like the 1990s in Latin America, was shaped by the de jure dismantling of racism and pluricultural recognition. With the creeping end of the "left turn" in Latin America, there now

214   *The Refeudalization of Society*

seems to be little state-regulated policy to democratize public spaces. The trend points to a reinforced refeudalization of space.

Communitization, especially regarding the use of space, is the central strategy to prevent and dismantle the walls and citadels in the course of re-feudalization. What is needed is a subsequent advocacy for public space. In this sense, the appeal to a public space guaranteed by the state and the administration remains an essential strategy, especially in times of a conservative wave. At the same time, privately and communally organized public spheres must be strengthened. In this context, the defense of everyday public places should also be considered. In many Latin American cities, for example, the plaza fulfills the function of a public place characterized by the encounter of different social groups.

In the political field, a tendency toward despotism can be discerned in the doubling of economic power into political power. Here, the rise of left-wing governments, all of which came to power only with massive popular support from the "third estate" of the 99%, has shown that it is quite possible to put the moneyed aristocracy with its lobby groups, spin doctors, and media moguls in their place. The popular, pluricultural, and plurinational democratic participation within the political process that has been gained is an achievement that must be defended, especially in the face of the massive erosion of political morality and the rise of whiteness and racism.

At the same time, the experience of the rise and subsequent creeping fall of pink tide governments has also made it clear that it is not possible to rely on hegemonic struggles alone. Authors from movements critical of globalization have rightly criticized the "hegemony of hegemony" in the thinking of the left and pointed out that it is equally necessary to pursue a politics of affinity. Here, it was a matter of building one's own affinity-based spaces and networks to live the alternatives already in the here and now.

Translation: Matti Steinitz

Notes

1. This passage from a section titled "Sumaria Revisión Histórica" was added posthumously to the Spanish editions of the *Siete ensayos de interpretación de la realidad peruana* but is not included in the English translation *Seven Interpretative on Peruvian Reality*.
2. These were: Bill Gates, Amancio Ortega Gaona, Warren E. Buffett, Carlos Slim Helú, Jeff Bezos, Mark Zuckerberg, Lawrence J. Ellison, Michael R. Bloomberg. In 2022 Elon Musk was the richest man in the world, while also Asian billionaires such as Mukesh Ambani and Gautam Adani entered the Top 10 of the Forbes Magazine.
3. The Gini coefficient is a statistical measurement of unequal distributions. It is based on a value between 0 (in the case of an even distribution, i.e., every individual in the group has the same share) and 1 (in the case of maximal unequal distribution, i.e., all values, for example, income or landownership, are concentrated in just one person).

The Refeudalization of Society 215

4. Only Germany, the country with the most billionaires in Europe (148 in 2013), has a similar ratio. Here, the wealth of 46% of billionaires is based on inherited assets; and only 33% of the German super-rich have built up their wealth themselves (Wealth-X 2013).
5. At this point, we will not delve into the discussion about genetic engineering in the agricultural industry. However, I would like to briefly address the counterarguments. From an ecological point of view, the criticism is that the consequences of outcrossing and outgrowth are not foreseeable, and that biological biodiversity is threatened by the combination of genetic engineering and agrochemicals. The legal situation for possible consequential damages is unclear. In addition, new relationships of dependency and considerable additional costs arise for farmers.
6. The Brazilian Odebrecht Group paid upon to 785 million U.S. dollars in bribes in twelve countries, mainly in Latin America, in order to obtain construction contracts. A clandestine "bribery department" was installed for this purpose only.
7. I thank Heinrich Schäfer for pointing me to this interesting construction project.
8. I deliberately refrain from illustrating the offensive and sexist images here. However, I refer to the analysis by Biroli (2016).

Bibliography

Agamben, Giorgio. 2014. "God didn't die, he was transformed into money" In: libcom.org, 10.02.2014. [https://libcom.org/article/god-didnt-die-he-was-transformed-money-interview-giorgio-agamben-peppe-sava].

Altvater, Elmar and Birgit Mahnkopf. 1996. *Grenzen der Globalisierung: Ökonomie, Ökologie und Politik in der Weltgesellschaft.* Münster: Westfälisches Dampfboot.

Bastos, Santiago. 2014. Multicultural Projects in Guatemala: IdentityTensions and Everyday Ideologies. In: Olaf Kaltmeier, Sebastian Thies und Josef Raab (Ed.): *The new dynamics of identity politics in the Americas: Multiculturalism and beyond.* London: Routledge, 78–95.

Bauman, Zygmunt. 1998. Das Jahrhundert der Lager? In: Mihran Dabagund Kristin Platt (Ed.): *Genozid und Moderne: Strukturen kollektiver Gewalt im 20. Jahrhundert.* Opladen: Leske und Budrich, 81–99.

Bauman, Zygmunt. 2005. *Vidas desperciadas. La modernidad y sus parias.* Buenos Aires: Paidós.

Bauman, Zygmunt. 2007. *Consuming Life.* Cambridge: Cambridge University Press.

Bauman, Zygmunt. 2017. *Retrotopia.* Frankfurt a.M.: Suhrkamp.

Beaverstock, Jonathan. 2012. "The Privileged World City: Private Banking, Wealth Management and the Bespoke Servicing of the Global Super-rich." In: Ben Derudder, Michael Hoyler, Peter J. Taylor and Frank Witlox (Ed.): *International Handbook of Globalization and World Cities.* Northhampton: Edward Elgar Publishing, 378–389.

Biroli, Flávia. 2016. "Political violence against women in Brazil: expressions and definitions." *Direito & Práxis,* 07, 15, 557–589.

Blakely, Edward J and Mary Gail Snyder. 1999. *Fortress America: Gated Communities in the United States.* Washington, DC: Brookings Institution Press.

216   The Refeudalization of Society

Blow, Charles. 2016. Trump reflects White Male Fragility. In: New York Times, 04.08.2016.[www.nytimes.com/2016/08/04/opinion/trump-reflects-white-male-fragility.html].

Boano, Camillo and Belen Desmaison. 2016. Lima's 'Wall of Shame' and the gated communities that build poverty into Peru. In: The Conversation, 11.02.2016. [http://theconversation.com/limas-wall-of-shame-and-the-gated-communities-that-build-poverty-into-peru-53356].

Bogan, Jesse. 2009. Cocaine King. In: Forbes, 20.03.2009. Online verfügbar unter [http://forbes.com/forbes/2009/0330/102-cocaine-king.html#sogace33c812].

Bogliacino, Francesco and Daniel Rojas Lozarno. 2017. The evolution of in-equality in Latin America in the 21st century: What are the patterns, drivers and causes? In: GLO Discussion Paper 57. [http://hdl.handle.net/10419/156723].

Boltanski, Luc and Armaud Esquerre. 2016. "The Economic Life of Things." *New Left Review*, 98, 8, 31–54.

Boltanski, Luc and Armaud Esquerre. 2017. "Enrichment, Profit, Critique. A Rejoinder to Nancy Fraser." *New Left Review*, 106, 67–76.

Boris, Dieter et al. 2008. *Sozialstrukturen in Lateinamerika: Ein Überblick.* Wiesbaden: VS Verlag.

Boym, Svetlana. 2001. *Future of Nostalgia*. New York, NY: Basic Books.

Brand, Ulrich. 2016. "Neo-Extraktivismus, Aufstieg und Krise eines Ent-wicklungsmodells." *Aus Politik und Zeitgeschichte*, 39/2016, 21–26.

Burchardt, Hans-Jürgen. 2016. "Zeitenwende? Lateinamerikas neue Krisen und Chancen." *Aus Politik und Zeitgeschichte,* 39/2016, 4–9.

Büschges, Christian. 1996. *Familie, Ehre und Macht: Konzept und soziale Wirklichkeit des Adels in der Stadt Quito (Ecuador) während der späten Kolonialzeit, 1765-1822*. Stuttgart: Steiner.

Bussolo, Maurizio, Maryla Maliszewska and Elie Murard. 2014. "The Long-Awaited Rise of the Middle Class in Latin America is Finally Happening." In: *Policy Research Working Paper 6912*. Washington, DC. http://hdl.handle.net/10986/18767 License: CC BY 3.0 IGO.

Butler, J. 2003. "Violence, Mourning, Politics." *Studies in Gender and Sexuality*, 4, 1, 9–37.

Capgemini. 2017. World Wealth Report. Latin America. [http://www.worldwealthreport.com/reports/population/latin_america[.

Capgemini. 2021. World Wealth Report 2021. [https://www.capgemini.com].

Castells, Manuel. 2001. *The rise of the network society*. Oxford: Blackwell.

CEPAL. 2016. Estudio Económico de América Latina y el Caribe 2016: La Agenda 2030 para el Desarollo Sostenible y los desafios del financiamiento para el desarollo. [https://www.cepal.org/en/publications/40327-economic-survey-latin-america-and-caribbean-2016-2030-agenda-sustainable].

Chavkin, Sasha and Emilia Diaz-Struck. 2017. *The Offshore Connections of Latin American Presidents, Ministers and Business Leaders Revealed*. ICIJ. [https://www.icij.org/investigations/paradise-papers/paradise-papers-offshore-connections-latin-american-presidents-ministers-business-leaders-revealed/].

CIA. 2018. World Factbook. [https://www.cia.gov/the-world-factbook/].

Ciudad Cayalá. 2018. [https://cayala.com.gt/nosotros/historia/].

Clement, Raquel and Jill. L. Grant. 2012. "Enclosing Paradise: The Design of Gated Communities in Barbados." *Journal of Urban Design*, 17, 1, 43–60. [https://www.tandfonline.com/doi/full/10.1080/13574809.2011.646249?needAccess=true].

The Refeudalization of Society 217

Conadecus. 2011. Trajetas de crédito: La esclavitud moderna. [https://www.conadecus.cl/tarjetas-de-credito-la-esclavitud-moderna/].

Continental Citizenship. [https://continental-citizenship.com/citizenship-by-investment/].

Corak, Miles. 2012. Great Gatsby Curve. [https://milescorak.com/2012/01/12/here-is-the-source-for-the-great-gatsby-curve-in-the-alan-krueger-speech-at-the-center-for-american-progress/].

Credit Suisse Research Institute. 2016. *Global Wealth Databook*. Zürich. [https://www.credit-suisse.com/media/assets/corporate/docs/about-us/research/publications/global-wealth-databook-2016.pdf].

Crouch, Colin. 2004. *Post-Democracy*. New York, NY: Wiley.

Da Silva, Costa and Carlos Henrique. 2015. Characteristics and Trends of Luxury Commerce in Sao Paulo (Brazil). In: Études caribéennes. Online verfügbar unter [https://journals.openedition.org/etudesca-ribeennes/7378].

Davis, Mike. 2007. *Planet of Slums*. New York, NY: Verso Books.

De Ferranti, David et al. 2004. Inequality in Latin America. *Breaking with History?* Washington, DC: World Bank.

Debord, Guy. 1967. *The Society of the Spectacle*. Paris: Buchet-Chastel.

Deininger, Klaus and Lyn Squire. 1996. "A New Data Set Measuring Income Inequality." *The World Bank Economic Review*, 10, 3, 565–591.

Del Cueto, Carla and Mariana Luzzi. 2010. "Betrachtungen über eine fragmentierte Gesellschaft. Veränderungen der argentinischen Sozialstruktur (1983-2008)." In: Peter Birle, Klaus Bodemer, Andrea Pagni (Ed.): *Argentinien heute: Politik, Wirtschaft, Kultur. Frankfurt a.M.*, 33–54. Frankfurt a.M: Vervuert.

Douzinas, Costas and Zižek Slavoj. 2012. *Die Idee des Kommunismus. Band 1.* Hamburg: Laika.

Dunker, C. 2015. *Mal-estar, sofrimento e sintorna*. São Paulo: Boitempo.

Edwards, Alberto. 1928. *La fronda. Aristocrática en Chile*. Santiago de Chile: Imprenta Nacional.

El Mercurio. 2007. "La historia del inmigrante italiano que llegó a ser le más rico de Chile". August 29, 2007.

Elwert, Georg. 1999. "Markets of Violence." In: Georg Elwert, Stephan Feuchtwang and Dieter Neubert (Ed.): *Dynamics of Violence. Pro-cesses of Escalation and De-Escalation in Violent Group Conflicts*. Berlin: Duncker & Humblot, 85–102.

Engels, Friedrich. 1972. *Die Lage der arbeitenden Klasse in England*. Dietz Verlag: Berlin.

Erdmann, Gero. 2002. "Neopatrimoniale Herrschaft—oder: Warum es in Afrika so viele Hybridregime gibt." In: Petra Bendel, Aurel Croissant and Friedbert W. Rüb (Ed.): *Zwischen Demokratie und Diktatur*. Wiesbaden: VS Verlag, 323–342.

Escobar, Germán. 2016. La relevancia de la agricultura en América Latina y el Caribe. In: *Revista Nueva Sociedad*. Buenos Aires, Argentina. https://static.nuso.org/media/documents/agricultura.pdf.

Espinoza, Fran. 2013. Bolivia, élite sectorial chola y élite política: las ambivalencias du su relación. In: *Anuario de Acción Humanitaria y de Derechos Humanos 1.* Bilbao: Universidad de Deusto, 141–160.

218 *The Refeudalization of Society*

Estrada Mejia, Rafael and Carla Guerrón Montero. 2016. Brazilian Elitist Gated Communities as the New Version of the Colonial Portuguese Fort. In: Panoramas, 04.10.2016. [https://www.panoramas.pitt.edu/health-and-society/ brazilian-elitist-gated-communities-new-version-colonial-portuguese-fort].

Evans, Michelle. 2014. Arrival of Financial Cards to Latin America Led to Credit Binge. [https://www.euromonitor.com/article/arrival-of-financial-cards-to-latin-america-led-to-credit-binge].

Evers, H.-D. 1987. "Subsistenzproduktion, Markt und Staat. Der sog. Bielefelder Verflechtungsansatz." *Geographische Rundschau*, 39, 136–140.

Fabian, Johannes. 1983. Time and the Other. *How Anthropology Makes Its Object*. New York, NY: Columbia University Press.

FAO. 2017. América Latina y el Caribe es la región con la mayor desigualdad en la distribución de la tierra. [www.fao.org/americas/noticias/ver/es/c/ 879000/].

Fischer, Karin. 2011. Eine Klasse für sich. Besitz, Herrschaft und ungleiche Entwicklung in Chile 1830-2010. Baden-Baden: Nomos.

Fischermann, Thomas. 2008. "Reich wie nie" Die Zeit, 4. September 2008. [https://www.zeit.de/2008/37/Superreiche].

Forbes. 2009. [https://www.forbes.com/consent/?tohttps://www.forbes.com/ business/lists/2009/10/billionaires-2009-richest-people_Joaquin-Guzman-Loera_FS0Y.html]

Frank, André Gunder. 1969. *Kapitalismus und Unterentwicklung in Lateinamerika*. Frankfurt a.M.: EVA.

Gamboa, José and Julián Dextre. 2016. *Estudio Inicial y Plan Maestro del Provecto de Playa de 'Las Calas'. Master Thesis*, Universidad Católica del Perú.

GCC. 2014. Wealth Insight Report. [https://www.eibank.com/assets/pdf/GCC_ Wealth_Insight_Report.pdf].

Gottdiener, Mark. 1995. *Postmodern Semiotics: Material Culture and the Forms of Postmodern Life*. New York, NY: Wiley-Blackwell.

Gottdiener, Mark. 2001. *The Theming of America: Dreams, Visions, and Commercial Spaces*. Boulder, CO: Westview Press.

Grain. 2016. The global farmland grab in 2016: how big? how bad? [https://www. grain.org/article/entries/5492-the-global-farmland-grab-in-2016-how-big-how-bad].

Greenpeace. 2005. Eklat bei der Verleihung der Goldenen Kettensäge: Preisträger auf der Flucht. [https://www.greenpeace.de/themen/waelder/eklat-bei-der-verleihung-der-goldenen-kettensaege-preistraeger-auf-der-flucht].

Grosfoguel, Ramón. 2008. "Developmentalism, Modernity, and Dependency Theory in Latin America." In: Moraña, Mabel, Enrique Dussel and Carlos C. Jáuregui (Ed.): *Coloniality at large*. Durham: Duke University Press, 307–333.

Gudynas, Eduardo. 2010. "Ten Urgent Theses about Extractivism in Relation to Current South American Progressivism. Americas Program Report, 14." In: Schuldt, Jürgen et al. (Ed.): *Extractivismo, política y sociedad*. Quito: Centro Andino de Acción Popular, 187–225.

Habermas, Jürgen. 1962. *Strukturwandel der Öffentlichkeit: Untersuchungen zu einer Kategorie der bürgerlichen Gesellschaft*. Frankfurt a.M.: Suhrkamp.

Hardt, Michael and Antonio Negri. 2000. *Empire*. Cambridge: Cambridge University Press.

The Refeudalization of Society 219

Hardt, Michael and Antonio Negri. 2009. *Commonwealth*. Cambridge: Cambridge University Press.

Harvey, David. 2001. Spaces of Capital. *Towards a Critical Geography*. London: Routledge.

Heeren, Anne. 2016. Commercialization of Biodiversity: The Regulation of Bioprospecting in Ecuador. In: Forum for Interamerican Research 9.2. [http://interamerica.de/wp-content/uploads/2016/09/06_fiar-Vol.-9.2-Heeren-94-117.pdf].

Hinkelammert, Franz. 2021. *La crítica de las ideologías frente a la crítica de la religión. Volver a Marx trascendiéndolo*, Buenos Aires: CLACSO.

Htun, Mala and Jennifer Piscopo. 2014. Women in Politics and Policy in Latin America and the Caribbean. In: CPPF Working Papers on Women in Politics 2. [http://webarchive.ssrc.org/working-papers/CPPF_WomenIn Politics_02_Htun_Piscopo.pdf].

ICIJ. 2017. Explore the Politicians in the Paradise Papers. [https://www.icij.org/investigations/paradise-papers/explore-politicians-paradise-papers]/.

ICSC 2009. 2008 Winners: ICSC 32nd Design and International Development Award. [https://www.yumpu.com/en/document/read/26249369/2008-winners-icsc-32nd-design-and-international-development-].

International Council of Shopping Centers. 2008. 32nd Design and International Development Awards. 2008. [https://www.yumpu.com/en/document/read/26249369/2008-winners-icsc-32nd-design-and-international-development-]

IPEA. 2018. Retrato das Desigualdades de Gênero e Raça. [www.ipea.gov.br/retrato/indicadores_populacao.html].

Iráabal, Clara. 2009. Revisiting Urban Planning in Latin America and the Caribbean. Regional study prepared for Revisiting Urban Planning: Global Report on Human Settlements 2009. [https://drum.lib.umd.edu/bitstream/handle/1903/26977/GRHS2009-RegionalLatinAmericaandtheCaribbean.pdf?sequence=1&isAllowed=y].

Jaramillo, Pedro. 2010. The Sustainability of Urban Heritage Preservation. *The Case of Quito*. New York, NY: Inter-American Development Bank.

Jijón, Victor H. 2013. "The Ecuadorian Indigenous Movement and the Challenges of Plurinational State Construction." In: Marc Becker (Ed.): *Indigenous and Afro-Ecuadorians Facing the Twenty-First Century*. Newcastle: Cambridge Scholars Publishing, 34–70.

Johnson, Cade. 2017. About 70 protest UG Berkeley professor Judith Butler's conference in Brazil. [http://www.dailycal.org/2017/11/08/protesters-gather-at-conference-organized-by-campus-professor-judith-butler-in-brazil/].

Kaltmeier, Olaf. 2009. "Das Land neu gründen: Gesellschaftliche Kon-texte, politische Kulturen und indigene Bewegungen in Südamerika." In: Mittag, Jürgen und Georg Ismar (Ed.): *El pueblo unido? Soziale Bewegungen und politischer Protest in der Geschichte Lateinamerikas*, Münster: Westfälisches Dampfboot, 339–363.

Kaltmeier, Olaf. 2011. "Urban Landscapes of Mall-ticulturality: (Retro-) Coloniality and Identity Politics in Quito: The Case of the San Luis Shopping Center." In: Olaf Kaltmeier (Ed.): *Selling EthniCity: Urban Cultural Politics in the Americas*. Farnham: Ashgate, 93–114.

220   The Refeudalization of Society

Kaltmeier, Olaf. 2013. "Soziale Ungleichheiten in Lateinamerika: Historische Kontinuitäten im sozialen Wandel." In: Olaf Kaltmeier (Ed.): *Soziale Ungleichheit in den Amerikas: Historische Kontinuitäten und sozialer Wandel von der Mitte des 19. Jahrhunderts bis heute.* Köln: KLA.

Kaltmeier, Olaf. 2015a. "Die Retro-Kolonialisierung der Stadt: Kulturerbepolitiken und Vertreibung im historischen Stadtzentrum von Lima." In: Hans-Jürgen Burchardt, Olaf Kaltmeier and Rainer Öhlschläger (Ed.): *Urbane (T)Räume: Städte zwischen Kultur, Kommerz und Konflikt.* Baden-Baden: Nomos, 71–88.

Kaltmeier, Olaf. 2015b. "En búsqueda de la ciudad perdida. Género, erotismo y nostalgia en el paisaje urbano de Quito." In: Sebastian Thies, Luzelena Gutiérrez de Velasco and Gabriele Pisarz Ramírez (Ed.): *De Patrias y Matrias: Gender and Nation in the Americas.* Trier: WVT, 187–200.

Kaltmeier, Olaf. 2016. Konjunkturen der (De-)Kolonialisierung. Indigene Gemeinschaften, Hacienda und Staat in den ecuadorianischen Anden von der Kolonialzeit bis heute. Bielefeld: Transcript.

Kaltmeier, Olaf. 2017. "On the Advantage and Disadvantage of Heritage for Latin America. Heritage Politics and Nostalgia between Coloniality and Indigeneity." In: Olaf Kaltmeier and Mario Rufer (Ed.): *Entangled Heritages. Postcolonial Perspectives on the Uses of the Past in Latin America.* London: Routledge, 13–35.

Kaltmeier, Olaf. 2019. "Invidious Comparison and the New Global Leisure Class: On the Refeudalization of Consumption in the Old and New Gilded Age." *Forum for Inter-American Research (fiar)*, 12, 1, 29–42.

Kaltmeier, Olaf. 2022. Resistencia mapuche. Reflexiones en torno al poder Siglos XVI a XXI. Santiago de Chile: Pehuén.

Kantorowicz, Ernst. 1957. "The King's Two Bodies. A Study in Mediaeval Political Theology. Princeton, NJ: Princeton University Press.

Kingman, Eduardo. 2004. "Patrimonio, políticas de la memoria e institucionalización de la cultura." *ICONOS: Revista de Ciencias Sociales*, 20, 26–34.

Koselleck, Reinhart. 1989. *Vergangene Zukunft: Zur Semantik geschichtlicher Zeiten.* Frankfurt a.M.: Suhrkamp.

Kotek, Joel and Pierre Rigoulot. 2001. *Das Jahrhundert der Lager. Gefangenschaft, Zwangsarbeit, Vernichtung.* Berlin: Propyläen.

Kron, Stefanie. 2004. "Guatemala: Paramilitarismus und sozialer Widerstand." In: Olaf Kaltmeier, Jens Kastner and Elisabeth Tuider (Ed.): *Neoliberalismus—Autonomie—Widerstand. Soziale Bewe-gungen in Lateinamerika.* Münster: Westfälisches Dampfboot, 101–119.

Krysmanski, Hans Jürgen. 2015. *0,1 Prozent—Das Imperium der Milliardäre.* Frankfurt a.M.: Westend Verlag.

Laclau, Ernesto. 1971. "Feudalism and Capitalism in Latin America." *New Left Review*, 67, 19–38.

Larrañaga, O. and M. E. Rodríguez. 2015. "Desigualdad de Ingresos y Poberza en Chile 1990 a 2013." In: Osvaldo Larrañaga and Dante Contreras (Ed.): *Las Nuevas politicas de proteccion social en Chile.* Santiago: Uqbar Editores.

Le Bot, Yvon. 1995. *La guerra en tierras mayas—Comunidad, violencia y modernidad en Guatemala (1970-1992).* Mexiko City: FCE.

Levine-Rasky, Cynthia. 2002. *Working through Whiteness.* New York, NY: Suny Press.

The Refeudalization of Society 221

Luxemburg, Rosa. 1923. Die Akkumulation des Kapitals. *Ein Beitrag zur ökonomischen Erklärung des Imperialismus*. Berlin: Vereinigung Internationaler Verlags-Anstalten.

Marcuse, Peter. 1997. "The Enclave, the Citadel, and the Ghetto: What has Changed in the Post-Fordist U.S. City?" *Urban Affairs Review*, 33, 2, 228–264. [https://journals.sagepub.com/doi/10.1177/107808749703300206].

Mariátegui, José Carlos. 2007. 7 Ensayos de interpretatión de la realidad peruana. [http://resistir.info/livros/mariategui_7_ensayos.pdf].

Martens, Helmut. 2016. Refeudalisierung oder Überwindung des Kapitalismus. Am Ende der industriekapitalistischen Wachstumsdynamik. Hamburg: VSA.

Martínez, Inés del Pino. 2009. *Centro Histórico de Quito. Una centraldad urbana en transformación bacia el turismo. 2001-2008*. Quito: Flacso.

Marx, Karl. 1978 [1852]. "Der achtzehnte Brumaire des Louis Bonarparte." In: *Karl Marx/Friedrich Engels - Werke 8*. Berlin: Dietz Verlag.

Mato, Daniel. 2008. "All Industries are Cultural: A Critique of the Idea of 'Cultural Industries' and New Possibilities for Research." *Cultural Studies*, 23, 1, 70–87.

MDMQ. 2010. *Invierta en Quito. Perfil de Turismo*. Quito: Dirección de Inversiones y comercio exterior.

Mignolo, Walter D. 2000. *Local Histories/Global Designs: Coloniality, Subaltern Knowledges, and Border Thinking*, Princeton, NJ: Princeton University Press.

Moraña, Mabel, Enrique Dussel and Carlos C Jáuregui. 2008. *Coloniality at large*. Durham: Duke University Press.

Moulian, Tomás. 1997. *Chile actual. Anatomia de un mito*. Santiago de Chile: LOM.

Moulian, Tomás. 1998. *El consumo me conume*. Santiago de Chile: LOM.

Murmis, Miguel and Juan Carlos Portantiero. 2004. *Estudios sobre los Origenes del Peronismo*. Buenos Aires: Siglo XXI.

Murray, Warwick E. 2006. "Neo-Feudalism in Latin America? Globalisation, Agribuisness, and land re-concentration in Chile." *The Journal of Peasant Studies*, 33, 4, S. 646–677.

Neckel, Sighard. 2010. "Refeudalisierung der Ökonomie: Zum Strukturwandel kapitalistischer Wirtschaft." MPIfG Working Paper, 10, 6. Köln: Max-Planck-Institut für Gesellschaftsforschung. [https://www.econstor.eu/handle/10419/41695].

Neckel, Sighard. 2013a. "Refeudalisierung. Systematik und Aktualität eines Begriffs der Habermas'schen Gesellschaftsanalyse." *Leviathan* 41, 1, S. 39–56.

Neckel, Sighard. 2013b. "Zukunft der Vergangenheit. Zur Refeudalisierung der modernen Gesellschaft." *Polar. Zeitschrift für politische Philosophie und Kultur*, 15. [www.polar-zeitschrift.de/position_kommentare.php?id-713].

Nozaki, William and Jessé de Souza. 2017. O Brazil não conhece o Brasil. [https://fpabramo.org.br/2017/04/20/o-brazil-nao-conhece-o-brasil/].

Nugent, José Guillermo. 1992. *El laberinto de la choledad*. Lima: Fundación Ebert.

Obermayer, Bastian and Frederik Obermaier. 2016. Panama Papers. *Die Geschichte einer weltweiten Enthüllung*. Köln: Kiepenheuer & Witsch.

222 *The Refeudalization of Society*

Oxfam. 2017. An Economy for the 99%. Oxfam Briefing Paper. [https://www.oxfam.org/sites/www.oxfam.org/files/file_attachments/bp-economy-for-99-percent-160117-en.pdf].

Oxfam. 2020. Latin American billionaires surge as world's most unequal region buckles under coronavirus strain. [https://www.oxfam.org/en/press-releases/latin-american-billionaires-surge-worlds-most-unequal-region-buckles].

Pierson, Paul. 2004. Politics in Time. *History, Institutions, and Social Analysis*, Princeton, NJ: Princeton University Press.

Piketty, Thomas. 2014. *Capital in the Twenty-First Century*. Cambridge, MA: Harvard University Press.

Planas, Roque. 2016. We're Starting To Get A Bad Feeling About Brazil's New Interim President. In: Huffington Post, 19.05.2016. [https://huffpost.netblog-pro.com/entry/michel-temer-brazil-president_n_573d99eee4b0aee7b8e91132]. Accessed in 2018.

Ponce Maldonado, Modesto. 2005. *El palacio del diablo*. Quito: Pan-Óptica.

Portes, Alejandro. 1985. "Latin American Class Structures: Their Composition and Change during the last Decades." *Latin American Research Review,* 20, 3, 7–39.

Portes, Alejandro and Kelly Hoffman. 2003. "Latin American Class Structures: Their Composition and Change during the Neoliberal Era." *Latin American Research Review*, 38, 1, 41–82.

Portocarrero, Gonzalo. 2007. "Racismo y mestizaje. *Y otros ensayos*. Lima: Fondo editorial del congreso del Perú.

Quijano, Anibal. 2008. "Coloniality of Power: Eurocentrism and Social Classification." In: Mabel Moraña, Enrique Dussel, and Carlos A. Jáuregui (Ed.): *Coloniality at Large: Latin America and the Postcolonial Debate*. Durham: Duke University Press, 181–224.

Rajeev, Syal. 2009. Drug money saved banks in global crisis, claims UN advisor. In: The Guardian. [https://www.theguardian.com/global/2009/dec/13/drug-money-banks-saved-un-cfief-claims].

Rinke, Stefan. 2015. Im Sog der Katastrophe. Lateinamerika und der Erste Weltkrieg. Frankfurt a.M.: Campus.

Rivero Villaverde, Polette. 2017. Territorialer Vertreibungskrieg und Landgrabbing. [https://amerika21.de/analyse/187047/territorialer-vertreibungskrieg].

Rosa Luxemburg Stiftung. 2021. *Atlas of Enslavement*. Berlin: Rosa-Luxemburg-Stiftung [www.rosalux.de/atlasofenslavement].

Roth, Julia. 2020. *¿Puede el feminismo vencer al populismo? Avances populistas de derecha y contestaciones interseccionales en las Américas*. Bielefeld: Kipu.

Rovira Kaltwasser, Cristobal. 2009. "Towards a Historical Analysis of Elites in Latin America." In: *21st World Congress of Political Science*, Santiago de Chile. [http://paperroom.ipsa.org/papers/paper_744.pdf]. Accessed in 2018.

Ruf, Werner (ed.). 2003. *Politische Ökonomie der Gewalt*. Opladen: Leske & Budrich.

Sacri, Diding, Andy Sumner and Arief Anshory Yusuf. 2022. "Whose intergenerational mobility? A new set of estimates for Indonesia by gender, geography, and generation. UNU-Wider Working Paper.

Schäfer, H. W. 2021. *Protestant "Sects" and the Spirit of (Anti-) Imperialism: Religious Entanglements in the Americas*. New Orleans, LA: University of New Orleans Press.

The Refeudalization of Society 223

Schetter, Conrad. 2004. Kriegsfürstentum und Bürgerkriegsökonomien in Afghanistan. In: AIPA - Arbeitspapiere zur Internationalen Politik und Außenpolitik 3 [https://nbn-resolving.org/urn:nbn:de:0168-ssoar-218458].

Schwarz, Moritz. 2020. *Interview with Leon Krier Entrevista a Léon Krier Entrevista com Leon Krier.* 11.

Segato, Rita. 2016. *La guerra contra las mujeres.* Madrid: Traficantes de Sueños.

Sennett, Richard. 2000. *Der flexible Mensch.* München: Siedler.

Seppänen, Maaria. 2003. "Historia local y patrimonio mundial. Ciudad letrada, arcadia colonial y el centro histórico de Lima". *Anuario Americanista Europe,* 1, 107–120.

Smith, Peter. 1979. Labyrinths of Power. Political Recruitment in Twentieth-Century Mexico. Princeton, NJ: Princeton University Press.

Sokoloff Kenneth L. and Stanley L. Engerman. 2000. "History Lessons: Institutions, Factor Endowments, and Paths of Development in the New World." *Journal of Economic Perspective,* 14, 3, 217–232.

Song, Lijie. 2022. Examining the Relationship Between Intergenerational Upward Mobility and Inequality: Evidence from Panel Data. *Social Indicators Research* 163, 1–27.

Stecchi, Diego. 2015. El perfil del nuevo consumidor del mercado de lujo en América Latina. [https://www.america-economia.com/analisis-opinion/el-perfil-del-nuevo-consumidor-del-mercado-de-lujo-en-america-latina]. Accessed in 2018.

Stern, Steve J. 1988. "Feudalism, Capitalism, and the World-System in the Perspective of Latin America and the Caribbean." *The American Historical Review,* 93, 4, 829–872.

Süddeutsche Zeitung. 2017. Panama Papers. Die Geheimnisse des schmutzigen Geldes. [http://panamapapers.sueddeutsche.de].

Supiot, Alain. 2013. "The Public-Private Relation in the Context of Today's Refeudalization." *International Journal of Constitutional Law, 11, 1,* 129–145.

Svampa, Maristella. 2001. Los que ganaron. *La vida en los countries y barrios privados.* Buenos Aires: Biblos.

Svampa, Maristella. 2008. "Kontinuitäten und Brüche in den herrschen-den Sektoren." In: Dieter Boris (Ed.): *Sozialstrukturen in Lateinamerika: Ein Überblick.* Wiesbaden: VS Verlag, 45–71.

Tanner, Jakob. 2015. "Refeudalisierung, Neofeudalismus, Geldaristokra-tie: die Wiederkehr des Vergangenen als Farce?" In: Giovanni Biaggini, Oliver Diggelmann and Christine Kaufmann (Ed.): *Festschrift für Daniel Thürer.* Zürich: Dike Verlag, 733–748.

The Guardian. 2017. Land defenders call on UN to act against violence by state-funded and corporate groups. [https://www.theguardian.com/environ-ment/2017/sep/21/land-defenders-call-on-un-to-act-against-violence-by-state-funded-and-corporate-groups].

Thorp, Rosemary. 1998. Progress, Poverty and Exclusion. An Economic History of Latin America in the 20th Century. New York, NY: Inter-American Development Bank.

Torche, Florencia. 2014. "Intergenerational Mobility and Inequality: The Latin American Case." *Annual Review of Sociology,* 40, 30.24.

224 The Refeudalization of Society

UBS. 2016. Billionaire Insights. [https://www.ubs.com/microsites/billionaires-report/en/feeling-the-pressure/_jet_content/mainpar/gridcontrol_2077236744/col/link-list/link.1943461365.file/bGluay9wYXRoPSojb25o/WsoLzRhb891-YnMvbWijem9zaXRIcygiaWxsaW9uZXItcmVwbaJoL3BkZigiaWxsa-W9uYWlyZXMtemVwb3/oLnBkZg-/billionaires-report.pdf]. Accessed in 2018.

UNDP. 2016. Human Development Report 2016. [www.undp.org/content/undp/en/home/librarypage/hdr/2016-human-development-report.html]. Accessed in 2018.

UNHCR. 2018. Colombia. [www.unhct.org/colombia.html].

Unmüßig, Barbara. 2012. "Einleitung." In: Silke Helfrich (Ed.): *Commons. Für eine neue Politik jenseits von Markt und Staat*. Bielefeld: Transcript, 1–13.

Vasella, Reto and Stefan Beutelsbacher. 2013. Brasiliens Ikarus vernichtet sein Vermögen. In: Handelszeitung, 08.08.2013. [www.handelszeitung.ch/unternehmen/brasiliens-ikarus-vernichtet-sein-vermoegen-480177].

Veblen, Thorstein. 2007 [1899]. *The Theory of the Leisure Class*. Oxford: Oxford University Press.

Vicuña, Manuel. 2001. La belle époque chilena. *Alta sociedad y mujeres de elite en el cambio de siglo*. Santiago de Chile: Editorial Sudamericana.

Wacquant, Loic. 2007. Los condenados de la ciudad. Gueto, periferias y Estado. Buenos Aires: Siglo XXI.

Wallace, Arturo. 2013. *Extorsión en Colombia: un negocio de más de US$1.000 millones al año*. In: BBC. [https://www.bbc.com/mundo/noticias/2013/12/131101_colombia_extorsion_negocio_gaula_aw].

Wallerstein, Immanuel. 1988. "The Bourgeois(ie) as Concept and Reality: From the Eleventh Century to the Twenty-First." *New Left Review*, 7167, 91–106.

Wealth-X. 2013. World Ultra Wealth Report. [http://wuwr.wealthx.com/Wealth-X%20and%20UBS%20World-1%2oUltra%20Wealth%20Report%20 2013.pdf]. Accessed in 2018.

Wealth-X. 2014. The Wealth-X and UBS Billionaire Census. [http://inequalities.ch/wp-content/uploads/2014/10/Census-2014_Jatest.pdf].

Wealth-X. 2016. Billionaire Census Highlights 2015-2016. Online verfügbar unter [https://www.agefi.fr/sites/agefi.fr/files/fichiers/2016/08/billionaire_census_2015-2016_highlights.pdf].

Weber, M. 2019. *Economy and Society: A New Translation*. Cambridge, MA: Harvard University Press.

Weber, Max. 1958. *The Protestant Ethic and the Spirit of Capitalism: Chapter V: Asceticism and the Spirit of Capitalism*. New York, NY: Charles Scribner's Sons.

Wichmann, Stefan. 1992. *Wirtschaftsmacht Rauschgift*. Frankfurt a.M.: Fischer.

Zarazúa, Ulises. 2011. "No-Go Areas and Chic Places: Socio-Spatial Segregation and Stigma in Guadalajara." In: Olaf Kaltmeier (Ed.): *Selling EthniCity. Urban Cultural Politics in the Americas*. Farnham: Ashgate, 261–274.

Zeller, Christian. 2004. "Die globale Enteignungsökonomie." In: Christian Zeller (Ed.): *Die globale Enteignungsökonomie*, Münster: Westfälisches Dampfboot, 9–20.

Zitzmann, Mare. 2015. Wird Denken jetzt Mode? Unternehmen wie Hermès, Louis Vuitton oder Chanel leisten sich Hausphilosophen—in verschiedenen Funktionen. Sie sind für das gewisse Etwas der Marken zuständig. In: Neue ZüricherZeitung, 14.08.2015.[https://www.nzz.ch/feuilleton/wird-denken-jetzt-mode-ld.737548].

Understanding Multiple Crises: Interview with Olaf Kaltmeier and Edgardo Lander

Interviewers: *Hans-Jürgen Burchardt and Jochen Kemner*
Interviewees: *Olaf Kaltmeier and Edgardo Lander*

Hans-Jürgen Burchardt & Jochen Kemner: After reading both essays, it seems clear that the planetary environmental crisis cannot be separated from the deepening socioeconomic disparities, which Olaf considers to be a process of refeudalization. How do you see the relationship between the ecological and the social question?

Edgardo Lander: Obviously the social and ecological dimensions cannot be separated in any way. Both have to do with the potential—or lack thereof—to preserve life on planet Earth. The capitalist logic of endless growth with an ever-increasing commodification of all aspects of existence is incompatible with life. In the neoliberal era, this logic has intensified, surpassing many of the obstacles that the practice of democracy had imposed to the primacy of accumulation regarding its legitimacy or any other consideration. The growth of profound inequalities and the advance toward planetary climatic collapse constitute a singular and inseparable dynamic. In the search for the maximization of short-term gains, the tiny fraction of humanity that today controls political and economic power, despite all the indisputable evidence that these processes are in reality suffocating the conditions that make life possible, continue blocking drastic decisions that must occur to stop and, if possible, reverse environmental devastation in some way. Those who have the most responsibility for the sustained war against nature are not the ones who will suffer its consequences, while those who have less responsibility for environmental destruction due to their cultural patterns or consumption habits are suffering with an ever-growing intensity and frequency the devastation caused by extreme climate events (droughts, hurricanes, floods, sea level rise, heat waves and forest fires, the loss of biological diversity), which destroy the conditions for reproduction of their cultures as well as their lives.

DOI: 10.4324/9781003308850-4

226　*Understanding Multiple Crises*

For all these reasons, the fight against environmental destruction and the fight for equality and democracy form the same battle.

Olaf Kaltmeier: I share Edgardo's diagnosis that we are living through a profound crisis of the civilizational patterns of the colonial modernity. This is a multiple crisis that finds its most concise and urgent expression in the age of the Anthropocene, which took hold with the Great Acceleration beginning in the 1950s. These epistemological and socio-cultural upheavals are central to the findings of the Anthropocene in the natural sciences and, above all, those surrounding the earth system, such as the transgression of planetary boundaries, especially regarding global warming, the sixth extinction, and the spread of the human-made technosphere. This means that our modern relationship to nature must be urgently rethought and fundamentally realigned. The massive consumption of natural resources, global pollution, and the threat of crossing tipping points are planetary challenges that fundamentally call into question the survival of mankind on Earth. Thus, modern capitalist forms of production and consumption, above all, are at the center of this crisis.

However, the responsibility, historical and current, for the multiple crisis in the Anthropocene has a highly uneven distribution. The ecological footprint of continents and states calculated by the Footprint Network provides information about the distribution of responsibility between the Global North and the Global South—due especially to its good visual representability in maps. Thus, North America, Western Europe, and Australia can be identified as the main contributors to the ecological crisis. This is important in order to demand political responsibility from the respective states. At the same time, this account runs into the trap of methodological nationalism. For in the global network society, the Global North has long since been located not only in the geographical North, but also in global cities of the South such as Sao Paulo, Mexico City, and Santiago de Chile in Latin America.

If we now look at the ecological footprint from the perspective of the refeudalization thesis, the focus shifts primarily to the refeudal cosmocracy. Oxfam has presented calculations on this in 2021. According to these, it is calculated that the richest 1% of the world's population will be responsible for 16% of total greenhouse gas emissions by 2030. This is mainly due to their neo-aristocratic lifestyle based on luxury consumption and the ostentatious display of wealth. This includes—in addition to private helicopters and jets—extravagant leisure competitions such as the rivalry in space between billionaires Jeff Bezos and Richard Branson. Here, not only is wealth demonstratively destroyed for reasons of prestige but emissions are also released and resources wasted. Why eliminate the multi? "Billionaires" no longer describes their level of accumulation of wealth. Edgardo.

I think Edgardo has also argued along these lines when he uses the term plutocracy to point out that this privileged and hyper-wealthy group not only excessively emits emissions and consumes resources, but

Understanding Multiple Crises 227

also sits at key political levers that make policies to address the multiple crises in the Anthropocene impossible.

A refeudalized society is structurally incapable of finding answers to the planetary environmental crises and the global crisis of social inequality. This group of the moneyed aristocracy has increasingly withdrawn from democratic decision-making processes, welfare state governance systems, and social norms. There is a strong tendency for this group to self-segregate in their "small principalities." Thus, this group is able to escape the ecological damage that it is largely responsible for. On the other hand, as proponents for approaches of environmental justice have pointed out, the poorest, who are particularly vulnerable, cannot escape these environmental consequences. With this powerful cosmocracy, alternative proposals that formulate a new human-nature relationship can hardly be implemented. Here it is obvious, especially in Latin America, that concrete perspectives for action to overcome the multiple crisis in the Anthropocene and the crisis of social inequalities are formulated precisely by peasant, indigenous, Afro-American, and chiefly, feminist movements. Concepts such as Buen Vivir or the formulation of the rights of nature and geographical entities, such as rivers, come to mind. It is the task of social science research, but also of democratic politics, to explicitly deal with this new social group of the globally networked refeudal plutocracy. And this does not only apply to research to North America and Western Europe. Especially in Asia, Arabia, and Latin America, the number of millionaires rapidly increases.

Hans-Jürgen Burchardt & Jochen Kemner: Both of you criticize antidemocratic tendencies in your essays that affect confidence in democratic processes and social cohesion. Why have authoritarian tendencies developed in various (progressive) governments in Latin America? And why have social movements and grassroots democratic initiatives not been able to assert themselves more strongly?

Olaf Kaltmeier: In my reflections on the refeudalization of society, the transformations in political culture occupy a central position. In Latin America, the revolutionary movements at the beginning of the 19th century did fight for independence from the Spanish crown and established republics. At the same time, however, these revolutions did not proceed to overcome the colonial social structure. In short, the social revolution failed to materialize. Instead, the wealthy and educated white man remained the prototype of the citoyen, while the popular majorities of these populations were excluded from political participation. Only with the massive mobilizations of indigenous movements in the 1990s, the subsequent constitutional changes recognizing the pluricultural or even plurinational character of the state, and the "pink tides" of left-wing governments in many Latin American countries was it possible to partially overcome the de facto exclusion of these populations. In this sense, the partially established antidemocratic tendency today is preceded by a

228   *Understanding Multiple Crises*

historically unprecedented regional process of democratization and the expansion of rights for the disadvantaged, which can be attributed to the successful mobilization of social movements. Politically and culturally, the interpretive authority of the "white man" has thus been challenged and partially overcome.

This loss of white, upper-class, and male authority is associated with fear and anger among this group, which historically considers itself elite. This manifests itself partly through aggression and misogynistic and racist forms of violence. Sectors of the middle class or the underclass who have risen to a lower middle status as a result of the social programs of leftist governments also participate here. "Whiteness" is not racially given, but still represents a status desirable to many, attainable through education and wealth. Similar to the U.S. under Trump, these sectors proclaim, "We want our country back." And similar to the U.S., in countries with strong evangelical movements, there are tendencies to resacralize that literally demonize dissenters.

Even representatives of left-wing governments, some of whom also came from the group of the historically privileged elite socio-structurally, were not immune to this political and cultural change. Racist statements can also be found in the case of Ecuadorian ex-president Rafael Correa, as well as in the case of the Nicaraguan presidential couple Daniel Ortega and Rosario Murillo. In addition, parts of the political leadership in the pink tide were also closely associated with the extractivist model and the associated plutocratic elites. Accordingly, the number of billionaires in Latin America increased precisely under left-wing governments. This produced conflicts with many social movements and local communities.

The refeudal plutocracy also benefited politically from these debates. With Mauricio Macri in Argentina, Guillermo Lasso in Ecuador, and Sebastián Piñera in Chile, multimillionaires were elected presidents. In the spirit of Habermas, we see here a colonization of the political public sphere by economic elites. But the political power of the elites is not uncontested. Under democratic conditions, the political field is a privileged space for the articulation of alternative projects, since the principle of "one citizen, one vote" still formally applies. The billionaire's single vote counts just as much as that of the impoverished indigenous peasant. That is why the political field in Latin America is currently such a privileged place for the struggle for hegemony of different, even antagonistic, projects. From a global perspective, this is unique. Unlike in other regions of the world, where there are no alternative social movements with mass impact or where the political field is closed in an authoritarian way, in Latin America alternatives to the multiple crisis of capitalism are being debated on a broad scale, implemented politically in part, and lived out socially in daily life.

Edgardo Lander: It is not possible to identify a single cause or reason for which authoritarian trends arise in various progressive governments

Understanding Multiple Crises 229

in Latin America. It is necessary to highlight that there was a wide range of experiences which have been named part of the first cycle or first wave of Latin American progressivism and this overly broad characterization could not possibly account for all the specificities of each case. We will note here, only as a rough outline, some issues that are of particular importance to an analysis of the failures from the experiences of Venezuela, Ecuador, and Bolivia as democratizing processes.

The influence of the Leninist heritage has been persistent in the Latin American left, although rarely in an explicit form. The projects formulated in part by the directors and parties that conduct these processes of constructing societies apart from capitalism are done without an adequate accounting of what the experience of real existing socialism in the 20th century was, in particular the severe limitations on the so-called proletariat democracy and the authoritarian consequences of the fusion of State and party. Based on the left's tradition of historical distrust in the practices of liberal democracy (transitions of power, separations of State powers, civil liberties, free elections, etc.), their exercise—despite being reaffirmed fundamentally in the respective constitutions—was declining without being replaced with other more democratic modalities of political organization of society. Continuity in power was becoming the principal objective of administration.

Associated with the above, there has been an intense pressure on state centric conceptions and practices and the attempts to produce the desired social changes from the centralized power of the state. The State (revolutionary?) is taken as the representative of the general interests of the society. The limited tolerance of autonomous forms of organization of society is directly derived from this assumption. In the cases of Bolivia and Ecuador, this is expressed in the search for divisions of social organization and movements, both to debilitate them and to rely on the support of the more favorable factions to the government. In the case of Venezuela, the experience of incorporating millions of people in popular organizational processes, in particular the *Consejos Comunales* and the *Comunas,* represented the search for alternative to the limitations of liberal democracy, and, as experienced, meant rich processes of solidarity-based participation and politization. Nevertheless, with few famous exceptions, these organizations had limited autonomy in relation to the State-party. They were highly regulated by the extensive judicial and administrative scaffolding of the so-called *Poder Popular* and their functioning depended on public financing. Once the severe economic crisis limited the capacity of the State to continue with the financing, the majority of these organizations languished or disappeared as a whole.

The *caudillismo* represented by Hugo Chávez, Rafael Correa, and Evo Morales had ambiguous, and even contradictory, effects in relation to democracy. On one side, in its initial phases it promoted elevated levels of mobilizations and participation from subaltern and previously politically

230 *Understanding Multiple Crises*

excluded social groups, expanding in a very significant way the subject of democracy. Nevertheless, with time, the manner by which it concentrated more power in the leader and surrounded them with groups of staunch supporters severely limited the spaces for open debate, the confrontation of diverse opinions, and the exploration of alternatives to the will of the leader. Add to this the known consequences of cults of personality. In this way, the spheres for democratic exercise were reduced, and the social sectors as a whole, far from participating effectively in decision-making, began to be informed about decisions already taken by the leader.

In the Venezuelan case, the weight of the military both in public administration (ministries, governors, presidents of state-owned enterprises, and autonomous institutes) and in the governing party (United Socialist Party of Venezuela) served as a strong curbing factor on the possibilities of democracy. The military culture of verticality and obedience represents the opposite of democracy and transparency in public administration. The wide-ranging military presence has had immense responsibility in the expansive trends that have been both authoritarian and corrupt in the Venezuelan process.

When extractivism, which implied a deepening of the subordinate role in the international division of labor, in the phase of the so-called commodity boom, became the main axis of the political economy of these countries, it entered into contradiction with the more democratic and transformative goals present at the beginning of these projects for change, as established in the constitutions and other legal norms of Ecuador and Bolivia, and more limitedly in the Venezuelan case. The notions of plurinationality, recognition of the territories of indigenous peoples, and the rights of Nature all became secondary when faced with the need to increase tax revenue through the expansion of the borders of extraction. In Venezuela, despite the critical discourse about the rent economy, during the years of the Chavez government the country had higher levels of dependency on petroleum than at any other moment in its history.

Hans-Jürgen Burchardt & Jochen Kemner: Latin America continues to rely heavily on the production/extraction and exportation of raw materials. This has the consequence both of environmental degradation and the growth of social disparities. What has to be done to halt or even overcome this dependency? Or do you see a possibility that this model can be transformed to be sustainable and distributive?

Edgardo Lander: The conditions of the subordinate role of Latin America in the international division of labor and nature has acquired different modalities through the course of the last five centuries. Nevertheless, in such subordination there have equally been basic structural continuities present, characterized in each phase for the lack of effective autonomy to define and implement independent economic policies on the part of the State of these countries. In the current phase, due to neoliberal globalization, mediated through free trade agreements, the norms of the World Trade Organization, and the policies of structural adjustment from the Washington Consensus, the instruments to define public policies from the basis of some definition of popular interest have been extraordinarily limited. Industrialization policies by way of import substitution, which appeared possible in the '60s and '70s of the 20th century, are not possible today without opposing such norms. When transformative and groundbreaking actions have been attempted in the search to move away from such narrow limits, the United States' imperial reaction has always been immediate. Take note of the cases of Guatemala, Brazil, Cuba, Nicaragua, and Chile.

In Latin America in the context of neoliberal globalization, there is today an extraordinary weakness both in the so-called progressive governments, as in the voices critical of extractivism and factory-work, in relation to alternative models of production capable of stopping environmental devastation, guaranteeing the rights of workers, and, at the same time, responding to the needs of populations for better living conditions.

Olaf Kaltmeier: The restriction of Latin American economies to the export of raw materials is historically closely connected with deep colonial structures, which are linked to dynamics in the capitalist world system, and various historical conjunctures of recolonization, such as in the so-called "Second Conquista" from the 1860s to the 1930s or the Third Conquista from the 1980s until today. This Third Conquest is related to the—often violent—imposition of neoliberal economic models in the region.

In a boom phase of international commodity prices in the 1990s and 2000s, leftist governments failed to overcome extractivism, but they were partially able to siphon off profits from commodity exports to finance social programs. This strategy, which some social scientists have called neoextractivism, was thus quite successful for short-term poverty reduction and the expansion of educational programs. However, in the subsequent phase of economic crisis, exacerbated by the COVID-19 pandemic, these populations that benefitted then largely descended again. Neoextractivism was also socially unsustainable.

A sustainable fight against social inequality and poverty would have to go hand in hand with redistribution policies. Latin America is the most socially inequitable region in the world. Possible measures include wealth and inheritance taxes, as well as tax collection systems that basically function at all. These measures are currently being discussed in Colombia and Chile, but the tax rate remains low. At the international level, measures would have to be adopted for the taxation of the super-rich, which would also close tax loopholes. Unfortunately, no fundamental changes can be expected in this area in the short term. Political pressure from social movements worldwide is needed here.

In Latin America, closing the social gap between rich and poor is not possible without agrarian reform. In view of the plantation economy and monoculture, an agrarian reform that favors small peasants is also

232 *Understanding Multiple Crises*

ecologically necessary. It must take ecology into account and focus on national food sovereignty, combined with regional economic cycles. Furthermore, international measures should be considered, according to which the non-exploitation and protection of planetary relevant ecosystems, such as the Amazon rainforest, should be understood as a human task and this care work should be rewarded accordingly.

Fundamentally, however, a break with refeudal value and norm structures, such as ostentatious consumption and self-segregation, is also necessary. The care debate, initiated by feminist and indigenous movements, opens up perspectives for developing a good life precisely through the relationships and care of others, including non-human living beings and entities.

Hans-Jürgen Burchardt & Jochen Kemner: Your original texts were written before the COVID-19 pandemic and the latest political turn in Latin America toward progressive governments. What lessons from the boom and bust of the first phase of progressive governance should the new governments have in mind? Is there evidence, for example, from Colombia or Chile that such lessons have been recognized and are leading to new policies?

Olaf Kaltmeier: The COVID-19 pandemic was a global event that highlighted the extent to which the conjuncture of refeudalization can be reinforced precisely by crises. In this context, the moneyed aristocracy is a crisis winner worldwide. In the peak period of the pandemic alone, between March 2020 and November 2021, the wealth of the ten richest billionaires doubled. In Latin America, a social-structural bungee effect has been evident. While under the pink tide there was an elevator effect in which all social classes experienced upward mobility, in the crisis, the hyper-rich have become richer, while middle-class sectors have descended into poverty. Furthermore, we see a greater private indebtedness which reinforces the refeudal trend toward a new debt bondage. At the same time, it is generally noted that the poorer and more ethnically marked people are, the worse their health outcomes have been in the pandemic. A clear racist and racialized biopolitics is visible here. The targeted lack of supplies for Brazil's indigenous peoples by the Bolsonaro government is worth remembering here.

Besides this pessimistic view, the COVID-19 pandemic also held important insights on the possibility of state interventions. Against the neoliberal idea of the weak state, the pandemics demonstrate that the state is an important instrument of intervention, especially in the economic sphere. In this sense, rigid measures to combat social inequality and ecological crisis are possible, if there the political will to do so exists.

In the face of a disastrous social and ecological situation in Latin America, many of the new left-wing governments—as in Mexico under Manuel López Obrador, Argentina under Alberto Fernández, Chile under Gabriel Boric, Bolivia under Luis Arce, or Peru under Pedro Csstillo—have limited themselves to national programs. In my opinion,

Understanding Multiple Crises 233

it is hardly possible to speak of a renewed tide so far, since—unlike the Latin American integration process under Chávez and Lula da Silva—no truly Latin American vision is being developed. The government often limits itself to preventing the worst of a possible shift to the right, as in Chile, for example, in view of the radical right-wing presidential candidate Antonio Kast. In Chile, the change does not come from the current Boric government, but from the social movements. After the social uprising in October 2019 and the subsequent convention to draft the New Constitution, a profound debate began on the reinvention of the social, the rights of nature, gender justice, and anti-neoliberalism. After the devastating defeat in the vote for the draft of the New Constitution on September 4, 2022, the democratization process in Chile came to an abrupt halt. The reasons for the electoral failure are many, but it is certain that the power of media corporations, right-wing think tanks, and an unequal campaign—80% of all campaign funds went to rejecting and maintaining the constitution from the Pinochet dictatorship—played a central role. The moneyed aristocracy successfully defended its interests in the political arena as well.

In Colombia, on the other hand, Gustavo Petro and Francia Márquez presented an ambitious government program in August 2022 that has a regional dimension and has indeed also drawn lessons from the analysis of the pink tide. The very name of the government program, "Colombia, potencia mundial de la vida," (Colombia, world power of life) makes clear the reformist aspiration, that were internationally oriented. The focus is on a life policy that encompasses all areas of society. Specifically, work is being done on redistribution through tax reform, focusing primarily on the taxation of the super-rich and big corporations. It also plans to implement agrarian reform, already included in the peace treaty with the FARC, but which, in addition to redistribution, will also have the function of securing food supplies. Further extractivist activities in the fossil energy sector are not planned. The ideas addressed to the international community for the protection of the Amazon region are also promising. However, real implementation will be difficult, given the political majority in the Senate, the power of the elite, and the polarization of society. For a real regional pink tide 2.0, the election result in Brazil in October 2022 will be crucial.

Edgardo Lander: This is a critical question for the future of the continent. The issues noted by the previous questions must be motive for reflection for these new processes since, obviously, learning from these experiences—having failed fundamentally in their attempt to reach their initial goals—is indispensable in avoiding the same failed paths. This refers as much to public policy as to the priorities made by social movements and organizations. A place of hope has opened in this sense with the government of Gustavo Petro and Francia Márquez pertaining to what probably has been the most decisive point of the confrontations

234 *Understanding Multiple Crises*

concerning the first wave of progressive governments: the environmental, political, social, cultural, and even civilizational implications of the extractivism that characterized each one of these administrations, without exception. A core axis of the policies that have been formulated by this new Colombian government establishes the clear priority to protect life over the exploitation of fossil fuels and other forms of extraction.

Translation (Edgardo Lander): Eric Rummelhoff

Index

accumulation 4, 9, 14, 24, 41, 48–49, 52, 88–89, 100, 123, 125, 134–135, 144, 148–149, 156, 159–166, 170–173, 211–212, 225

afrodescendant 152, 161, 174, 194, 201, 208, 212

Amazon 22, 43, 53, 56, 63, 70, 85, 96, 161, 163, 232, 233

Andean 70, 140, 183, 202

Anthropocene 14–15, 28–29, 226–227

Argentina 1, 2, 69, 71, 98, 104, 123, 136–138, 140–141, 143–145, 147, 153, 159–161, 168–169, 178, 187, 194, 195, 201, 206, 228, 232

aristocracy (moneyed) 3, 124–127, 132–134, 139– 155, 161, 165–175, 190–199, 206, 210–214, 226, 232–233

Bachelet, Michelle 1, 68, 159, 195, 201

Bahamas 167

Barbados 104, 167, 183, 193

Belize 161

Bermuda 140–141, 168

billionaire 88, 124–125, 132–149, 155–156, 160, 164, 169, 173, 192–193, 213–215, 228, 232

biopolitics 189, 209, 232

Bolivia 1, 3, 6, 16, 37, 39–44, 49, 52, 56–61, 68–69, 79–80, 85, 99, 104, 123, 138, 140, 142, 144–145, 160, 161, 196, 200–202, 206, 209, 212, 229–230

Bolsonaro, Jair 100, 158, 202, 205, 209, 232

Boric, Gabriel 1, 123, 232–233

bourgeoisie/bourgeois 41, 71, 148–156, 209–210

Brazil 1–2, 61, 69–71, 86, 98, 100, 104, 123, 127, 132, 133–147, 149–154, 159–161, 168, 175, 178, 183, 195–196, 200–209, 231, 233

buen vivir 7, 39–40, 52, 56, 58, 70, 208, 211, 227

Canada 55, 60, 150, 156, 160–161

Cárdenas, Lázaro 136

Caribbean 68–69, 84, 87, 89, 97, 132–134, 138, 141, 157, 177, 182–183, 193

Cayman Islands 167–168, 193

Central America 15, 68, 157

Chávez, Hugo 1, 62–63, 70, 81–83, 91, 97, 138, 198, 229–233

Chile 1–2, 68, 69, 71, 123, 135, 138, 140–147, 149, 150, 152, 153, 159, 168, 175, 178–179, 194–195, 201, 209, 212, 228, 231–233

China 30, 36, 53, 66, 67, 69, 87–92, 132, 150, 161, 180

civil society 180, 198–199

civilizational crisis 2, 4, 5–9, 37–38, 100, 104

climate change 2, 10–24, 27–31, 35, 37, 61–63, 67, 83–84, 100, 102–103

Colombia 1–2, 4, 69, 71, 97, 104, 123, 135–136, 140–141, 145, 154, 160–161, 165, 168, 175, 178, 198, 209, 231–233

coloniality 6, 77, 80, 102, 129–131, 142, 143, 157, 177, 182–183, 187–188, 202–203

commons 14, 26, 30, 71, 79, 91, 210–213

consumerism 148, 213

Correa, Rafael 52–56, 138, 197, 202, 208, 228–229

Costa Rica 104, 136, 168

Cuba 63, 91–92, 104, 212, 231

236 *Index*

debt bondage 125, 170, 178–179, 213, 232
Dominican Republic 105
drugs 164, 166, 213

ecological footprint 13–14, 226
Ecuador 1, 6, 37, 39–41, 44, 52–56, 67, 69, 79, 80, 85, 99, 103, 104, 123, 138, 140, 144, 152, 160, 163, 179, 183, 185–187, 194, 196, 197, 202, 208, 210, 212, 228–230
El Salvador 104, 141, 157, 166
environmental justice 52, 227
estate 135, 148–155, 172, 210, 214
Europe 72, 79, 98, 101, 126, 128, 132, 135, 139, 146, 147, 153–157, 162, 173–176, 180–182, 188, 198, 210, 215, 226–227
extinction 14–16, 226
extractivism 3, 7, 40, 47–52, 56, 60, 62, 66–67, 80–81, 83, 103, 139, 156–160, 230–231, 234

Fernández de Kirchner, Cristina 123, 138, 195, 201
feudalism 122, 124, 126–129, 154, 161–162, 165, 188, 209, 211
Fordism 134, 154
France 143, 150, 161, 175

García Linera, Álvaro 49–50, 56–57, 79–80
Gates, Bill 125, 148, 214
gender 85–86, 132, 151, 201, 204–206, 233
gentrification 125, 177, 188–190
geoengineering 27, 28, 102, 112
geopolitics 67, 73, 87
Germany 132, 140, 144, 147, 150, 154, 161, 180, 184, 191, 211, 215
Gilded Age 131, 134, 170
Great Britain/England 143, 211
Greece 181
green economy 24–26, 102
Grenada 193
Guatemala 104, 141, 168, 178, 184–187, 207, 231
Guianas 140

Haiti 104, 154, 198, 205
heritage 32, 42, 59, 77, 79, 82, 130, 176–177, 183, 187–190, 213, 229
Honduras 104, 160, 192, 200, 207, 209

human rights 42–43, 54–56, 75, 85, 89, 95, 105–106, 153, 202, 205

indigenous peoples 22–23, 40–43, 48, 54, 56, 58–60, 63, 65–66, 70, 76, 83, 152, 154, 161, 163, 185, 208, 230, 232
Italy 76, 147, 150, 161, 197

Jamaica 161
Japan 103, 132, 150, 161

Kirchner, Néstor 138, 195

land 12–13, 16–17, 22, 39, 44, 46, 53, 58, 59, 61, 76, 125–126, 137, 146, 148–149, 156–163, 187–189, 193, 202, 205, 208, 211–212
LGBT/LGBTQ+ 86, 99, 201, 206
López Obrador, Andrés Manuel 1, 123, 232
Lugo, Fernando 1, 195
luxury 125, 134, 170–176, 179, 184, 189, 190, 213, 226

Macri, Mauricio 4, 158, 168, 194–195, 200, 206, 228
Maggi, Blairo 161, 168
Mariátegui, José Carlos 126
Martinique 104
Marx, Karl 130, 157, 177, 211
Marxist 76, 101, 126, 150, 154, 162, 209
Mexico 2, 79, 104, 123, 132, 136, 140–144, 146, 149, 154, 157, 165, 170, 175, 182, 196, 212, 226, 232
middle class 19, 133, 135–138, 151–155, 160, 184, 188, 203, 207
migration 16, 96, 137, 146, 180–181
military 28, 36, 67, 90, 95, 97, 98, 105, 122–123, 145–146, 147, 151, 165, 181, 187, 194, 197, 200–204, 208, 230
millionaire 4, 29, 126, 134, 140, 142, 145, 147, 169, 170–171, 173, 192, 194–196, 202, 208, 227
modernity 5, 8–9, 19, 20, 27, 29, 40–41, 73, 77, 78, 80, 99, 102, 122, 124, 130, 179, 181, 225
Morales, Evo 1, 57, 59, 61, 68–69, 138, 142, 196, 198, 200, 202, 229
multiculturalism 41, 204
Mujica, José 1, 138

nature 7, 9, 13, 17, 20, 21, 24–28, 31, 36, 38, 40, 45–56, 59, 60, 67, 70–74,

77–78, 87, 88, 100–101, 131, 162, 173, 188, 199, 200, 212, 225–227, 230–233
neoliberalism 48, 54, 66, 70, 80, 123, 151, 233
Netherlands 14, 161
Nicaragua 3, 93–95, 104, 123, 157, 178, 206, 209, 231
nostalgia 129, 182, 184, 188

Obama, Barack 33, 103, 181, 194
Ortega, Daniel 87, 93–95, 228
Oxfam 29, 132–133, 157, 226

Panama 104, 136, 157, 166–168, 195, 197, 201
Paraguay 1, 69, 71, 105, 140, 160, 161, 178, 195–196, 200
Perón, Juan Domingo 136, 144
Peru 1–2, 16, 69, 71, 105, 123, 136, 140–141, 143–145, 150, 154, 161, 178, 182, 206, 232
Petro, Gustavo 1, 4, 123, 233
Pinochet, Augusto 123, 135, 144, 146, 147, 159, 202, 208, 233
pink tide 1, 3, 138, 152, 214, 227–228
Piñera, Sebastián 4, 143, 158, 194–195, 200, 228
planetary boundaries 12, 47, 226
plurinationality 39–41, 48, 52, 54, 56, 67, 123, 230
plutocracy 28, 29, 226–228
populism 39, 198, 206
Portugal 161
post-democracy 122, 124–125, 129, 193
privatization 1, 16, 66, 76, 137, 145–146, 151, 163, 192, 211–212
protest 56, 58, 90, 96, 197, 200, 205, 208–209
Puerto Rico 16, 105

Quijano, Aníbal 77–78, 102, 104, 131, 142

racism 6–7, 37, 44, 73, 74, 80, 102, 142, 183, 201–202, 208, 213–214
religion 93, 200
revolution 32, 36, 39, 71, 74, 80, 88, 90, 94, 98, 100, 129, 130, 135, 144, 145, 153–154, 157, 162, 173, 198, 208–210, 212–213, 227
rights of nature 7, 21, 40, 46, 56, 60, 67, 70, 227, 230, 233
Rousseff, Dilma 1, 168, 195–196, 200–201, 205
Russia 30, 36, 66, 87, 167

Sao Paulo Forum 7, 82–87, 89, 90, 94, 95, 97–99, 104, 110
Silva, Luis Ignacio da 1, 86, 138, 168, 176, 198, 233
slavery 127–128, 179
Slim, Carlos 132, 146, 214
social inequality 1–2, 24, 98, 122, 124, 132, 135–142, 149, 226, 231
social movements 2, 81, 98, 227–231
socialism 5, 8, 38–40, 49, 72–73, 76, 78, 80–82, 88, 91, 99–101, 104, 210, 229
Spain 143, 150, 181
St. Kitts 193

taxes 32, 81, 139, 167, 197
telecommunications 70, 96, 146
Temer, Michel 4, 158, 161, 168, 196, 201, 203
TIPNIS 58–60, 85, 109, 111, 118
Tobago 105
transnational corporations 17, 26, 66, 81, 90, 163, 195
Trinidad 105
Trump, Donald 33–37, 96, 103, 153, 167, 171, 181, 194, 197, 201, 228

UNASUR 51, 68, 70, 71, 104, 108, 117, 119, 195
United States of America 6, 9, 10, 19, 29–38, 59, 67, 69, 74, 83, 87–89, 93–94, 98, 103, 105, 131–136, 145, 148–150, 154, 156, 161, 164, 170, 171, 175, 178, 182–183, 194, 195, 201–204, 231
Uruguay 1, 69, 105, 123, 136, 138, 140, 161, 195

Venezuela 1, 3, 6, 37, 40, 42, 62–66, 68–69, 81–82, 85, 89, 91, 93–100, 104–105, 123, 136, 138, 141, 145, 161, 178, 229–230

Weber, Max 149–150, 172
Whiteness 126, 202–204, 207, 214, 228

Xenophobia/xenophobic 5, 37, 98, 204

Yasuní 52–53, 85, 109–110, 114

Zapata, Emiliano 103
Zapatista 79
Zuckerberg, Mark 148, 171, 214

Printed in the United States
by Baker & Taylor Publisher Services